BANK FRAUD:

Exposing the Hidden Threat to Financial Institutions

BENTON E. GUP
University of Alabama
Tuscaloosa, Alabama

BANKERS PUBLISHING COMPANY
Rolling Meadows, Illinois

Library of Congress Catalog Card Number: 88-082155

Printed in the United States of America.

No. 300

To Jean, Lincoln, Andy, and Jeremy

CONTENTS

V

FOREWORD

Most of this book was written while I was on sabbatical from the University of Alabama doing research on the growth and profitability of financial institutions. One aspect of growth was the large number of failures of banks and thrifts in which fraud and insider abuse played a significant role. Although there was widespread knowledge that such frauds occurred, there was nothing published in one place about the nature of the frauds and insider abuse or how to prevent them. This book provides a partial remedy for that situation. However, it is only a partial remedy for several reasons. First, there are structural problems within our financial system that provided the setting for fraud and abuse to occur. Some of these structural problems involve reform of federal deposit insurance, laws dealing with the powers of financial institutions, and the role of regulators. Obviously this book cannot resolve those problems and it does not deal with them. Second, as long as there is greed and money, someone is going to figure out a way to "beat the system." Therefore, it would be presumptuous for me to suggest that what is written here will put an end to fraud at financial institutions. Instead, the aim of this book is modest. It is written to inform readers about major frauds that have contributed to the failure and financial distress of financial institutions and to suggest ways to help prevent such occurrences in the future. The basic idea is that it is easier to prevent frauds than it is to uncover and successfully prosecute them.

In order to prevent them, we must understand how they happen. Therefore, major types of frauds, and some minor ones, are covered in the book.

In one sense, nothing in this book is new. All of the information presented here was taken from published articles, books, documents, and interviews—sources that are believed to be reliable. Some articles from trade publications, local newspapers, and U.S. House Reports, for example, are not widely circulated. Therefore, although information about major frauds at financial institutions was available in widely scattered sources, it has never been compiled into one convenient source, until now—in this book.

Because the names of many individuals and institutions are mentioned, great care was taken to cite the principal sources of information about them. Some of the individuals mentioned are being tried for their alleged crimes as this book is being written, and they may be found innocent. Some are appealing their convictions, and their convictions may be overturned. Others may be brought to trial at later dates. In any case, I tried to do a thorough and careful job of research and reporting the information that was available to me. As both an academic scholar and, in writing this book, an investigative reporter, I know that a potential for error exists. Therefore, I want to take this opportunity to apologize in advance for any that may be found. They were not intentional.

Benton E. Gup

INTRODUCTION

I thought about calling this book *How to Rob Banks for Fun and Profit*, but decided against that title in favor of *Bank Fraud: Exposing the Hidden Threat to Financial Institutions*. The term "bank" refers to a variety of financial institutions. The types of crimes described in this book occur in banks, thrifts, insurance companies, and other types of financial institutions. After reading cases of outrageous frauds and insider abuses, and learning that some crooks spent millions of dollars on yachts, jets, vacations, and personal luxuries, it became clear that some of these criminals had fun and lived outlandish life-styles. Therefore, was the fraudulent and abusive activity profitable? You bet—at least in the short run for some of the crooks. In 1988, fraud and embezzlement at U.S. institutions amounted to $2.2 billion and contributed to the failures of hundreds of banks and thrifts, which will cost the U.S. taxpayers more than $150 billion. While we—U.S. taxpayers—must pay the bill for the bail out, we can still take actions at the level of each financial institution to avoid similar problems in the future. We can take preventive measures to deter fraud and insider abuses from occurring, and we can attempt to detect them in the incipient stage when they do occur. These are the two themes of this book—detection and prevention.

This book is divided into nine chapters. Chapter 1 provides background information on the causes of the current epidemic of bank fraud and insider abuse. Chapter 2 describes various types of major crimes and schemes used to defraud banks.

Chapter 2 also explains some of the difficulties in prosecuting these crimes. Chapter 3 deals with the detection of frauds. "Profiles" of crooks, as well as red flags used to uncover their activities, are presented. Chapters 4 and 5 contain case studies of crimes by "outsiders"—those people who are not officers, directors, or employees of the bank. Many crimes against banks are perpetrated by outsiders who prey on vulnerable banks and bank employees, and some of these outsiders are linked to organized crime and international crime organizations. Chapter 6 examines case studies of crimes by insiders in banks. With this background, we next turn to prevention. Chapter 7 deals with the role of bank directors because they are the key to preventing bank fraud and insider abuse. Chapter 8 is about internal controls and audits. These are the tools that are used to deter and detect fraud and insider abuse. Chapter 9, the final chapter, is called "Point of View." It contains the point of view of regulators, investigators, and others on what individual institutions can do to prevent fraud. Appendices at the end of the book contain "reg flags" and sample loan policies.

Writing this book would not have been possible without the aid of many people who provided me with information, ideas, suggestions, and materials. This is the appropriate place to thank them. Four people who deserve special thanks are Christopher A. "Kip" Byrne (Federal Deposit Insurance Corporation); James Horner (Office of the Comptroller of the Currency); Stephen R. McSpadden, (Counsel, U.S. House Commerce Consumer, and Monetary Affairs Subcommittee on Government Operations); and Gregory D. Meacham (Federal Bureau of Investigation). A special thanks is also due to Sara B. "Sally" Reeves and her staff at the University of Alabama Library who provided many of the government documents used in the preparation of this book. Others include: Anthony Adamski, Jr. (Federal Bureau of Investigation); Pat Allen (U.S. League of Savings Associations); Skip Baird (First Alabama Bank); Pete Brewton (*Houston Post*);

Philip F. Bartholomew (Federal Home Loan Bank Board); Dan Brigham (VISA); Dennis Brosan (VISA); Pamela H. Bucy (University of Alabama); John J. Byrne (American Bankers Association); Janet Campbell (AmSouth); Kenneth Cline (*American Banker*); William J. Crawford (Savings and Loan Commissioner, California); Frank Donaldson, (U.S. Attorney, Northern District of Alabama); Donald Drummand (International Association of Credit Card Investigators); Harold W. Eavenson (NCNB Texas); Richard Fishkin (Dallas Task Force); Carey Gillam (*Kansas City Business Journal*); Tim Gruber (First Alabama Bank); Susan G. James (Attorney, Alabama); Mark Holder (OCC); Tim James (Attorney, Texas); George F. Klersey, Jr. (University of Alabama); Sue Lindsay (*Rocky Mountain News*); Bruce Maffeo (Organized Crime Strike Force, Booklyn); Charles A. McNelis (Attorney, Washington, D.C.); Bill Newman (VISA); William N. Noonan (MasterCard); Lawrence T. Oden (AmSouth); Ricardo R. Pesquera (Assistant U.S. Attorney Office, Middle District of Florida, Orlando Division); Kurt T. Peters, (*Credit Card News*); Richard Ringer (*American Banker*); Bob Serino (Office of the Comptroller of the Currency); Charles A. Sittason (First Alabama Bank); Rosemary Stewart (Federal Home Loan Bank Board); Sara L. Strait (Office of the Comptroller of the Currency); Zack Thompson (Superintendent of Banks, Alabama); Jack D. Walker (The Home Bank of Guntersville, Alabama); Michael Violano (*Bankers Monthly*); Joseph T. Wells (National Association of Certified Fraud Examiners); Steven R. Woods (Marion, Ross, Woods, Inc., Washington, D.C.); Charles A. Worsham (Louisiana Bankers Association).

1

INSIDER ABUSE AND CRIMINAL MISCONDUCT AT BANKS

BAD GUYS USED TO WEAR BLACK

Bank robbers in old cowboy movies were portrayed as tall, dark strangers who wore black outfits and carried large revolvers. They rode lean horses into frontier towns and sacked the local banks. Modern bank robbers, however, are more likely to be well-dressed insiders (officers, directors, and principal stockholders). Instead of carrying guns and stealing thousands of dollars in coin and currency, they develop complex manipulative schemes and steal millions of dollars. In one large heist, insiders (and others) looted more than $100 million in about a one year period from Empire Savings of Mesquite, Texas.[1] Outsiders, of course, still rob banks, and they too develop schemes that net them millions of dollars.

Most bank crimes do not yield such large sums, but the sums are nevertheless substantial. Table 1-1 shows the distribution of estimated dollar losses from 520 criminal referrals from commercial banks, savings and loans, and credit unions. For convenience, the term *bank* is used to describe these institutions unless referring to a specific type of institution or to a specific bank by name.

Since *banks* hold most of the money, it makes sense to steal large amounts of it. As shown in the table, almost 70 percent of the losses amount to $250,000 or more. Almost 30 percent amount to *$1 million or more*. When there is a known or sus-

TABLE 1-1   ESTIMATED DOLLAR LOSS FOR CRIMINAL REFERRALS FOR 520 FINANCIAL INSTITUTIONS, 9/30/1987*

ESTIMATED LOSS			NUMBER	PERCENT
Unknown			40	7.7%
$0	-	$99,000	39	7.5
100,000	-	249,999	85	16.3
250,000	-	499,999	109	21.0
500,000	-	999,999	93	17.9
1 million or more			<u>154</u>	<u>29.6</u>
	Total		520	100.0%

Source: U.S. House, *Adequacy of Federal Efforts to Combat Fraud, Abuse, and Misconduct in Federally Insured Institutions,* Hearing before the Commerce, Consumer and Monetary Affairs Subcommittee of the House Committee on Government Operation, 100th Cong., 1st. Sess., November 19, 1987, p. 562 - 563.
*Total includes 439 banks, 60 savings and loans, 21 credit unions.

pected financial criminal activity, other than robberies or burglaries, which are reported directly to appropriate law enforcement agencies, many banks are required to file Criminal Referral Forms with their primary regulators. National banks, for example, file with the Comptroller of the Currency.[2] However, not all state-chartered banks have a similar requirement.

According to the Federal Bureau of Investigation, total losses recorded from completed investigations of bank fraud and embezzlement in 1988 amounted to $2.1 billion. This compared to $861 million in the previous year and $280 million in 1983.[3] The FBI reported that in the 16,037 incidents where federal violations occurred in 1988, 63 percent of them involved internal frauds. These figures understate the amount of crime because they do not include 1,027 incidents that were investigated but not deemed federal violations. Many crimes go unreported because banks do not want adverse publicity, and the loss is written off as a bad loan. Even if crimes are reported, the FBI may not complete the investigation. In regions where the FBI's case load is extremely heavy, they may not have the manpower to deal with all their cases. In addition, national banks are not required to report "mysterious disappearances or unexplained shortages" of $5,000 or less. Finally, the rules for state-chartered institutions reporting financial crimes vary from state to state; so there is no way to estimate the full extent of fraud.

The epidemic of insider fraud and abuse contributed to the sharp increase in the failures of commercial banks and savings and loan associations in recent years. In 1982 there were 10 failed commercial banks. In 1983, 48 banks failed. Every year thereafter the number of bank failures has increased, reaching 221 failed commercial banks in 1988, and 101 in the first half of 1989. Perhaps more banks would have failed if there had been a sufficient number of bank regulators to close them.

Between 1980 and 1988, fraud and insider abuse contributed to 33 to 50 percent of the commercial bank failures and to 25 to 75 percent or more of saving and loan association failures.[4] The extent of the fraud and the degree to which it contributed to these bank failures varied from case to case. In some cases it played only a minor role, while in others, however, it played a major role. The growth of criminal misconduct and the increase of bank failures go hand in hand, and it has always been a major contributing factor in bank failures.[5] Fraud contributes to unsafe and unsound banking practices, even when the banks do not fail.

Heads I Win, Tails the Insurance Funds Lose

Let's examine the reasons for the epidemic of fraud, insider abuse, and bank failures. To do that, we must go back before 1973 when the Organization of Petroleum Exporting Countries (OPEC) demanded and received higher prices for crude oil.

Higher Energy Prices and Real Estate.   For years prior to 1973, the average price of imported crude oil was $1.80 per barrel. Then OPEC forced prices higher. In 1974 the price per barrel went to $12.52, and by 1981 it had reached $35. During this period of rising energy prices and the subsequent inflation, many banks made two assumptions concerning their lending policies. First, they assumed that inflation was here to stay, and second, they assumed that oil prices would continue to rise. They were wrong on both accounts. Nevertheless, the influx of petrodollars from OPEC countries and the wealth generated from oil and gas production in the United States fueled a boom in real estate construction and speculation, especially in those states that produced oil and gas.

During the early 1980s, when energy prices and inflation rates were high, some banks adopted risky lending policies and speculated in loans for acquisition, development, and construction of real estate projects. Market interest rates soared—the Treasury bill rate increased from about seven percent in 1980 to over 16 percent in 1981. Some banks that borrowed short-term funds at high rates of interest and loaned them for long periods at lower rates of interest did not survive the negative spreads; that is, costs exceeded returns, and they failed.

Federal and State Regulation.   A study by the Federal Home Loan Bank Board put the blame for the failures on a rigid institutional design of fixed-rate mortgage loans and variable rate deposits that set the stage for failures of thrifts.[6] To forestall failures and to promote growth in the housing industry, Congress enacted the Depository Institutions Deregulation and Monetary Control Act (1980) and the Garn-St Germain Depository Institutions Act of 1982 permitting deregulation of banks. The acts gave federally insured thrifts greater flexibility in deciding how to acquire and invest their funds. The Monetary Control Act provided for the gradual elimination of Regulation Q that set interest rate ceilings on deposits and opened the door for banks to pay higher rates on deposits.

Garn-St Germain also provided for thrift institutions to broaden their investment powers by allowing up to 20 percent of their assets in consumer loans, commercial paper, and corporate debt securities. Garn-St Germain further liberalized a bank's powers by allowing S&Ls to engage in commercial lending. It also permitted the interstate acquisition of failing institutions. Some state laws were changed to encourage the growth of thrifts. In California, the Nolan Bill liberalized state law to "allow state chartered thrifts authority to do anything and everything they wanted to do—no holds barred—using federally-insured deposits," said Edwin Gray, former Chairman of the Federal Home Loan Bank Board.[7]

Deposit Insurance.   To facilitate the survival and growth of S&Ls, the minimum regulatory capital on savings and loans (S&Ls) was reduced from five percent to three percent (from 1981-1983). This, according to Gray, caused a perverse incentive to grow excessively and gamble the store. There were great opportunities to make a killing on the upside, with little or no downside risk because of deposit insurance. The presence of deposit insurance provided little incentive for depositors to be concerned about the financial condition of the banks that held their fully insured funds deposits, or how they invested those funds. Therefore, the deposit insurance actually helped contribute to the failure of many financial institutions by shielding them from the volatile financial markets that would have normally signaled unsound investments. Market investors in uninsured loans to banks would have required progressively higher returns on loans to banks taking on increasingly risky loans and investments. Hence, deposit insurance provided little incentive for management to worry about risk when they had little or no equity capital to lose. One role of equity capital—the owner's investment—is to absorb losses. When there is no equity capital, there is nothing for the owners to lose when losses occur. Someone else, namely, the insurance funds and the public, had to absorb the losses.

Low Capital Requirements.   Another reason for the increasing financial institution failure was the difference between regulatory accounting principles (RAP), promulgated by the Federal Home Loan Bank Board, and generally accepted accounting principles (GAAP). According to a congressional report,

"Regulatory and statutory accounting gimmicks included permitting thrifts to defer losses from the sale of assets with below-market yields; permitting the use of income capital certificates, authorized by Congress, in place of real capital; letting qualifying mutual capital certificates to be included as RAP capital; allowing FSLIC insured members to exclude from liabilities in computing net worth, certain contra-accounts, including loans in process, unearned discounts, and deferred fees and credits."[8]

In 1984, the RAP method overstated the GAAP net worth by $9 billion. At the end of 1988, the difference was $14.9 billion. This difference masked the true extent of the thrifts' problems and enabled weak institutions to continue to operate when they should have been closed.

In addition, because banks are not required to evaluate their loan portfolios at market value, some banks that appeared to be solvent (have a positive equity capital or net worth) were actually insolvent. As their capital declined or became negative, there was even greater incentives for the owners to speculate and engage in risky loans. The attitude of the day was "Heads I win, tails the insurance funds loses."

Recognizing this profit opportunity with little or no risk, some real estate developers bought control of banks and S&Ls. One FSLIC official said that "For the unscrupulous developer, owning a thrift was a dream come true—a virtual printing press to provide money to develop his real estate."[9] Such S&Ls adopted a strategy of rapid expansion. In fact, S&Ls were encouraged by the Federal Home Loan Bank Board to grow faster to enhance their earnings to relieve their financial distress. To do this, they turned to "brokered deposits" as a source of funds. These were insured certificates of deposit that were sold to investors through brokerage houses such as Merrill Lynch and others. The CDs carried high rates of interest to attract investors. To pay for the high-cost deposits, S&Ls invested in increasingly risky projects that promised high returns. The more brokered deposits they sold, the more they invested in risky projects, and the faster they grew. From December 1982 through December 1986, the assets of 40 risky

Texas S&Ls grew 299 percent, compared to 99 percent for other Texas thrifts and 55 percent average growth in the United States. Therefore, federal and state regulations, the federal deposit insurance, and capital requirements (RAP vs GAAP) all contributed to the demise of many financial institutions, as well as created a climate where both inside and outside abuse could flourish.

THE THIN LINE BETWEEN ABUSE AND FRAUD

Insider abuse frequently leads to criminal misconduct. *Insider abuse* is a technical term that "refers to a wide range of misconduct by officers, directors and insiders of financial institutions committed with the intent to enrich themselves without regard for the safety and soundness of the institutions they control, in violation of civil banking laws and regulations and perhaps also in violation of criminal banking laws. The term *criminal misconduct* refers strictly to criminal acts committed by such insiders against the institutions they control."[10] Thus, insider abuse does not necessarily involve criminal misconduct. However, there is usually a very thin line between insider abuse and bank fraud. The difference between fraud and abuse is a "thin" line because what is abuse—which is legal but not good—and what is fraud—which is illegal is a narrow matter of interpretation. It is up to a jury to decide which side of the line the accused is on; and the so-called bad guys frequently get off, despite the best efforts of the FBI, regulators, and others. Equally important, insider abuse and fraud lead to "unsafe or unsound" banking practices, such as extending credit that is inadequately secured, failing to maintain internal controls, and paying excessive cash dividend.[11]

Self-dealing is a common form of insider abuse. It refers to insiders putting their own self-interest above the interest of the bank. One form of self-dealing is when an insider uses his or her authority to grant loans to oneself, or a related business, at preferential terms or buys using lower credit standards, with the intent of making profit in that business. For example, banking regulators sued the National Bank of Georgia, Calhoun

First National Bank, and T. Bertram (Bert) Lance, an insider, for engaging in certain unsafe and unsound banking practices that violated federal securities laws. Bert Lance was the former Carter Administration budget director who resigned that post because of his banking practices.[12] The complaint alleged that credit (loans and overdrafts) was extended to Lance, his relatives, and his friends on preferential terms and without regard to their creditworthiness. The extension of the credits caused liquidity problems at Calhoun bank. To solve the problems, Calhoun bank transferred troubled loans to other banks, but Calhoun bank concealed the transfers by making misleading entries on its books. The loans were not reflected on Calhoun's financial statements, and no adjustment was made to the provision for loan losses for some of the transactions. The result was that earnings and assets were overstated, and the bank failed to disclose its true financial state to banking regulators and investors. The National Bank of Georgia also extended credit to Lance, his relatives, and his friends on preferential terms so that they could pay on the loans and overdrafts at Calhoun bank. The National Bank of Georgia also failed to reserve properly for loan losses. The problems at both banks were corrected.[13]

A related form of self-dealing is when directors and principal shareholders become dependent on fees and income from providing outside dealings with the bank (that is, legal services) to such an extent that their interests come ahead of the banks. Other types of insider abuse include:

- Paying high cash dividends when the bank is insolvent.
- Payment of personal trips to Europe or elsewhere.
- Putting friends and relatives on the bank's payroll.
- Directing the bank's business to friends and relatives.
- Unwarranted fringe benefits to insiders.
- Kickbacks from customers in return for granting loans or low interest rates on loans.

To further illustrate insider abuse, consider the case of Manhattan Beach Savings and Loan Association, Manhattan Beach, California, that was owned by Peter Sajovich.[14] About one year before Manhattan Beach was closed, Sajovich "contributed" to it a company that he owned called National Home Equity Corporation (NHEC). The contribution was made on the condition that Manhattan Beach would recapitalize NHEC with an infusion of $4.5 million in cash, which exceeded the S&L's equity capital. The day before he made the contribution to the S&L, Sajovich received a check for $3 million from NHEC. Of that amount, $2.515 million was a "dividend" representing the entire net worth, and the remaining $485,000 was a noninterest-bearing loan, resulting in NHEC having a negative net worth. NHEC went bankrupt, and Manhattan Beach Savings and Loan failed.

Since 1984 there has been an increased amount of fraud and abuse involving outsiders—borrowers, brokers, dealers, and crooks. Consider the case of Consolidated Savings Bank, Irvine, California. Consolidated made a $9 million loan to a corporation owned by a convicted felon, Charles J. Bazarian, who, no doubt, promised them large returns; and they were greedy enough to believe him. The loan was made without any loan application or financial information. There was, however, a one page opinion from appraisers concerning the value of the property being used as security for the loan. Not one payment was made on the loan, and it appears to have been a substantial or total loss.[15] Bazarian was also connected with the failure of Florida Center Bank. His role in this failure is discussed in Chapter 4.

Butterfield Savings and Loan Association, Santa Ana, California, is a similar example of faulty appraisal practices and lack of proper internal controls by the S&L. Butterfield was in financial difficulty when its capital declined sharply. The holding company that owned Butterfield issued new stock and contributed the proceeds to Butterfield, which used the funds to purchase 40 parcels of real estate at a cost in excess of $80 million. Management wanted to record the highest possible purchase price to inflate the book net worth figures and to relieve the pressure from regulators; therefore, the appraisals were made at grossly inflated figures. Unfortunately, one parcel purchased for development was a swamp and another parcel was a forest preserve. Needless to say, Consolidated Savings Bank failed, too.

A 1989 U.S. Government Accounting Office study of 26 failed thrifts found that they all changed from traditional home lenders to higher risk lending activities.[16] Moreover, indications of fraud and insider abuse were evident in all of them. Most of the criminal misconduct involved officers and directors who violated the following laws and regulations:

- Seventeen had inaccurate appraisals for real estate projects.
- Twenty-three exceeded the legal limits of loans available to one borrower.
- Twenty-one conducted business with prohibited persons or entities affiliated with the thrifts.
- Twenty-four did not adequately assess the borrower's financial condition.

BANK FAILURES

The end of the speculative bubble came in the early 1980s when the Federal Reserve put the brakes on the economy to slow the rate of inflation, and when oil prices plummeted from $35 per barrel to $10 per barrel. As cash flow dwindled from oil and gas production, a domino effect began in the economy that resulted in deflation, or falling prices. The agricultural export boom came to a halt when the price of farmland declined, especially in the Midwest. The prices of residential and commercial real estate declined in cities, such as Houston, Texas, where there was overcapacity because of speculation. Many loans linked to energy and real estate went into default. Some home mortgage loans were jokingly called "jingle loans" because a substantial number of borrowers abandoned their properties and sent their jingling keys to the lenders instead of sending monthly payments to amortize mortgage loans.

Furthermore, falling energy prices contributed to the international "debt crisis" where lesser developed countries and developed countries were unable or unwilling to honor their debts. Mexico, one of the major trading partners of the United States, devalued the peso and took other actions that negatively impacted the economies of Texas, California, and other states.

Most of the commercial banks that failed between 1985 to 1987 came from oil-producing states [Texas (88), Oklahoma (60), Colorado (26), Louisiana (22)] and from farm belt states [Kansas (35), Iowa (27), Nebraska (25), and Minnesota (21)]. A complete listing of bank failures by state is presented in Appendix 1-A.[17]

Many S&Ls failed in these same states. One factor that contributed to the S&L failures was a lack of supervision. In 1983 the Federal Home Loan Bank of Little Rock, Arkansas, moved to Dallas, Texas. Thirty-seven of the bank's 48 employees quit rather than move. Only two of the eleven employees who moved were examiners, and their responsibility covered 480 S&Ls.[18]

Restricted Branching and the Small Bank.   Most of the states where the largest number of failures occurred had laws that restricted branch banking. Ninety percent of the banks that failed in 1987 were in such states.[19] As a result of the banking structure, states such as Texas had a large number of small unit banks. At the end of 1987, Texas had 1,766 banks of which 1,081 had total assets of less than $50 million.[20] Five hundred and sixty-one banks had assets of less than $25 million. The large number of small banks is important because small banks cannot afford a large write-off as well as a large bank. A bank with $25 million in assets may have about $1.5 to $2 million in capital (six to eight percent). As mentioned previously, a significant portion of the criminal referrals resulted in losses over $1 million. Large losses destroy the capital of small banks. In addition, small-unit banks have less opportunity to diversify geographically, and they have fewer opportunities to achieve economies-of-scale through branching. In addition, their resources for qualified management and directors are stretched. For example, 10 unit banks require 10 boards of directors, while one bank with 10 branches requires only one board. Thus, restrictions on branch banking contributed indirectly to the failures by fostering a large number of small-unit banks rather than large banks with many branches.

Small banks in financial difficulty were easier targets than large banks for insiders that wanted to manipulate them for their own purposes. Table 1-2 shows the average asset size of 426 banks that had criminal referrals filed with the Department of Justice by regulatory agencies. There were relatively few referrals at large banks. However, the criminal referrals may not reveal the extent of crime at large banks. They are better able to cover up losses from financial crimes by writing them off as bad loans or by some other means. Nevertheless, the largest concentration of criminal referrals was in small banks, those with assets of $50 million or less. Although not shown in Table 1-2, 116 of the 426 banks with referrals were closed.

TABLE 1-2   FINANCIAL INSTITUTIONS THAT FILED SIGNIFICANT CRIMINAL REFERRALS WITH THE DEPARTMENT OF JUSTICE 1/1/86 TO 3/30/87*

ASSET SIZE			NUMBER	PERCENT
$0	-	$50 million	164	38.5%
51	-	$100 million	73	17.1
101	-	750 million	109	25.6
751	-	10 billion	54	12.7
10	-	250 billion	25	5.9
Information not provided			1	0.2
	Totals		426	100.0%

Source: U.S. House, *Adequacy of Federal Efforts to Combat Fraud, Abuse, and Misconduct in Federally Insured Institutions,* Hearing before the Commerce, Consumer and Monetary Affairs Subcommittee of the House Committee on Government Operation, 100th Cong., 1st Sess., November 19, 1987, p. 562 - 563.

*The term "Significant" means a uniform referral form filed by a regulatory agency and supervised financial institutions.

One reason for the concentration of criminal referrals in small banks is that they are targets and less costly for crooks to acquire than large banks. A 1964 congressional study revealed that 56 percent of all banks had fewer than 50 stockholders, and 75 percent had less than 10,000 shares.[21] Although that study is dated, the figures probably have not changed very much.

LEADING THE LAMBS TO SLAUGHTER

Greed is the motive for bank crimes. Greed is a double-edged sword. Those who commit bank crimes are greedy, and many of the so-called victims are greedy. Dishonest loan and deposit brokers showed eager and willing lenders how to make a financial killing on large deals that sounded to good to be true. To paraphrase one crook, "It was like leading lambs to slaughter." The lenders, wanting to reap huge financial gains, overlooked obvious flaws in underwriting speculative loans because they were not only greedy, but careless. They were careless because they didn't do their homework. They ignored the five "Cs" of credit for making sound loans: character, capacity, capital, collateral, and conditions. The following case illustrates the point.

The Office of the Comptroller of the Currency (OCC) published a "Banking Issuance" concerning annuity contracts from American Teachers Life Insurance Company, Humble, Texas, and General Mercantile Finance Corporation, Houston, Texas. At the same time they published an "OCC Advisory" that stated an insurance company sold single premium insurance annuities (for example $100,000) to individuals for a small down payment. The remainder of the cost of the annuity was financed by a promissory note with a finance company. The buyers were told that interest on the note would cost them $6,000 per year, but that the annuity would pay them $7,000 at the end of the year, resulting in a nice profit. Most of the individuals lacked the financial resources to make the note payments without the annuity income. A finance company packaged the promissory notes and sold them at discounts to banks or used them as collateral for bank loans. The banks did their credit checks on the individuals who signed the notes and paid the finance company. However, they failed to check the insurance company that issued the annuities. The banks assumed that the Texas Board of Insurance guarantee fund would insure the insurance policies. However, the guarantee fund does not insure fraudulent deals. Subsequently, the annuities, which were worthless or grossly overvalued, were not honored, so those individuals who bought them were defrauded. The banks that held the notes may suffer a loss.[22] The OCC was careful not to include those firms named in the Banking Issuance in its advisory. Nevertheless, the implication was clear that those firms named were involved in the annuities fraud. Hence, the banks that bought the promissory notes were careless and did not do their homework.

IN SUMMARY

There are many ways to steal from banks. Bank crimes have not, and will not end. People will always rob and steal from banks because that's where the money is. But there are things we can do to prevent some bank crimes. Those who were inclined to commit crimes during the 1970s and 1980s were given a golden opportunity and the means "on a silver platter." First, high energy prices fueled a speculative boom in real estate and land values. Second, federal and state laws fostering deregulation opened the door for speculative investments and brokered deposits that weak institutions used to their advantage, although some lawmakers and regulators claimed that industry lobbying groups deceived them into a political black hole.[23] Third, depositors, because of their insured deposits, had no incentive to know it. Fourth, regulators imposed low capital requirements and had lax standards for regulating banks. Fifth, bank directors, officers, and shareholders were either ignorant or frequently chose to ignore the condition of their bank, especially in regard to its safety and soundness. Sixth, restrictive state laws on branch banking nurtured a large number of small banks that were ripe for picking. (In Texas, for example, control of state-chartered thrifts could be effectuated by buying their stock in the marketplace, with no regulatory controls.)

The largest bank crime wave in our history was uncovered when the speculative bubble in real estate burst and banks began to fail in large numbers. The problem was exacerbated by the Tax Reform Act of 1986 which made real estate investments less attractive. Had economic activity not declined, many of the crimes involving real estate would have been covered up by economic prosperity and inflation.

APPENDIX 1-A   FAILED COMMERCIAL BANKS BY STATES, 1985-1987

State	1987	1986	1985	Total
Alabama	2	1	1	4
Alaska	2	1	0	3
Arkansas	0	0	1	1
California	8	8	7	23
Colorado	13	7	6	26
Florida	3	3	2	8
Idaho	0	1	0	1
Illinois	2	1	2	5
Indiana	3	1	1	5
Iowa	6	10	11	27
Kansas	8	14	13	35
Kentucky	1	2	0	3
Louisiana	14	8	0	22
Massachusetts	2	0	0	2
Minnesota	10	5	6	21
Mississippi	1	0	0	1
Missouri	4	9	9	22
Montana	3	1	0	4
Nebraska	6	6	13	25
New Mexico	0	2	3	5
New York	1	0	2	3
North Dakota	2	0	0	2
Ohio	1	0	0	1
Oklahoma	31	16	13	60
Oregon	1	1	2	4
Pennsylvania	1	0	0	1
South Dakota	2	1	0	3
Tennessee	0	2	5	7
Texas	50	26	12	88
Utah	3	3	1	7
Wisconsin	0	1	1	2
Wyoming	4	7	5	16
Puerto Rico	0	1	0	1
Totals	184	138	116	438

Source: Federal Deposit Insurance Corporation, *1987 Annual Report*, p.6.

Notes

1. Dennis Cauchon, "S&L Fraud Trial Opens in $136M Vanishing Act," *USA Today,* February 22, 1989, B1. Empire Savings and Loan is examined in Chapter 6.
2. Comptroller of the Currency, "Criminal Referral Form (Short Form) 1557-0069. Under 12 C.F.R. #21.11, National banks are required to file within 30 days following the detection of a loss or suspected violation of all known or suspected crimes/losses involving financial transactions. A long form is used when executive officers, directors, or principal shareholders are involved (12 C.F.R. #215.2). Also see 12 C.F.R. #21.5(c), 17 C.F.R. #240.17f-1.
3. U.S. Department of Justice, Federal Bureau of Investigation, "Bank Crime Statistics (BCS), Federally Insured Financial Institutions, 1988 estimate, January 1, 1987 to December 31, 1987, January 1, 1983 to June 30, 1983, July 1, 1983 to December 31, 1983. Although the data are not strictly comparable from period to period due to changes in definition, the increased crime from 1983 to 1987 is real.
4. Federal Deposit Insurance Corporation, *1987 Annual Report,* Washington, D.C., FDIC, 1988, pp. xiii, 6; FDIC News Release, "Interagency Cooperation Controls Fraud and Insider Abuse, But More Action is Needed, FDIC Chairman Says," PR-2-3-87, November 11, 1987; U.S. House, *Combating Fraud, Abuse, and Misconduct in the Nation's Financial Institutions: Current Federal Efforts are Inadequate,* 72nd Report by the Committee on Government Operations, House Report 100-1088, 100 Cong., 2nd Sess., October 13, 1988, pp. 10-11; U.S. House, *Federal Response to Criminal Misconduct and Insider Abuse in the Nation's Financial Institutions,* 57th Report by the Committee on Government Operations, House Report 98-1137, 98th Cong., 2nd Sess., October 4, 1984, p. 7; U.S. House, *Financial Institutions Reform, Recovery and Enforcement Act of 1989,* Report of the Committee on Banking, Finance and Urban Affairs, Report 101-54, Part 1, 101st Cong., 1st Sess., May 16, 1989, 300.

5. Bank failures in earlier periods were analyzed by Joseph F. Sinkey, Jr., *Problem and Failed Institutions in the Commercial Banking Industry*, Greenwich, CN: JAI Press, Inc., 1979; Also see Irvine H. Sprague, *Bailout: An Insider's Account of Bank Failures and Rescues*, New York: Basic Books, Inc., 1986; George J. Benston, *An Analysis of the Causes of Savings and Loan Failures*, Monograph 1985-4, New York: Salomon Brothers Center for the Study of Financial Institutions, New York University, 1985; Richard L. Peterson and William L. Scott, "Major Causes of Bank Failure," Appears in *Proceedings, Bank Structure and Competition*, Federal Reserve Bank of Chicago, May 1-3, 1985, 166-183; Gregory R. Gajewski, *Bank Risk, Regulator Behavior, and Bank Closure in The Mid-1980s,: A Two Step Logit Model*, Unpublished Dissertation, George Washington University, 1988, Chapter 2.

6. James R. Barth, Philip F. Bartholmew, and Carol, J. Labich, *Moral Hazard and the Thrift Crisis: An Analysis of the 1988 Resolutions*, Research Paper #160, Federal Home Loan Bank Board, May 1989, 13.

7. Edwin J. Gray, "Statement of Edwin J. Gray, Past Chairman, Federal Home Loan Bank Board, before the Committee on Banking, Housing and Urban Affairs, Senate, August 3, 1988. Also see Council of Economic Advisers, *Economic Report of the President*, Washington, D.C.: U.S. Government Printing Office, 1989, pp. 200-205, for a discussion of the impact of regulation and deposit insurance.

8. U.S. House, *Financial Institutions Reform, Recovery and Enforcement Act of 1989*, ibid., 298; For details on how RAP differs from GAAP, see, U.S. General Accounting Office, *Bank Regulation, Information on Independent Public Accountant Audits of Financial Institutions*, GAO/GGD-86-44FS, April 1986.

9. Black, William K., and William L. Robertson, "State-

ment of the Federal Home Loan Bank submitted by William K. Black, Deputy Director, FSLIC and William L. Robertson, Director ORPOS, before the Subcommittee on Financial Institutions, Supervision, Regulation, and Insurance of the Committee on Banking, Finance, and Urban Affairs, House of Representatives, 100th Cong., June 9, 1987.

10. U.S. House Report 98-1137, p. 2, n.5; U.S. House Report 100-1088, p. 7-9; U.S. House, *Fraud and Abuse by Insiders, Borrowers, and Appraisers in the California Thrift Industry*, Hearing before the Commerce, Consumer, and Monetary Affairs Subcommittee of the Committee on Government Operations, 100th Cong., 1st Sess., June 13, 1987, Testimony of William K. Black, Federal Home Loan Bank Board, pp. 188-191; The Comptroller of the Currency has a different definition of insider abuse and fraud which may be found in *Bank Failure: An Evaluation of the Factors Contributing to the Failure of National Banks*, Washington, Comptroller of the Currency, June 1988, 45-46.

11. Additional examples of "Unsafe or Unsound" practices are listed in the FDIC's *Manual of Examination Policies*. They are also shown in U.S. House, *Federal Response to Criminal Misconduct and Insider Abuse in the Nation's Financial Institutions, Part 2*, Hearings before the Commerce, Consumer, and Monetary Affairs Subcommittee of the Committee on Government Operations, 98th Cong., 2d Sess., May 2 and 3, 1984, 1384.

12. Bert Lance in also mentioned in Chapter 6 in connection with UAB Knoxville and Jake Butcher's financing the World's Fair.

13. Hearings, Part 2, ibid., 1573-1574.

14. *Fraud and Abuse by Insiders*, ibid., 188-189.

15. *Combating Fraud*, House Report 100-1088, ibid., 185-186.

16. U.S. General Accounting Office, *Thrift Failures: Costly Failures Resulted From Regulatory Violations and Unsafe Practices*, GAO/AFMD-89-62, June 1989, 3.

17. Most insolvent savings and loan associations were located in Texas, California, Illinois, Louisiana, Florida, and Oklahoma. For details, see U.S. General Accounting Office, *Thrift Industry: Forbearance for Troubled Institutions 1982-1986*, GAO/GGD-87-78BR, May 1987, 20; Also, U.S. Government Accounting Office, *Thrift Failures*, ibid., 92-93.

18. Rick Atkinson and David Maraniss, "Only Ambition Limited S&L Growth," *The Washington Post*, June 12, 1989, A1.

19. U.S. General Accounting Office, *Bank Failures: Independent Audits Needed to Strengthen Internal Control and Bank Management*, GAO/AFMD-89-25, 33.

20. The number of banks by size for each state can be found in FDIC, *Statistics on Banking, 1987*.

21. U.S. House, *The Market for Bank Stock*, Subcommittee on Domestic Finance, Committee on Banking and Currency, 88th Cong., 2d Sess., 1964, 1.

22. Comptroller of the Currency, "OCC Advisory", "OCC Banking Issuance," 1989.

23. Brooks, Jackson, and Paulette Thomas, "As S&L Crisis Grows, U.S. League Loses Lobbying Clout," *The Wall Street Journal*, March 7, 1989, A1, A18.

2 TYPES OF CRIMES

There is a saying that one cannot see "the forest through the trees." So it is with bank fraud because it is a covert activity. Unless one knows what to look for, only those who are involved are aware of it. Bank frauds can go on for years before they are detected, if ever. Certain frauds, however, are more prevalent and preventable than others. In this chapter, we will examine the most prevalent types of fraud and learn why they are difficult to detect, and even more difficult to prosecute.

RELATIVELY SMALL FRAUDS

There are many types of criminal misconduct involving banks. Table 2-1 lists the principal federal criminal statutes involving banks and some of the crimes. Rather than analyze each type of violation, bank fraud—the general term—is divided into two broad criminal categories: those that involve large dollar amounts and may or may not contribute to bank failures (major frauds), and those that involve relatively small dollar amounts and do not cause bank failure (relatively small frauds). As explained in the previous chapter, a $2 million loss from fraud has a different impact on a large than on a small-size bank. It may have little or no effect on the capital of a large bank, but it may erase the capital of a small bank, thus causing it to fail. Consequently, a fraud's impact is relative to the asset size of the banks involved. Finally, although a bank has failed and fraud was present, the fraud may not have been the major cause of the failure.

TABLE 2-1   PRINCIPAL FEDERAL CRIMINAL STATUTES INVOLVING BANKS

18 U.S.C. Section 215; kickbacks and bribes prohibition; making it unlawful for any officer, director, employee, agent, et al. (insiders) of a financial institution to solicit, accept, or give anything of value in connection with a transaction or the business of the institution.

18 U.S.C. 656; 961(c); theft, embezzlement or misapplication of bank funds willfully by an insider with the intent to injure or defraud the bank.

18 U.S.C. 1344; financial institution fraud; scheme or artifice to defraud a federally insured institution to take money, funds, credits, assets, securities, or other property by misrepresentation.

18 U.S.C. 1001; general false statements statute: knowingly and willfully falsifying or concealing a material fact or making a false statement, etc.

18 U.S.C. 1005; false entries in bank documents including material omissions, with the intent to injure or defraud the commercial bank regulatory agencies' examiners or other individuals or companies.

18 U.S.C. 1014; false oral or written statements, such as a loan application, an agreement with the financial institution or another document, made knowingly for the purpose of influencing federally insured institutions.

18 U.S.C. 1341 and 1343; mail and wire fraud, respectively: a scheme or artifice to defraud that makes use of either the U.S. mail or electrical transmission.

18 U.S.C. 2, 371; the general Federal aiding and abetting statute and general Federal conspiracy statute, often applicable when two or more persons are involved in the commission of an offense.

Source: U.S. House, *Combating Fraud, Abuse, and Misconduct in the Nation's Financial Institutions: Current Federal Efforts are Inadequate,* 72 Report by the Committee on Government Operations, House Report 100-1088, October 13, 1988, 193; Financial Institutions Reform, Recovery and Enforcement Act of 1989. For 18 U.S.C. 215, 656, 657, 1005, 1006, 1007, 1014, 1341, 1343, 1344, and other sections, not all of which were discussed previously. The Act amends the civil penalties, criminal penalties, and it contains other revisions including civil and criminal forfeiture of assets.

Small frauds can be committed by trusted employees in any department of a bank. For example, computer related crimes are hard to detect because there are no witnesses or hard copy records.

Computer Fraud.   Computer crimes can be as simple as crediting a small fraction of interest payments to the perpetrator's account, or as complex as an elaborate computer scheme. For example, one elaborate computer scheme involved a senior computer operator on a bank's night shift of the main computer facility who used information from recently closed demand deposit accounts (DDAs) to open fictitious new ones. He had access to the correct passwords and personal identification numbers (PINs) to do it. He credited various funds to the new accounts by debiting one of the bank's "suspense accounts." Funds were credited to the suspense accounts from inactive savings accounts and high balance DDAs. He also withdrew funds from the new accounts using counter checks and the accounts' PIN numbers and used the home-banking telephone service to instruct the bank to pay for his various purchased goods and services. Over the seven months that he operated the scheme, the number of accounts and the amount of money in each account increased. His undoing occurred at a major gambling resort where he met a bank auditor whom he knew. The bell captain addressed the perpetrator by the wrong name, and the auditor became suspicious and investigated. The loss in this scheme was about $200,000.[1] The following cases also illustrate small frauds and abuses by insiders.

Automatic Tellers. Consider the case of an assistant supervisor of the automatic teller machine (ATM) department who had 27 years service, but who also was a gambler. Over the years he had won large sums, but had lost even more. Eventually, he was unable to pay off his gambling debts, so he gambled even more with the hopes of winning. When he was deep in debt to his bookies, they allowed him to satisfy his gambling debts by providing them with security information about his bank's ATM system. Shortly thereafter, thefts occurred at the ATMs, and he knew that his information had contributed to them. He became depressed, and his work and home life suffered. His wife, who was concerned about his health and his role in the thefts, reported him to bank authorities. The total loss to the bank was an estimated $135,000.[2]

Travelers' Checks. The next case of small bank fraud concerns an 11-year veteran employee who worked as a customer representative. Part of her job was to sell savings bonds and travelers' checks to bank customers. Eventually, she created false records to make it appear as if the $175,000 that she had received over a period of time had been sent on to American Express, but actually she had kept the money and had used part of it to pay for her mother's medical expenses. However, the total amount stolen far exceeded the medical expenses. Gradually the paperwork involved in the "cover up" became so time consuming that she was unable do her job. She turned herself into her attorney, and then contacted federal authorities.[3]

Withdrawing from Trust Accounts. Finally, there is the small fraud case of F. Ray Harvard, a vice president in the trust department of a large bank.[4] He had 18 years of service, but it is alleged that over a period of a decade Harvard had misapplied trust funds by withdrawing large sums from certain accounts that had been entrusted to him. To cover the withdrawals, he had allegedly sent inaccurate and deceptive financial statements to the account holders. He also had told them that selected investments had increased in value to a greater extent than they had. Harvard had used some of the funds to speculate in the stock market, and eventually had lost more than $1 million.

The day after returning from a two-week vacation, Harvard followed his usual routine and left for work in the morning, but he never arrived at the bank. Following an extensive search, his body was discovered near a hunting club where he was a member. He had committed suicide, and his death had occurred after stock prices had declined sharply in August 1987, but before "Black Monday," when the stock market had eventually "crashed." Perhaps the falling stock prices forced him to realize that his crimes were going to be discovered. Unfortunately, we will never know.

Check Kiting. The previous frauds were all committed by bank insiders. Check kiting, however, is a type of small bank fraud that's perpetrated by an outsider. Check kiting is a scheme to create false bank balances without sufficient funds to cover them and involves two or more accounts at different banks. The perpetrator writes a check for an amount sufficient to overdraw the account on which it was written. For example, if there is $100 in the account, the perpetrator would write a check for $1,000. The overdraft is covered by depositing a similar check drawn on another bank and deposited before the first check has been returned for payment. The result of the continuous interchange of worthless checks is that artificial balances are created in the accounts of the banks involved in the scheme.

Two conditions must exist for a successful check kiting scheme. First, there must be a period of several days in the collection process before the depository bank can present the check to the drawee bank. Second, the banks must be willing to pay checks drawn against uncollected funds—items in the process of collection.

The "Expedited Funds Availability Act," (12 U.S.C. 4001) gave the Board of Governors of the Federal Reserve System the authority to regulate the availability of funds deposited in depository institutions. Federal Reserve Regulation CC calls for next business day availability for wire transfers, government checks, certified checks, and cashiers' checks, and for longer periods for other types of deposits. In many cases, it takes more than one day to determine if a certified or another type of check is good. It remains to be seen what impact Regulation CC will have on check kiting.

MAJOR FRAUDS

The greatest dollar losses from bank fraud come from large commercial and real estate transactions, and they frequently involve insider participation. The five most common types of schemes that result in major frauds, according to the Federal Bureau of Investigation (FBI), are summarized here, and are examined in detail in later chapters.[5]

Nominee Loans.   These are loans obtained by one person on behalf of another undisclosed person. The nominee, or "straw borrower," may have no involvement in the loan transaction other than to obtain the funds and pass them on to someone else who does not want their identity known.

Double Pledging of Collateral.   The same collateral is used at two or more financial institutions to obtain loans. The lenders are unaware that the collateral is pledged on another loan. The combined amount of the loans exceeds the value of the collateral.

Reciprocal Loan Arrangements.   These are loans made between insiders in different financial institutions that lend funds to each other. A variant of this device is to sell loans to other institutions with the agreement to buy loans from that institution. The purpose of such agreements is to conceal the loans or sales from bank examiners.

Land Flips.   This refers to the transfer of land between related parties in order to inflate the value of the underlying property fraudulently. The land with the inflated values is used as collateral for loans. The amount of the loans frequently exceeds the actual value of the underlying property.

Linked Financing.   Large amounts of funds are deposited in a financial institution, using brokered deposits or some other means, with the understanding that the institution will make a loan conditioned on the deposit. The loans may be used to finance land flips or other types of deals.

Some of these schemes, such as linked financing and land flips, are not necessarily illegal by themselves. However, they usually occur in connection with willful misapplication of funds, making false statements, willfully overvaluing property, and other illegal activities that were outlined in Table 2-1. Although these types of transactions are presented separately, they often occur in combination. For example, large-scale fraud involving real estate requires two misrepresentations. The first essential misrepresentation is that the value of the property is inflated. The second misrepresentation concerns the creditworthiness of borrowers. The crooks misrepresent their own creditworthiness, the creditworthiness of the buyers they control, and the value of the properties by using false income tax returns and false financial statements. Property values are usually inflated by using a "double escrow" or a "straw buyer."

In a double escrow, the same property is sold simultaneously to two separate parties controlled by the perpetrator. The first transaction is from a legitimate seller at a fair market price to a buyer who is controlled by the perpetrator. The second sale is from the first buyer to a second, both of whom are controlled by the perpetrator. The second sale is made at two or three times the fair market price. In some cases the value is inflated as much as 20-fold by using improper appraisals.[6] This type of operation is also used in connection with a land flip. If a straw buyer is used, the straw buyer buys the property from the legitimate seller at the fair market price. Then the property is sold again, but at a higher price to a buyer who will qualify for a loan on the property at an inflated value.

To obtain inflated appraised property values, the perpetrators hire real estate appraisers from distant locations who want to increase their fee income, or who may be criminals, too. The appraisers, who are not familiar with the property, are provided with false information about the comparable worth of properties in the area. To illustrate this process, one bank loaned over $54 million on an office complex and relied on a borrower-ordered appraisal. The appraisal did not consider that more than one-half of the rentable space was leased at rates that were 50 percent below the current market prices, or that occupancy levels were low in nearby comparable properties due to overbuilding.[7] The result of such actions is faulty and inflated appraised values.

Then "loan packages," including financial statements, appraisals, and other information are presented to prospective buyers by "loan brokers" or others pretending to be independent and objective third parties.[8] The buyers of the overvalued real estate are individuals, limited partnerships, or financial institutions who rely on the honesty and thoroughness of the independent and objective third parties. Rarely do the buyers do their own credit analysis or appraisals, especially if the property is at a distant location. Their failure to do so puts them at substantial risk if and when the deals fail.

In some cases, the perpetrators sell funds (brokered deposits) to the financial institutions and link the sale of funds to real estate deals of the type described previously. As demonstrated, there are an infinite number of ways to commit bank frauds.

OBSTACLES TO PROSECUTING MAJOR FRAUDS

According to Gregory C. Jones, First Assistant U.S. Attorney for the Northern District of Illinois (Chicago), major frauds "are sophisticated crimes that by their very nature are designed to disguise and conceal the financial relationships that exist between the offenders."[9]

Even when a fraud is discovered, banks may choose not to report it, or federal authorities may decline to prosecute, which makes it an attractive option for perpetrators, especially if they know beforehand that there is little risk in being reported and prosecuted. For example, a member of the board of directors of a bank was suspected of kiting $373,000. The United States Attorney declined to prosecute because restitution was being made. That means that technically the theft was converted into a loan and that there was no loss to the bank.[10]

Negative Bank Publicity. Why didn't the bank prosecute the director? Part of the answer is given by Robert Serino, deputy chief counsel of the operations section of the Comptroller of the Currency, who said in a discussion about bankers' ethics that individual bankers should not do anything that they would be embarrassed about having on the front page of the morning paper.[11] This so-called embarrassment test applies to both banks and individuals. Therefore, many bankers unfortunately interpret this to mean that they should not expose the criminal activities in their banks because it might tarnish the bank's image, especially if a member of their top management is involved.

The Right to Financial Privacy Act.   Another reason for not reporting bank fraud is that some bankers interpret the Right to Financial Privacy Act in such a way that prevents them from providing details about suspected crimes. The act deals with the disclosure of financial information about their customers, which include all borrowers and savers (except corporations). However, the act was liberalized (in the Anti-Drug Abuse Act of 1986, Title 12, U.S.C. 3403c) to facilitate criminal investigations. Nevertheless, some bankers are reluctant to provide law enforcement officials with information about the crime for fear of being sued. For these and other reasons, some banks wait long periods of time before reporting crimes. For example, in California a loan officer altered loan documents and received kickbacks from a loan broker in 1981 and 1982, yet the crime was not reported until 1985.[12] Furthermore, it may take the FBI 20 to 24 months to investigate a complex financial crime. Therefore, the long delay between the commission of a crime and the time when it is reported, and then finally brought to trial, may invoke the five-year statute of limitations on certain crimes, thus ensuring that the criminal will not be prosecuted.

A corollary to the "untarnished image" that banks like to maintain is that they are unwilling to share information with other banks about former employees or customers who are suspected or convicted of criminal misconduct. Similarly, regulators and law enforcement agencies do not share the information. Subsequently, the result is that criminals can operate their schemes in one bank after another with impunity.

Bank Regulators Delinquent Reporting.   Bank regulators may also drag their heels when it comes to making timely criminal referrals to the FBI. This is demonstrated by the Ramona

Savings and Loan failure. Donald P. Mangano, Sr. and John L. Molinaro acquired Ramona Savings and Loan Association in Orange, California, and transformed it from a traditional S&L that served the local population into a real estate development company. In one transaction, Ramona sold 173 units of Cherokee Village condominium in Palm Springs, California, to associates of Molinaro for $29.4 million. Ramona loaned the buyers the funds to pay for the transaction, secured by first and second trust deeds on the units. However, no payments were required on the first note for three years and not one was required on the second note for five years. In fact, the buyers were really strawmen who had no responsibility or control over the units. This and similar transactions made Romana's bank appear profitable. Ramona, concurrently, entered into an agreement with the buyers to operate Cherokee Village as a hotel and to pay all the expenses for three years. The accounting adjustments changed Ramona's apparent profit on the deal from $6.9 million to $0. Michael Sage, the auditor for Ramona, issued a fraudulent financial statement that the S&L had a net worth of $8.3 million, when its net worth was actually a negative $19.6 million, which allowed it to pay a $2 million cash dividend to John Molinaro. Sage, who was Molinaro and Mangano's personal tax accountant, was paid two checks of $75,000 and $45,000 for his tax services. Sage had a background in engineering before switching to accounting in 1975. According to California Savings and Loan Commissioner, William J. Crawford, Sage cashed the checks and exchanged them for $100 bills; therefore, Sage had to have known about the scheme said a FSLIC fee attorney.

Supervisory Letters covering Reports of Examination criticize Ramona's aggressive growth strategy, funding with large CDs, and requesting information about contracts signed with Mangano & Sons were sent to the S&L in 1984 and 1985. In August 1986, a Supervisory Directive imposed restrictions on Ramona's growth because it was insolvent. It went into receivership the following month.

In October 1986, the District Accountant for the Federal Home Loan Bank of San Francisco wrote a memo detailing the allegations and possible violations, and recommended that a formal investigation be implemented. But the FHLBSF, FSLIC, and fee counsel did not notify the FBI. Instead, the fee counsel told the District Accountant to forget it until he had made a complete analysis, and that he wanted to work out a settlement agreement with the principals. The referral was not made and Sage fled. Then, instead of notifying the FBI, the FHLBSF and the FSLIC hired a private detective to find him, which he did not do. In June 1987 the matter had still not been referred to the FBI. In mid-July 1987, Molinaro tried to flee the country and was arrested by a customs agent at an airport on a false passport charge. He was brought to trial in mid-1989; Sage, however, is believed to be in Mexico. Commissioner Crawford has also heard rumors that he was in Australia, or even in the United States with a changed identity. Wherever Sage's whereabouts, he is facing several criminal indictments if and when he returns.[13]

Criminal Referral to the FBI. Calling the FBI to make a criminal referral is not necessarily a simple task. California Savings and Loan Commissioner William J. Crawford wanted to refer an incident concerning North American Savings and Loan Association to the FBI. He made 17 calls over 8 days to Orange County and Los Angeles County FBI offices, the Federal Home Loan Bank of San Francisco, and a United States Senator trying to initiate an FBI investigation.[14] The FBI had more cases than they could handle at that time, which made it more difficult. The Los Angeles office had 32 agents and 450 bank fraud cases. Another difficulty was that Crawford's calls did not reach the right people in the FBI until almost his last telephone call. Crawford said that once the FBI got on the case that they did an excellent job.

Bankers and others can avoid problems like those experienced by Commissioner Crawford by establishing a working relationship with their local FBI agents. Alternatively, if they want to report of crime, they should contact the bank fraud supervisor in their local FBI office. This procedure avoids the complaint clerk and the paperwork that follows before it gets to the bank fraud supervisor.

Will the FBI Investigate? Despite the FBI being alerted, it does not mean that the crime will be investigated. Because of man-power limitations, the FBI prioritizes investigations according to the amount of the bank's loss, the number of victims, the nature of the crime, the position of the insiders involved, and other factors. In Los Angeles, for example, losses below $100,000 that have no prosecutive merit are not investigated. Losses between $100,000 and $250,000 are opened and investigated. Losses above $250,000 are given the highest priority.[15] How-ever, the amount of the loss necessary to trigger an investiga-tion varies in other areas.

For instance, the FBI is more likely to prosecute insiders in banks that fail than in those that remain solvent and open for business. It is easier to convince a jury that harm has been done when a bank has failed than it is when it remains open. In one such case, senior bank officials were involved in kickbacks, falsifying loan applications and bank records, double mortgag-ing of property, granting loans in excess of the legal lending limits, embezzlement, and false statements to the government. Nevertheless, the U.S. Attorney "did not feel that extensive investigation revealed any prosecutable violations."[16]

Some other reasons given for declining to prosecute cases include lack of gain by the insider, no loss to the bank, lack of criminal intent, lack of evidence, and other available civil remedies. Former Assistant U.S. Attorney, Southern District of Illinois, Theodore J. McDonald, Jr. once said that the prospect of the FBI having to expend funds and manpower for several years to analyze financial statements to catch two or three sophisticated bank manipulators is not as appealing to them as the public relations gained from standing next to 500 bales of marijuana, a briefcase full of money, and a speed boat on the beaches of Florida.[17]

It is not surprising, therefore, that two-thirds of insiders who are suspected of criminal misconduct in solvent institutions escape criminal and civil sanctions. Nor is it surprising that many major frauds are not prosecuted. Beverly Hills Savings and Loan is one such case. There were four sets of allegations of criminal misconduct associated with the failure of the Beverly Hills Savings and Loan, and the estimated loss to the FSLIC was about $800 million. The FBI had the manpower to investigate the $400 million Stout-Newberry Apartment loan, so the FBI told the FSLIC that they wanted criminal referrals on other parts of the transaction. However, FSLIC's fee counsel, who was busy dealing with civil cases, did not believe it appropriate to look for criminal misconduct.[18] Since then the policy has changed and fee counsels have been informed that it is their obligation to make criminal referrals. Nevertheless, from the Federal Home Loan Bank Board's point of view, seeking civil money damages through litigation to help prop up the beleaguered FSLIC insurance fund may have been a higher priority than seeking criminal prosecutions. Unfortunately, the record for collecting civil money penalties has not been good.[19] The FDIC has collected 21 percent of the civil money penalties assessed open banks and 2 percent from failed banks.

Will the Government Prosecute?   Even when the FBI "finds their man," the story is far from being over. Bank frauds are usually tried under Title 18, U.S.Code 656 and other sections of the Code.[20] Section 656 of the U.S. Code applies to insiders of federally connected banks who willfully misapply funds for their own use or that of a third party. Assistant U.S. Attorney Jones goes on to say that "Insider offenses are difficult to prosecute because the government bears the burden of proving beyond a reasonable doubt that the loan officer acted with the specific intent to injure and defraud the financial institution."

It is not good enough to prove that the loan officer demonstrated bad judgement, stupidity, or complete incompetence. To prove what knowledge a bank official had or with what intent he acted when he approved a loan several years before can be a burdensome if not impossible task. By the time a criminal investigation is initiated, financial records necessary to prove the offense may have already been removed or destroyed. It is not uncommon in these cases to find that entire bank files are missing. In addition relevant witnesses may be difficult to locate and even when located may have little recollection of events that occurred years before.

> "One way of establishing fraudulent intent is to show that the loan officer received a concealed financial benefit for approving the loan. To prove this, however, may require a time-consuming analysis of a loan officer's personal finances as well as tracing of the loan proceeds to determine how they were disbursed and by whom they were ultimately received. If kickbacks were paid in cash or through nominees, it may be impossible to prove a criminal offense without the cooperation of another participant in the scheme. To obtain the cooperation of others involved in a scheme, it may be necessary to enter into a plea agreement with them or give them immunity. All of these investigative avenues take time and there is no assurance that even if they are explored that they will be fruitful. Many individuals refuse to cooperate with the government even if offered immunity. Many defendants recognize that if none of them cooperate with the government it may be impossible for the government to convict any of them. Unfortunately therefore, despite a thorough investigation, the government may be unable to come up with sufficient evidence to prove the crime."[21]

Bringing a bank fraud case to trial is analogous to directing a movie and presenting the facts in a dramatic fashion. The complex plot, consisting of 90 counts of fraud must be condensed into a few counts that the jury will be able to understand. Therefore, the prosecutors seek "interesting examples" of frauds that will keep the judge and jury awake. Consequently, they are seemingly more interested in frauds involving topless dancers than those involving mundane real estate loans. Prosecutors also prosecute frauds that are clearly illegal, such as misapplication of funds and making false statements, rather than those involving business judgements, which may be wrong but not necessarily illegal. Prosecutors may find securities violations and tax frauds associated with the bank frauds, so they may decide they have a stronger case by prosecuting securities violations rather than under banking laws violations. Finally, they have to convince the jury beyond a reasonable doubt that someone is guilty as charged.

The defense, which helped select 12 people least likely to understand the complex transactions, does its best to obfuscate the crime. Part of this includes convincing the jury that the accused, who is a pillar of the community, is of such fine character that he would never do anything wrong. It was his own bank, his own castle, and he should be able to do what he wants with its funds. Consider the jury in the "I-30" condominium trial that involved D. L. "Danny" Faulkner and six others who were accused of stealing $135 million from Empire Savings and Loan Association (Mesquite, Texas) and other savings and loans. (Empire S&L is examined extensively in Chapter 6). After several years of investigation, seven months of trial, 3,000 separate pieces of evidence, and 17 days of deliberating, the jury remained deadlocked 11 to 1 in favor of conviction on 88 counts, and the judge declared a mistrial. The jury consisted of 11 women and one man, who was the holdout. He said that being the only male he felt isolated. Moreover, he understood business and the women didn't. Previously, another male on the jury was dismissed because of an alleged social relationship with Faulkner's daughter.[22]

Defendants use influential character witnesses to dispel the notion that they are criminals. The fraud case against Thomas M. Gaubert, a Texas real estate developer, S&L owner, and Democratic fund-raiser, was lost after both a federal judge and the Texas state treasurer testified on his behalf. These testimonials concerning his reputable character and other evidence were considered by the jury that acquitted him. In another case, television personality Art Linkletter helped convince a federal judge to go easy on his son-in-law who had pleaded guilty to kickbacks on real estate loans. Linkletter's testimony helped to get the sentence reduced from seven years to six months.[23] However, such pleas from notables are no guarantee of being acquited. Lady Bird Johnson, Walter Cronkite, and Liz Carpenter asked for leniency for former United Bank (Texas) Chairman Ruben Johnson. According to Lady Bird, he was "a worthy citizen who practiced love and mercy;" and Walter Conkite said that "Locking him away would deprive the community of one who contributes much to it."[24] The judge and jury disagreed and Ruben Johnson received an eight-year sentence and was ordered to pay $4.5 million in restitution on his conviction for bank fraud.

Compromise Agreements. Sometimes the bank regulatory agencies enter into a formal agreement, or issue a cease and desist order that essentially tells the criminal who stole millions of dollars not to do it again and to figure out a way to repay the bank for its loss. However, if a bank robber who stole $3,000 is caught, the penalty may be 20 years. There is something inequitable about an insider who steals millions of dollars and gets a minimal sentence, and a bank robber who steals a few thousand dollars and gets 20 years. Some small equity, however, is granted because insiders may be tried under other laws as well (see Table 2-1).

Once a case has been prosecuted under Title 18 U.S.C. 656, which was enacted in its basic form in 1877, the *maximum* penalty was $5,000 and/or imprisonment for not more than five years. In 1989, Congress enacted the the Financial Institutions Reform, Recovery and Enforcement Act of 1989 that increased criminal and civil penalties for certain financial institutions offenses. For 18 U.S.C. 656, for example, the criminal penalty was increased to a fine of $1 million and 20 years imprisonment.

The civil penalty may be $5 million or more. The act also has provisions for criminal and civil forfeiture in connection with Title 18 U.S.Code offenses affecting financial institutions. Here are several examples of losses and penalties given insiders given before the passage of the 1989 Act[25]:

- Gary Lewellen embezzled $16.7 million from the First National Bank, Humbolt, Iowa. No money was recovered, no fine imposed, and no restitution was made, but he was sentenced to 20 years in prison. If he serves the full sentence, which is not likely, that works out to $835,000 per year.
- Harry Fagen embezzled $4.8 million from Guaranty Bond State Bank, Redwater, Texas. No money was recovered, no fine imposed, no restitution was made, and he was sentenced to eight years, which amounts to $600,000 per year.
- John Vergo, President of Midtown National Bank of Pueblo, Colorado, received two years for a $1.6 million loss to the bank ($800,000/year).
- Jake Butcher and C.H. Butcher, Sr. caused the failure of 11 banks in Tennessee and Kentucky and hundreds of millions of dollars of losses to the FDIC. Jake was sentenced to two concurrent 20-year sentences. C.H. Butcher and others were ordered to pay $19.3 million in damages for a plot to hide his wealth when the banking empire collapsed. Their banking activities are examined in Chapter 6.

A 1989 study of 44 criminal convictions of insiders of failed institutions revealed widely disparate sentences.[26] Burton M. Bongard, former president and director of Home State Savings Bank in Cincinnati, Ohio, was ordered to repay $114 million in restitution and $800,000 in court costs. He is serving six years in prison. Jeffery A. Levitt, former president of Old Court Savings, Baltimore, Maryland, ordered to pay $14.6 million in restitution, is serving a 30-year term in prison. These are the upper extremes. At the other end of the spectrum fines were as low as $50, and there were work release programs and community service in lieu of jail.

RICO. Recently, bank frauds have been tried under authority of the Racketeer Influenced Corrupt Organization Act of 1970 (RICO, Title 18, Section 1961 and other sections), which broadly interpreted includes most ongoing patterns of racketeering (criminal) activities.[27] The key features of this law are that the fraud must involve an organization (two or more people) and a pattern of criminal activities (two or more crimes). U.S. Attorneys must get permission from the Department of Justice before prosecuting a case under RICO. The logic behind this is that a U.S. Attorney in Jackson, Mississippi, may want to charge someone whom he considers a world class racketeer, but in the overall scheme of things does not qualify under RICO. The first bank related case tried under RICO involved Mario Renda, his wife, and the 14 corporations they controlled.[28] Renda and others were prosecuted for bank fraud. Under an agreement that settled the charges, the FDIC obtained $10.5 million in property for liquidation, which included funds from a Swiss bank account, an apartment building on Park Avenue in New York City, a shopping center in Hawaii, a 101-foot yacht, a 26-passenger executive jet, two Persian rugs, a silver inkwell, and a silver cigar box.[29] Mario Renda's escapades will be examined in Chapter 4.

The maximum sentence that can be given under RICO is 20 years and a $250,000 fine on each count. But the convicted felon can get a life sentence if the RICO offense is linked to another predicate crime that calls for a life sentence. Given the sentencing guidelines, however, it is not likely that a bank robber would get that harsh of a sentence.

Conviction of a criminal is not the end of the story. Some convictions are overturned on appeal. For example, an Ohio appeals court overturned the conviction of Marvin L. Warner. He was convicted on felony charges in connection with the failure of Home State Savings Bank in Cincinnati, Ohio, and

E.S.M. Government Securities in Ft. Lauderdale, Florida. Lawrence A. Kane, Jr., special prosecutor for the state of Ohio, said the court's decision was based "on technical and procedural issues, not the merits of the charges or the innocence of the defendants."[30] One of the grounds for reversal was that one of the jurors had been a depositor in a failed thrift. Other grounds concerned instructions to the jury and the application of certain statutes. One attorney said, "It's exciting and it's justice."

This chapter has shown that crime does pay. Major frauds against banks are profitable for perpetrators because they are relatively easy to commit, hard to detect, difficult to prove and prosecute, and the penalties can be minimal. Major frauds will continue as long as there are people, greed, and money in our system; and the likelihood of that changing is also minimal. The best solutions to the problem are early detection of fraud and its prevention. Early detection is the subject of the next chapter and prevention is covered later.

NOTES

1. "Bank Fraud: Bulletin of Fraud and Risk Management," Rolling Meadows, IL: Bank Administration Institute, Vol 4., No. 1, February 1989.
2. "Bank Fraud: Bulletin of Fraud and Risk Management," Rolling Meadows, IL: Bank Administration Institute, Vol 4., No. 2, March 1989.
3. "Central Bank Worker Sent $175,000 to Self," *Birmingham Post Hearald*, March 8, 1989.
4. This is based on various news articles by Tom Jennings, Herb Jordan, and others, that appeared in *The Mobile Press Register*, October 10, 1987 - February 11, 1988.
5. U.S. House, *Adequacy of Federal Efforts to Combat Fraud, Abuse and Misconduct in Federally Insured Financial Institutions*, Hearing before the Commerce, Consumer, and Monetary Affairs Subcommittee of the Committee on Government Operations, 100th Cong., 1st. Sess., November 19, 1987, p. 605.
6. U.S. House, *Fraud and Abuse by Insiders, Borrowers, and Appraisers in the California Thrift Industry*, Hearing before the Commerce, Consumer, and Monetary Affairs Subcommittee of the Committee on Government Operations, 100th Cong., 1st. Sess., June 13, 1987, prepared statement from John K. Van De Kamp, State of California, Attorney General, pp. 81-82.
7. U.S. General Accounting Office, *Failed Financial Institutions: Reasons, Costs, Remedies and Unresolved Issues*, Statement of Frederick D. Wolf, before the Committee on Banking, Finance and Urban Affairs, House of Representatives, January 13, 1989, (GAO/T-AFMD-89-1).
8. The operations of loan brokers and deposit brokers are explained in Chapter 4.
9. U.S. House, *Federal Response to Criminal Misconduct by Bank Officers, Directors, and Insiders, Part 2*, Hearings before a Subcommittee of the Committee

on Government Operations, 98th Cong., 1st. Sess.,
May 2 and 3, 1984, 30.

10. U.S. House, Hearing, November 19, 1987, p. 934.

11. Ada Focer, "Bank Insiders Who Bend to Greed,"
Bankers Monthly, September 1988, 16; Conversation
with Robert Serino, June 29, 1989.

12. U.S. House, Hearing, June 13, 1987, 370.

13. U.S. House, Hearing, June 13, 1987, 455; U.S. House,
*Combating Fraud, Abuse, and Misconduct in the Na-
tion's Financial Institutions: Current Federal Efforts are
Inadequate,* 72 Report by the Committee on Government Operations, House Report 100-1088, October
13, 1988, 95-96; U.S. House, Hearing, June 13, 1987,
320-323, 553-555; Lee Berton, "An S&L in California Dumped Peat Marwick for Congenial Auditor,"
The Wall Street Journal, May 9, 1989, A1, A11; Conversation with William J. Crawford, 5/17/89.

14. U.S. House, Hearing, June 13, 1987, 456; U.S. House,
House Report 100-1088, 149.

15. U.S. House, Hearing, June 13, 1987, 367, 427: Also
see U.S. House, *Federal Response to Criminal Misconduct and Insider Abuse in the Nation's Financial Institutions,* 57th Report by the Committee on Government Operations, House Report 98-1137, 98th Cong.,
2d Sess., October 4, 1984, 8.

16. *Ibid.,* 135, 114-115.

17. U.S. House, *Federal Response to Criminal Misconduct
by Bank Officers, Directors, and Insiders (Part 1),* Hearing before a Subcommittee of the Committee on
Government Operations, 98th Cong., 1st. Sess., June
28, 1983, 26.

18. U.S. House, Hearing, June 13, 1987, 456. Also see
471-472, 482-486, 516-518; U.S. House Report 100-
1088, 95-101.

19. U.S. House, House Report 100-1088, October 13,
1988, 84-85.

20. See U.S. Department of Justice, *United States Attorneys' Manual, Criminal Division, Title 9,* for details.

21. U.S. House, Hearings, Part 2, May 2 and 3, 1984, 31-32.

22. Allan Pusey, "I-30 Juror Tells Why He Voted for Acquittal," *Dallas Morning News*, October 26, 1989; "FBI: Jury Tampering May Be Cause of Mistrial," Bryan, Texas *Eagle*, Sept. 26, 1989; Dennis Cauchon, "FBI Probes Jury in Big Texas S&L Trial,"*USA Today*, Sept. 27, 1989; Holden Lewis, "Judge Rules Mistrial in I-30 Condo Case with Jury Deadlock," Jacksonville, TX, *Daily Progress*, Sept. 17, 1989.

23. Liz Galtney and Thomas Moore, "The Judicial Aftermath," *U.S. News & World Report*, January 23, 1989, 43; Kathleen Day, "S&L Fraud Seen Going Largely Unpunished," *The Washington Post*, February 4, 1989, A 14.

24. "Former Bank Chairman Sentenced to Prison," *Times*, Kerville, Texas, July 21, 1989.

25. U.S. House, Hearing, November 19, 1987, 1087-1088.

26. Pat Allen, "The Verdict's In: Crooks Are Out," *Savings Institutions*, March 1989, 36-42; Also see U.S. General Accounting Office, *Thrift Failures: Costly Failures Resulted From Regulatory Violations and Unsafe Practices*, GAO/AFMD-89-62, June 1989, 52-53.

27. Some states are passing RICO laws. See Fred Strasser, "Rico and the Man," *The National Law Journal*, March 20, 1989, 1,34; Richard S. Dalebout and K. Fred Skousen, "RICO and Accountants," *CPA Journal*, August, 1987, 83-87. RICO is Title 18, Sect. 1962.

28. *Federal Deposit Ins. Corp.* v. *Renda*, 692 F.Supp. 128 (D.Kan. 1988).

29. FHLBB and FDIC Joint News Release, PR-42-89 (2-28-89).

30. Martha Brannigan and Gregory Stricharchuk, "Court in Ohio Overturns Marvin Warner's Conviction," *The Wall Street Journal*, November 16, 1989, B8.

DETECTING FRAUD

PROFILES OF INSIDERS WHO ABUSE AND ROB BANKS

Insiders who abuse and rob banks tend to have certain patterns of behavior that collectively form a profile. The following case studies of abuse and fraud illustrate these profile patterns.

Edwin T. McBirney III. Edwin T. McBirney III was an insider who abused his position as chairman of Sunbelt Savings Association of Texas; but whether he crossed the line between insider abuse and criminal misconduct will be up to the courts to decide.[1] He used brokered deposits and high-risk loans to fuel Sunbelt's growth from $90 million in assets to $3.2 billion within four years. Sunbelt expanded geographically and had real estate and other interests in California, Florida, Georgia, and Illinois. McBirney and the owners of a network of S&Ls allegedly wrote $100 million loans on butcher paper, while they were eating in restaurants, and sold parts of the loans (participations) to each other to avoid restrictions on making loans greater than the net worth of their respective institutions. The originator of the loans earned from 5 percent to 10 percent ($5 million to $10 million) on the front end for making the deals. The more deals they made, the more money they earned. In 1985 and 1986, Sunbelt paid more than $12 million in cash dividends, over half of which went to McBirney. To some extent he shared the wealth with others. Sunbelt paid $1.3 million for Halloween,

43

Christmas, and theme parties. One party had a jungle theme, including a live elephant. Lion and antelope meat were served to the guests, and McBirney was dressed as a king. Another party theme was a Russian winter with waiters dressed as serfs. McBirney also flew important guests to Las Vegas on a borrowed Boeing 727 for weekends of gambling and entertainment, including sexual favors for some. Amid all this extravagance, Sunbelt set an industry record by losing $1.3 billion in the first three quarters of 1988. Shortly, thereafter, the government took control of it.

In a civil court action to recover $500 million and get $100 million in punitive damages, the FSLIC alleged that McBirney and other officers had mismanaged Sunbelt and had engaged in illegal activities. In addition, they had made loans to cover interest payments as well as the principal, thereby creating artificial profits to mislead bank examiners and others.

Donald A. Regar.   Donald A. Regar was known as an aggressive, dynamic individual who promoted the idea of a king-sized bank for himself and the community.[2] Regar was the president of Metropolitan Bank & Trust Company in Tampa, Florida, that had $261 million in assets when it failed due to mismanagement and fraud. The federal indictment of Donald Regar and Alan Z. Wolfson, the "wheeler-dealer mastermind" behind the fraud, charged that they overvalued the property pledged for loans and misrepresented the purposes of the loans. Wolfson had been convicted previously for defrauding another Florida bank. Nevertheless, through a private stock placement, he gained virtual control of the bank, and he became Regar's bad loan work-out specialist. Wolfson and his friends accounted for almost half of the bank's $160 million loan portfolio, which was backed with grossly inflated real estate appraisals. Metropolitan made unsound loans to Wolfson and others to invest in a Miami option traders' get-rich scheme that cost the bank millions in losses. Wolfson and Regar also conspired to borrow funds from the bank to purchase the bank's stock illegally.

The Wheeler-Dealers of Penn Square.   "The Swinger Who Broke Penn Square Bank" and "Wheeler-dealers lead to Penn Square Bank" are the titles of articles that appeared in *Fortune* and *The Tulsa Tribune* after the Penn Square Bank failed.[3] These titles provide clues about the personalities of William G. Patterson, the 33-year-old director and senior executive in charge of Penn Square's (Oklahoma) oil and gas division, and Bill P. (Beep, or Billy Paul) Jennings, Penn Square's chairman. Jennings was an unindicted coconspirator in the Four Seasons Nursing Centers of America stock scandal in the 1970s, although officially he was not guilty of anything. He was described as an cherubic, amiable, cigar-smoking entrepreneur. In an attempt to grow the bank rapidly, and faster than any other bank in Oklahoma, Jennings turned to Patterson.

Patterson, it was said, knew the oil business and was such a good salesman that he "could sell snowmobiles to Okies." He was not the stereotypical banker: He engaged in food fights in restaurants and drank beer from his boots. He occasionally appeared at the bank dressed in a Tyrolean outfit, a foam rubber lobster hat, or a Nazi helmet. Despite these personality quirks, Patterson was very good at selling energy participation loans to large banks, and sell he did.

When making energy loans, however, Patterson ignored engineering estimates that resulted in oil and gas reserves being grossly overstated. For example, Penn Square loaned Kenneth E. Tureaud, president of Sket Petroleum Co., $27 million that was secured by leases on reserves that the bank's petroleum engineers appraised at $7 million, and Tureaud appraised at $33 million. According to Jennings, their engineering estimates occasionally differed from the estimates of their counterparts at other banks, but the differences were usually resolved in favor of the upstream banks when they sold participations. In another deal (Professional Oil Management, Inc.), Tureaud got into trouble with the Securities and Exchange Commission for overvaluing oil and gas property, diverting proceeds from the sale of securities for purposes other than drilling, failing to escrow drilling funds, and paying secret fees and commissions.

Under Patterson's reign, the bank's assets grew from $30 to $525 million in a six-year period, and the loan portfolio exceeded $2.5 billion. Part of the growth was financed by Mario Renda, a money broker who was later convicted of fraud in connection with other banks. He was sued for fraud in connection with selling Penn Square's CDs to credit unions, but he won that case. The actions of Mario Renda and some of his associates will be examined in Chapter 4.

To get around the legal lending limits to one customer, which was about $3.5 million, Penn Square originated large loans in excess of that amount, sold 80 percent or more of them to other banks, and kept the remainder. In doing so, they earned 0.5 percent to 1 percent origination fees when the loans were sold. The fees were not tied to the long-term performance of the loans. Thus, the front-end fees served as an incentive to sell more loans without regard to quality.

Penn Square had loaned oilman Carl W. Swan large sums to wildcat drill for oil. Swan was cochairman of Continental Drilling Company and a director of the bank. He was also Jennings' partner in deals outside of the bank. When Swan hit too many dry holes, the scheme to grow Penn Square rapidly by selling energy loan participations started to fall apart. For awhile, the bank shuffled the bad loans around, trying to hide them from examiners, but it didn't work, and the bank failed.

There are interesting similarities between the failure of Metropolitan Bank of Tampa and Penn Square Bank of Oklahoma City.[4]

- Both were suburban banks.
- Both were the fourth largest banks in their respective cities.
- Both had highly concentrated loan portfolios—energy for Penn Square and real estate for Metropolitan—and both were criticized for being overextended in those areas.

- Both had about 28,000 accounts.
- Both experienced phenomenal growth.
- Management caused the failure of both.
- Wolfson was involved directly with the failure of Metropolitan.
- Metropolitan was linked indirectly to Penn Square.[5]

A sad ending to the Penn Square failure is that none of the principals involved went to jail because the government failed to prove Patterson had intended to defraud the bank.[6] In short, it was a complex financial crime that baffled the jury.

Orrin Shaid, Jr. Orrin Shaid, Jr., a 300-pound flamboyant Texan was paroled after serving a five-year sentence for bank fraud at the Chireno State Bank (Texas), where he was the chairman. While on parole, he took control of the Ranchlander National Bank in Melvin, Texas. Not wanting to use his name in the deal, he claimed to be a financial consultant for Lynn Carruth Maree, a tall, attractive blond. Acting in her behalf, he purchased the troubled Ranchlander Bank for $186,000, although her annual salary as a secretary was $7,200. Shaid financed the deal by purchasing two $1,000 CDs from Ranchlander. He altered the certificates to show a value of $100,000 each and used the bogus CDs as collateral for a $200,000 loan from Chandler State Bank. The alterations took place in front of Jean Moon, a former waitress and the next president of Ranchlander. As president, Moon made fictitious loans and cattle loans with nonexistent collateral. Shaid used the same CD alteration scheme to purchase two Rolls Royce automobiles, two airplanes, and a yacht. He also diverted $6 million to the Cayman Islands where he eventually intended to escape, and acquired control of First State Bank, Wells, Texas, by paying a $50,000 kickback to obtain a fraudulent loan at that bank to finance its purchase.

When Shaid told Moon to destroy Ranchlander's records, she thought that he was going to kill her, and she went to the FBI. His pyramid crumbled when FBI agents arrested him one month before the end of his parole from the previous conviction.[7] He was convicted of mail fraud and was sentenced to 35 years in prison while Moon planned to go back to work as a waitress in a truck stop.

Ernest "Pug" Vickers.   Ernest "Pug" Vickers committed fraud.[8] After serving as a pilot in World War II, Pug became an automobile dealer and the mayor of Huntingdon, Tennessee. He borrowed money to buy an 80 percent controlling interest in the Carroll County Bank of Huntingdon, which had about $8 million in assets. Pug installed his own people to run the bank, and they ran it into the ground. When Pug faced serious financial problems, he stole money from the bank using nominee loans and continuing overdrafts. He also used his friends, including an auto mechanic at his dealership, to sign more than $500,000 in personal notes from the bank and give the proceeds to him with the assurance that he would repay the loans. When neither Pug nor his friends were able to pay back the loans, the bank failed.

A Typical Profile.   Keeping these cases in mind, a better understanding of a typical profile of a modern bank robber can be gained. "The `typical' insider bank thief . . . is a male officer, director, or majority stockholder of a commercial bank, who either commits his crimes alone or in association with a few close associates or bank employees. He is often an outgoing, flamboyant businessman who runs his bank as if it were a sole proprietorship, such as a real estate office or automobile dealership. He spends, borrows, and lends money freely, often single-handedly exercising control over the bank. The criminal schemes he uses may be simple or complex, depending upon his own ingenuity, but they usually involve a continuing series of related transactions that extend over a substantial period of time. The activities he engages in, while hidden from public view, are usually so abusive and involve such large sums of money that any reasonably alert board of directors should discern what is really going on inside the bank. Insider abuse and fraud cannot flourish in a vacuum."[9]

Let's elaborate on the last point about fraud not operating in a vacuum. The Comptroller of the Currency found that policies, planning, and management were problems in 89 percent of the failed national banks they examined.[10] Poor management led to poor asset quality, which caused the failures. The boards of directors at the failed banks took one of two courses of action. First, they were uninformed, had nonexistent or poorly followed loan policies and inadequate systems for compliance with policies and laws. And second, they were overly aggressive, had liberal lending policies (that is, making 10-year loans on equipment that had a life expectancy of five years), and fostered excessive loan growth. The latter policies went hand-in-hand with making loans that were not supported by current financial statements of the borrower, poor collateral documentation, and overlending. In either case, the directors being uninformed or being overly aggressive contributed to the bank failures.

Most of the 162 national banks that failed were small; 79 percent had assets of less than $50 million, and 64 percent had assets of less than $30 million. A surprise finding of the study was that a disproportionately large number of recently chartered banks had failed. Small banks have fewer stockholders than large ones. Therefore, it is easier for a criminal to install a friendly board of directors in a small bank that has a few passive stockholders than it is in a large bank that has actively traded stock and is closely watched by analysts and investors. However, the stockholders and directors of large banks can be duped too. Consider Jake Butcher's United American Bank in Knoxville, Tennessee, which had $838 million in assets when it failed. A congressional investigation of that bank failure found "The UAB board of directors was, by every measure, a weak board that at no time provided an independent and critical review of bank management's actions."[11] Butcher minimized his contact with the board and the information that they received about the bank's condition. Basically, the board "rubber stamped" whatever Butcher wanted to do. More will be said about Butcher's and the directors' responsibilities in Chapters 6 and 7.

LOOKING FOR FRAUD AND ABUSES

Most major frauds and insider abuse involve more than one party and do not occur overnight. They consist of a series of financial transactions over an extended period of time. As they develop, clues can emerge about their existence. These clues, called *red flags*, are warning signs that a further investigation is warranted. But unless someone observes the clues, and then does something about them, the fraud and abuse continue. This was the case for Butcher's United American Bank in Knoxville, Tennessee. Federal bank regulators knew that the bank had engaged in unsafe, unsound, and possibly unlawful activities for more than six years before it failed, but they failed to act decisively to eliminate the abusive practices until it was too late. Substantial time lags also occurred before the federal bank regulators took action at Franklin National Bank, Penn Square, and Empire Savings and Loan.[12]

Reducing the Time Lag.   To reduce the time lag between the recognition of fraud and abuse and the actions necessary to correct them, regulatory agencies, academicians, and consulting firms are trying to develop systems to predict which banks may fail and to thwart fraud. For example, efforts are under way at regulatory agencies to detect red flags by using statistical techniques to analyze financial statements that the banks are required to submit to them on a regular basis. David Cates, a financial analyst who had analyzed the data for Empire Savings and Loan before it failed, observed that it was (1) growing too fast to maintain sound credit administration, especially because many of its loans were of a commercial character. (2) The growth was heavily funded by jumbo CDs ($100,000 or more). (3) And the growth was so rapid that it could not occur within its natural market. Cates went on to say that Empires' financial performance "appeared to us so widely irregular—and so reminiscent of prefailure performance at Penn Square, Midland, Abilene, etc.—that I promptly dubbed Empire `the Penn Square of the thrift industry.'"[13]

Although Cates was able to predict the failure of Empire, a recent study dealing with the statistical analysis of S&L failures concluded that the financial characteristics associated with failures are not constant over time.[14] Variables that were significant predictors in some studies were not significant predictors in others. The record high interest rates and negative spreads that caused bank failures in the early 1982s affected balance sheet data differently than the sophisticated, fraud-related failures. Therefore, such models can be of limited value in detecting failures in general, as well as failures associated with fraud. Empire Savings and Loan, which is examined in Chapter 5, gave the illusion of profitability until the day before its failure. Nevertheless, the OCC believes that off-site monitoring of a bank's balance sheet changes may lead to some early detection of problems.[15] Such balance sheet changes include:

- Increased past-due loans.
- Loan growth.
- Increased volatile liability dependence.
- Change in loan mix.
- Change in investment portfolio.
- Increase in other real estate owned.

Some additional early indicators of vulnerable or corrupt institutions are[16]:

- A rapid growth of deposits.
- Recent changes of control.
- Making out-of-territory loans.
- An absence of outside audits.

In terms of deterrents, bank regulators are also trying to develop an artificial intelligence (AI) computer program for use by bank examiners. The AI program will give bank examiners working in banks the insights of experienced examiners in the examination process. The FDIC has proposed requiring insured banks that are anticipating rapid growth of nine percent or more in three months to give the agency advanced notice. And the Government Accounting Office (GAO) has proposed independent audits. Finally, bank examiners and accountants should also be aware of the possibility of fraud.

Conducting an Audit with a Possibility of Fraud.   Conducting an audit while being aware of the possibility of fraud is not the same thing as doing one with the intent of looking for fraud. If the cost of a regular audit is $100,000, the cost of one to detect fraud may be triple that amount. In addition to cost, audit problems arise when there are multiple, independent institutions involved in transactions. Auditors may not be able to track certain transactions in others institutions. Finally, the Right to Privacy Act stands as a barrier to such audits.

The fact that an audit is conducted by an independent certified public accountant (CPA) does not guarantee the quality of the audit or the auditor's ability to detect fraud. The GAO reviewed the quality of audit reports performed by CPAs on 11 S&Ls before they failed.[17] According to the audit reports, which ranged from 5 months to 17 months before failure, the S&Ls had a combined net worth of $44 million. When they failed they had a combined negative worth of $1.5 billion. (More is said about auditing in Chapter 8.)

Profits and net worth can be overstated in several ways. One way is for an S&L to make a 100 percent loan (no down payment) on acquisition, development, and land loans (ADL) that cover all of the points, fees, and the first few years interest (retained as interest reserve), plus an "equity kicker" (a share of the profits of the project). Because ADLs are risky, they carry high interest rates. They are frequently made on a "without recourse" basis, which means that there is no personal guarantee by the borrower; and they may only require interest payments to be made in the early years. Because of the high interest rates and interest reserves, the S&L gives the appearance of being profitable in the first few years, although the reserve is being drawn down as interest income. Moreover, the loans cannot become delinquent until the reserve is exhausted. Before that occurs, the loan can be sold. By using such devices,

S&Ls appear to be profitable. In fact, Empire Savings and Loan in Mesquite, Texas, was one of the most profitable thrifts in the country until it failed.[18]

According to the GAO study, the CPAs did inadequate audits on evaluating loan collectability and did inadequate reporting on regulatory compliance and internal controls. For example, in one audit a CPA firm was aware of a $30 million past-due loan that was guaranteed by two principal sharehold- ers, but there was little evidence in their working papers that the S&L had evaluated the collectability of that loan. In another audit, the working papers did not indicate that $625 million in loans had been restructured during the period covered by the audit. Another CPA firm did not disclose that the S&L had several hundred million worth of loans to the principal share- holders, secured by property in a limited geographic area. Finally, in two cases, CPAs did not point out that S&Ls had materially misstated their income. In fact, one of the S&Ls actually lost four times as much as it had reported.

Why Don't Employees Say Something?   One may wonder why employees who have knowledge of insider abuse or criminal misconduct don't do anything about it. When this question was asked to groups of bank employees, the answer was that they believed that such reports would cost them their jobs. Therefore, they were unwilling to report fraud and abuse to their superiors, to officers and directors, or to the FBI. Job security was more important to them than honesty and justice, and this type of defensive posture is common in most organi- zations. According to Chris Argyris, an expert in organiza- tional behavior, such "defensive routines are powerful and omnipresent," and they can have a counterproductive impact on the organization.[19] To change such defensive behavior re- quires changes in the culture of the organizations, as well as changes in our general culture. Since neither of these changes is likely to occur to a great degree in the short term, efforts to encourage "whistle-blowing" will probably not meet with any great success.[20]

Fast Frauds. Most frauds take time to develop, which gives examiners, auditors, and others time to discover them. However, some frauds occur virtually overnight, making it difficult to detect and deter them. For example, some individuals seek out small, weak banks that are in danger of failing. Specifically, these individuals want to acquire banks that are financed with loans secured by the bank's stock. Subsequently, the group goes to the correspondent bank that has loaned the funds, and offers to buy the stock at 20 to 50 cents on the dollar. The correspondent is glad to make the sale because if the bank fails, it gets nothing. Once they have control of the bank, the group installs their own officers and directors. Money brokers are used to pump up deposits. Then fraudulent loans are made, backed by debentures of worthless corporations they control, falsified personal financial statements, and zero-coupon Treasury bonds. Once this is done, the newly acquired bank's funds are wired to the group's accounts in other banks located elsewhere. Consequently, the withdrawal of funds could result in the newly acquired bank's failure in a very short time frame.[21] In one case, an alert cashier notified an OCC examiner that something was wrong. The OCC visited the bank that same day, traced the funds, and blocked the accounts.

RED FLAGS

In an effort to detect bank fraud and insider abuse at an early stage, the Federal Deposit Insurance Corporation published a list of red flags (warning signs) in its *Manual of Examination Policies (Appendix A)* (1987) to be used by their bank examiners. The following red flags were taken verbatim from the FDIC's manual. They are listed for specific areas that represent potential problems. Keep in mind that red flags are indicators for possible cause for concern. The manual, however, is careful to point out that generic terms widely used in law, such as "fraud," have a central meaning that must be applied to constantly changing factual circumstances. It goes on to say that many violations of laws and regulations are subject to legal interpretation.[22] Therefore, the presence of red flags does not mean that fraud or insider abuse is present. The subject areas covered by the red flags include:

- Linked financing and brokered transactions.
- Loan participations.
- Secured lending—real estate and other type of collateral.
- Insider transactions.
- Credit card and electronic funds transfer.
- Wire transfers.
- Offshore transactions.
- Third-party obligations.
- Lending to buy tax shelter investments.
- Money laundering.
- Corporate culture ethics.
- Miscellaneous.

The red flags for linked financing and brokered deposits are presented here. The red flags for the other are subject areas presented in Appendix A. Red flags for linked financing and brokered transactions include:

1. Out-of-territory lending.
2. Loan production used as a basis for officer bonuses.
3. Evidence of unsolicited attempts to buy or recapitalize the bank coupled with evidence of a request for large loans at or about the same time by persons previously unknown to the bank. Promise of large dollar deposits may also be involved.
4. Promise of large-dollar deposits in consideration for favorable treatment on loan requests. (Deposits are not pledged as collateral for the loans.)
5. Brokered deposits transactions where the broker's fees are paid from the proceeds of related loans.
6. Serious consideration by a bank of a loan request where the bank would have to obtain brokered deposits to be able to fund the loan.

7. Solicitations by persons who purportedly have access to multimillions of dollars from confidential sources that are readily available for loans and or deposits in U.S. financial institutions. Rates and terms quoted are usually more favorable than funds available through normal sources. A substantial fee may be requested in advance or the solicitor may suggest that the fee be paid at closing but demand compensation for expenses, often exceeding $50,000.
8. Prepayment of interest on deposit accounts where such deposit accounts are used as collateral for loans.

Some additional red flags that apply to white-collar crime in general that are also applicable to banks include[23]:

- Employees exceeding their scope of responsibilties.
- Failure to rescreen employees.
- Marked changes in the life-style of employees.
- Open-ended contracts with suppliers.
- Outside business interest of employees.
- Personal financial pressures of employees.
- Poor money management by employees.
- Unexplained rising costs or declining revenues.
- Unusual reductions in, or loss of, a regular customer's business.

NOTES

1. Thomas Moore, "The Bust of '89," *U.S. News & World Report*, January 23, 1989, 36–43; Liz Galtney and Thomas Moore, "The Judicial Aftermath," *U.S. News and World Report*, January 23, 1989, 43; Kathleen Day, "S&L Fraud Seen Going Largely Unpunished," *The Washington Post*, February 4, 1989, A1, A15; McBirney is also mentioned in Chapter 4 in connection with stock loans at Vernon S&L.

2. U.S. House, *Federal Response to Criminal Misconduct by Bank Officers, Directors, and Insiders, Part 1*, Hearing before a subcommittee of the Committee on Government Operations, 98th Cong., 1st. Sess., House Report 98–1137, 69–75; Oct 4, 1984 466–482; U.S. House, *Federal Response to Criminal Misconduct by Bank Officers, Directors, and Insiders, Part 2*, Hearings before a Subcommittee on Government Operations, 98th Cong., 2d. Sess., May 2 and 3, 1984, 1904–1945.

3. Roy Rowan, "The Swinger Who Broke Penn Square Bank," *Fortune*, August 23, 1982, 122–126; Hearings, Part 2, 2027-2029; also see U.S. House, *Federal Supervision and Failure of the Penn Square Bank, Oklahoma City, Okla.*, Hearing before a Subcommittee of the Committee on Government Operation, 97th Cong., 2d. Sess., July 16, 1982, 457–460.

4. *Ibid.*, 2025.

5. Wolfson was an investor in Chilcott Portfolio Management, Inc., which was involved in commodities fraud in Colorado. Chilcott had various loans and notes from Penn Square. Wolfson also tried to borrow from Penn Square but was denied a loan. Wolfson also was linked to Tureaud, who was a large borrower from Penn Square. *Ibid.*, 2028–2029.

6. Mark Singer, *Funny Money*, New York: Alfred A. Knopf, 1985. See Chapter 21 for a discussion of the Patterson trial.

7. U.S. House, Hearings, Part 2, 1954–1962; U.S. House, *Federal Response to Criminal Misconduct and Insider Abuse in the Nation's Financial Institutions*, 57th Report by the Committee on Government Operations, House Report 98–1137, 98th Cong., 2d Sess., October 4, 1984. 36-37, 45.

8. U.S. House, House Report 98-1137, 25; U.S. House, Hearings, Part 2, 2032.

9. U.S. House, House Report 98-1137, 26.

10. *Bank Failure: An Evaluation of the Factors Contributing to the Failure of National Banks*, Washington: Comptroller of the Currency, June 1988; Susan F. Krause, Fred C. Graham, and James E. Horner, "An Evaluation of the Factors Contributing to the Failures of National Banks," presented at the Conference on Bank Structure and Competition, Federal Reserve Bank of Chicago, May 13, 1988; Fred C. Graham and James E. Horner, Bank Failure: An Evaluation of the Factors Contributing to the Failure of National Banks, appears in *The Financial Services Industry in the Year 2000: Risk and Efficiency*, Proceedings of a Conference on Bank Structure and Competition, Federal Reserve Bank of Chicago, May 11-13, 1988, 405-435. There are some differences in the various versions of this study as different phases of it were released. An early draft of this study was dated January 1988.

11. U.S. House, *Federal Supervision and Failure of United American Bank (Knoxville, Tenn.)*, Hearing before the Commerce, Consumer, and Monetary Affairs Subcommittee of the Committee on Government Operation, 98th Cong., 1st. Sess., November 18, 1983, 45.

12. U.S. House, *Federal Supervision and Failure of United American Bank in Knoxville, Tenn., and Affiliated Banks*, 23rd Report by the Committee on Government Operations, House Report 98-573, 98th Cong., 1st.,

Sess., November 18, 1983, 16-29; U.S. House, *Federal Home Loan Bank Board Supervision and Failure of Empire Savings and Loan Association of Mesquite Tex.*, Report by the Committee on Government Operations, House Report 98-953, 98th Cong., 2d Sess., August 6, 1984, 9.

13. U.S. House, House Report 98-953, 38.
14. Patricia M. Rudolph and Bassam Hamdan, "An Analysis of Post-Deregulation Savings-and-Loan Failures," *AREUEA Journal*, Vol. 16, No. 1, Spring 1988, 17-33; Also see: "Warning Lights for Bank Soundness: Special Issue on Commercial Bank Surveillance," *Economic Review*, Federal Reserve Bank of Atlanta, November 1983; Booth, David E., Perzaiz Alam, Sharif N. Ankam, and Barbara Osyk, "A Robust Multivariate Procedure for the Identification of Problem Savings and Loan Associations," *Decision Sciences*, Vol. 20, 320-333.
15. Robert L. Clarke, Comptroller of the Currency, Response to the Honorable Doug Barnard, Jr. concerning U.S. House Report on Combating Fraud, March 10, 1989, Major Findings, page 5.
16. William F. Weld, Assistant Attorney General, Criminal Division, U.S. Department of Justice, Remarks before The Banking Law Institute, 4th Annual Bank and Savings and Loan Supervision, Enforcement and Compliance Conference, Washington, D.C., September 21, 1987.
17. U.S. General Accounting Office, *CPA Audit Quality: Failures of CPA Audits to Identify and Report Significant Savings and Loan Problems*, GAO/AFMD-89-45, February 1989. U.S. General Accounting Office, "The Need to Improve Auditing in the Savings and Loan Industry," Statement of Frederick D. Wolf before the Committee on Banking, Finance and Urban Affairs, House of Representatives, GAO/T-AFMD-89-2, February 21, 1989.

18. William K. Black and William L. Robertson, "Statement of the Federal Home Loan Bank, before the Subcommittee on Financial Institutions, Supervision, Regulation, and Insurance of the Committee on Banking, Finance, and Urban Affairs, House of Representatives, 100th Cong., June 9, 1987.

19. Chris Argyris, *Strategy, Change and Defensive Routines*, Boston: Pitman Publishing Inc., 1985, 34.

20. Janet P. Near, "Whistle-Blowing: Encourage It!" *Business Horizons*, January/February 1989, 2-6.

21. OCC Advisory, November 21, 1988.

22. U.S. House, Hearings, Part 2, 1384. This section covers administrative actions by the FDIC.

23. Joseph T. Wells, "Red Flags: The Key to Reducing White-Collar Crime," *Corporate Accounting*, Spring 1987, 51-53; Robert J. Lindquist and James E. Baskerville, "To Catch a Thief," *World*, July-August 1985, 32-35.

4 CASE STUDIES OF CRIMES BY OUTSIDERS—PART 1

INTRODUCTION

This is the first of two chapters dealing with crime by outsiders. It examines the patterns of deception by outsiders who prey on financial institutions throughout the country. The same groups of outsiders are involved in crimes nationwide. Usually, the crimes are committed by both national and international networks of criminals and organized crime figures who find flaws in our financial institutions and then exploit those flaws which, in turn, sometimes results in bank failures. In most cases, it is not the familiar names of organized crime, such as La Cosa Nostra, Mafia, Triad, "the mob," or drug dealers, who cause the failures. These groups, according to the President's Commission on Organized Crime, are criminals bound together by enthnicity and kinship and united in their drive for power and profits. They, in addition, maintain their power through protectors, including financial institutions, lawyers, politicians, and others.[1]

Money Laundering. There is no doubt that organized crime is connected with some banks and that these connections have existed for many years. This is partly because organized crime uses banks to launder their funds and for other purposes. Laundering refers to the process of concealing the existence or sources of funds to make them appear legitimate. About $100 billion or more in illegal money from drugs is laundered each year through the international banking system.[2] For example, People's Bank of Covington, Kentucky, laundered funds for Luis Pinto, a Columbian citizen, who was involved in a cocaine ring. Pinto made large cash deposits of about $300,000 and withdrew numerous bank checks and cashiers checks in amounts small enough to avoid reporting requirements under the Bank Secrecy Act. Therefore, the bank never had to report Pinto's transactions.[3] In 1988, the Bank Secrecy Act was amended by the Bank Records and Foreign Transaction Act, which changed the reporting requirements for depository insitutions. Now, Currency Transaction Reports (CTRs) are required on cash transactions of $10,000 or more and on certain other transactions. The CTRs must be filed with the Internal Revenue Service. Failure to make CTR reports can result in fines up to $10,000 per day for each violation and prison terms of up to 20 years. The largest fine to date was $4,750,000 at Bank of America.

Outside Foreign Conspiracy. There is the tendency for the public to think of bank crimes in terms of a sinister foreign conspiracy. This is because the media have convinced the public that every crime committed by two or more people who eat in a pizza parlor and drink Chianti is Mafia related. However, there is no compelling evidence that a "conspiracy" by organized crime exists to systematically steal from banks or to cause their failure.[4] On the other hand, if they had an opportunity to make a profit from a quick scam on a bank, they would probably do it. Finally, not all outsiders who commit bank crimes are connected with the crime network. Some are ordinary and extraordinary individuals who have figured out a way to steal from the system.

Similarly, there are international networks at work stealing from banks and businesses. In Nigeria, for example, it is rumored that there are training schools that teach foreign nationals how to commit various small-scale bank frauds involving checks and credit cards.[5] (An example of a Nigerian flim-flam operation is presented in the next chapter.)

Our primary concern, however, is with individual crooks who know each other, or who know how to contact each other when an opportunity arises to rape a bank financially. To some extent, there is "guilt by association" between some of these criminals and organized crime. However, the guilt by association gives the misleading impression that there is a closer connection between bank failures and organized crime than may actually exist.

The Distance Factor. Another difference concerning crimes by outsiders is that the institutions they exploit may be thousands of miles apart and seemingly unrelated, making it difficult to uncover the link between the various crimes. Regarding this connection, this chapter focuses on Mario Renda and some of his associates, who were involved in varying degrees in bank frauds and bank failures in Florida, Kansas, New York, Wyoming, and elsewhere. Renda and his associates, however, are by no means unique in their geographic dispersion of activities. For example, Frank Domingues and Jack Bona were real estate developers from California who made fraudulent loans from a number of California and Texas S&Ls by pledging properties with overinflated values as collateral.[6] These loans contributed directly to the failure of the San Marino S&L, San Marino, California. Participations in the fraudulent loans contributed to the financial distress of S&Ls in Florida, Massachusetts, Oregon, Pennsylvania, and elsewhere. Domingues and Bona were also under criminal investigations in connection with their takeover of South Bay S&L, Newport Beach, California, which also failed. Domingues also borrowed $815,000 from Vernon S&L (which is examined in the next chapter) to buy stock in South Bay S&L. He was also a part owner of San Diego National Bank and a co-owner of the Atlantic City Dunes Hotel and Casino.

The Sequence of Events. Some of the same individuals are involved with institutions located throughout the United States because of the way they find their prey. Hypothetically, the sequence of events may begin with a corrupt loan broker who wants to find a bank to take loans on a $5 million real estate project that is probably (or definitely) going to be a bad loan. Loan brokers may be either individuals or firms who sell loans to banks; most are honest, but here we are interested in the crooked ones.

The ideal bank to buy a bad loan is a small bank in trouble because of inadequate capital, or for some other reason. It needs loans to grow. To find weak banks, loan brokers use bank financial data that are published in *Polk's Bank Directory* and in other sources. A list of weak banks is selected, and the broker calls each of them, talking to senior officers and directors to learn more about the bank and to determine what kind of loans they can sell to that bank. Once the bank has been selected, the loan broker explains that he has certain loans that he is willing to place with that bank. Moreover, he will also arrange for the "loan package" to include funds—brokered deposits—to finance the loans. The acquisition of loans conditioned on the purchase of brokered deposits is commonly called *linked financing*. The loans may be for 10 years or longer, while the deposits may only be in the bank 90 days or less. At this point, the loan broker is counting on the cooperation of the banker who is grasping at straws to keep his bank from failing. The banker sees an infusion of funds, fees, and loans. To get the loans and funds, some bankers may be willing to overlook correct underwriting procedures and ignore sound controls that are in place.

To avoid the appearance of out-of-territory loans, local escrows and nominees may be used. If the bankers used common sense, they probably would not make such loans. However, they are under pressure to improve the performance of their bank. The loan brokers and crooks require the voluntary cooperation of some insiders and the unwitting help of others to close their deals. The loan brokers believe that bankers in this position are generally dumb, have ego problems, and are greedy. The fact that many bankers have fallen for such deals suggests that the brokers are correct in their assessment. When the deal is closed, the loan broker gets paid by the borrower, gets paid a finder's fee from the deposit broker, and then he is no longer associated with the deal, leaving the bank holding loans that will go bad and that are financed with short-term brokered deposits. A weak bank, bad long-term loans, and hot money (short-term deposits) are the essential ingredients for failure. Even when regulators suspect something is wrong, there may be little they can do about it until it is too late to save the bank.

THE ESCAPADES OF MARIO RENDA

Mario Renda, president and founder of First United Fund, Ltd., Garden City, New York, was a major player in various bank failures and frauds.[7] First United Fund was a holding company engaged in money brokerage, investments in government securities, real estate lending, discount brokerage, and other activities.

Renda—First United Fund—was a source of brokered deposits for the failed Penn Square bank (described in Chapter 3), for the failed Empire Savings and Loan and Mainland Savings (described in Chapter 6), for the failed San Marino S&L (mentioned at the beginning of this chapter), and for failed banks in Kansas, Maryland, and Florida. He was also involved in one of the nation's largest pension fund scams; therefore, we will examine several of his escapades and those of his associates.

Deposit Broker. First United Fund was one of the five most active deposit brokers, dealing with more than 1,000 financial institutions. A *deposit broker* is defined as "any person or entity engaged in the business of placing deposits for others, or in placing funds in accounts to be sold to others, an agent or trustee who established a deposit or member account in connection with an agreement with the institution to use the proceeds in the account to fund a prearranged loan."[8] This definition, however, excludes banks.

First United Fund brokered investments in the following manner. Employees, officers, and agents of First United Fund solicited banks and other financial institutions and negotiated rates of interest and related terms on deposits. Then First United, or its agents, contacted its clients, advised them of the terms, and arranged for the investments to be made. When the deal was closed, First United demanded payment from the banks issuing the CDs. For example, suppose a credit union wanted to invest $5 million in CDs. The credit union would then wire the funds to a deposit broker who would then wire it in fully insured $100,000 blocks to the 50 banks paying the highest rates. Some brokers often invest more than $100,000 in banks and then subdivide the funds into amounts that provide full insurance coverage. Other brokers invest more than $100,000 and accept the risk of uninsured deposits. CDs of $100,000 or more with maturities in excess of one year are called *long-term jumbo CDs.*

Deposit brokers get better rates than individual depositors because of the large amounts of money they control. The credit union in the previous example gets insured deposits and the deposit broker earns up to $50,000 in commissions for the transaction. Deposit brokers' commissions usually range from 25 to 100 basis points, or $250 to $1,000 for each $100,000 of funds placed. In 1983, it is estimated that First United Fund placed over $2.5 billion in bank certificates of deposit and earned more than $3.2 million.

Deposit brokers may work with loan brokers to find target banks, or they may select their own targets. One way in which First United allegedly defrauded clients was with their so-called special deal. One of the brokers selected a target bank to make a loan. The broker then solicited customers to invest in that bank by misrepresenting the rate of interest that they would receive. First United would procure the loan and make up the difference in interest rates paid by the bank and what was promised the investor with funds from the loan.[9]

In a 1985 survey by the FDIC of the largest suppliers of fully insured deposits to *troubled* insured banks, Merrill Lynch ranked first with $771.3 million and First United Fund ranked 13th with $28.1 million.[10] The survey did not include institutions that were financially sound.

There is nothing illegal about brokered deposits. They serve a function in financial markets of facilitating the flow of capital. However, abuses can occur and Renda and associates excelled in this area. Similarly, there is nothing illegal about linked financing, but it too can lead to abuses that can affect the soundness of a bank, as illustrated by Indian Springs Bank. Renda's First United Fund engaged in linked financing with 17 other banks, 14 of which ultimately failed. The combined deposits for all the banks was over $2 billion. Many, but not all, linked financing deals are associated with real estate. For example, First Federal Savings and Loan Association of Beloit, Kansas, used brokered deposits to invest $5.6 million in a Hungarian movie called "Predator," which was about a rock band being chased by a man-eating bear. The movie was never finished and the loan went into default. Clifford R. Roth, esquire, an officer of First Federal Savings and Loan, was also the former general counsel at Indian Springs Bank.

LINKED FINANCING: THE CASE OF INDIAN SPRINGS BANK

Indian Springs Bank was a small, one-office bank located between Wig City and Athlete's Foot on the lower level of a shopping center in Kansas City, Kansas. William Lemaster, president of the bank, wanted it to be a big bank. He hired Anthony R. Russo as a bank officer to help the bank grow. Russo, a former prominent criminal lawyer who represented reputed mobsters, was a convicted felon who had served a 16-month prison term in Leavenworth Penitentiary for conspiracy to bribe and for promoting prostitution. Within an eight-month period after being hired by the bank, Russo was promoted from vice president to executive vice president. Because Russo was a convicted felon, the bank required FDIC approval for his employment. The FDIC gave its approval, but restricted Russo's

Russo's activities to new business development. The new business that he generated included accounts and loans to reputed organized crime figures in Kansas City and Chicago. When a number of these loans failed, the FDIC put pressure on Lemaster to get rid of Russo. One such loan was for $300,000 and made to Carmen Civella, son of Kansas City mob leader Carl Civella. To get around the FDIC, Russo was elected chairman of Indian Springs' holding company. In that position he was not an employee of a federally insured institution and was outside the FDIC's jurisdiction.[11]

While on vacation in Hawaii, Russo met real estate developers Franklin Winkler and Sam Daily. Mario Renda had a social and business relationship with Winkler and Daily in First United Management Co. Ltd. First United Management's articles listed Renda as president, Winkler as executive vice president, and Daily as executive vice president and secretary. The company received $25,000 in management fees for managing the Hawaiian real estate development partnerships. Renda was also partners with Winkler and Daily in First United Partners Four, another real estate partnership.

Winkler and Daily arranged a linked financing deal between their real estate development in Hawaii, First United Fund, and Indian Springs Bank. Brokered deposits from First United Fund were the key to the deal. In the early 1980s, Indian Springs' assets grew from about $6 million to more than $50 million. The growth was financed largely by brokered deposits. When the bank did not roll over maturing CDs, its assets shrank to $27 million in 1984—the same year it was closed. The bank's deposits included $9.3 million in brokered deposits, of which First United Fund provided about $6 million.

Indian Springs Bank agreed to accept $6 million in brokered deposits from Renda's First United Fund if certain loans were made on favorable terms in connection with the Hawaiian real estate development. The commissions on the brokered deposits were paid to First United Fund from an account set up by Winkler and Daily to distribute loan funds to the limited partners, instead of the commissions being paid by the bank.

Also, First United Fund made payments to Indian Springs Bank to subsidize the high cost of the CDs, thereby creating an artificial market for them.

Indian Springs Bank got around its legal lending limit on large loans of 15 percent of capital, surplus, and undivided profits, plus half of the loan loss reserve to a single borrower, by making relatively small unsecured loans to individual investors. The investors used the funds to invest in a Hawaiian real estate development, instead of making large loans to the real estate partnership. Indian Springs legal lending limit ranged from about $250,000 to $350,000. The bank loaned $3.7 million to about 30 individuals, who invested the funds in speculative real estate partnership's in Hawaii and to the partnership's organizers. Some of these borrowers were paid $2,000 to $3,000 by the real estate developers to apply fraudulently for the loans and then make the funds available to Winkler and Daily. This method of getting around the bank's legal lending limit is called *mortgage pulling*. Renda was the president of Southbrook Inc., which was one of the limited partners in the real estate development. The total loans in this venture exceeded Indian Springs Bank lending limit by about 10 times! And they accounted for about 16 percent of the bank's total loans. Of the $3.7 million loaned by the bank, Daily and related companies received about $930,000; Winker and related companies and trusts got $603,500; and Renda's First United Fund and Southbrook got $78,000. That left $2 million for investments in real estate.

An FDIC examination of Indian Springs Bank in December 1982, uncovered large loans made outside its normal market area, and it ordered accelerated repayments of the Hawaiian real estate development loans. At a meeting between the FDIC and the bank's board of directors, the directors were told that the bank was near insolvency as a result of the loans on the Hawaiian real estate development. Until then, the directors were unaware of the details of these loans. Part of the bank's plan to resolve their problem consisted of making more loans on similar real estate development projects in Hawaii and

Missouri that were organized by some of the same characters. The maturity on the original loans was approaching and the bank was not going to renew them.

The private placement memorandum for one of the limited partnerships advised prospective investors that the Hawaiian real estate development was a speculative security, and that it was going to purchase residential real estate that was subject to large cash flow deficits. The funds raised would permit the properties to be carried until they could be liquidated satisfactorily. Three limited partners in the real estate development refused to repay the loans to the bank, claiming that they were told by the general partners that the loans would never have to be repaid. Moreover, Lemaster told them that the loans would be rolled over when they matured at the end of one year, and that it was the general partners—not the limited partners—who would repay the loans. In July 1983, five days before the loans matured, Lemaster was killed in an automobile accident. His son thought that he might have been murdered. The problem loans were written off when the bank could not collect on them, and the Kansas Banking Department closed the bank in January 1984.

The Federal Deposit Insurance Corporation and the Federal Home Loan Bank Board brought charges against Renda, his wife, and their related companies for bank fraud under the authority of the Racketeer Influenced and Corrupt Organizations Act (RICO). The FDIC claimed that the partnership interests were securities, and that through the use of mortgage pullers, securities were sold in violation of securities and racketeering laws. False representations were made to obtain the loans. There was a "conspiracy" and a "pattern of racketeering" to defraud Indian State Bank. The bank's failure was a direct result of the failure to repay the loans of the Hawaiian and Missouri real estate partnerships. As noted in Chapter 2, The FDIC and the FHLBB sought treble damages of $63.5 million, but settled with the Renda's for $10.4 million. The FDIC was also awarded treble damages of $61.2 million against Winkler. Collecting that amount is another matter. Daily filed for bankruptcy in Hawaii. He cannot be sued without the bankruptcy court's permission.

The linked financing schemes described in the Indian Springs Bank case also caused the failures of Coronado Federal Savings and Loan, which was located in the same shopping center as Indian Springs Bank, and Rexford State Bank, Rexford, Kansas. Indian Springs was the "pilot project" for the fraudulent schemes.

LINKED FINANCING: THE CASE OF FLORIDA CENTER BANK

The principal participants in this case are Michael Hellerman, Charles J. Bazarian, John A. Bodziak, and Mario Renda. For simplicity, not all of the individuals involved in these and other schemes described in the book are mentioned by name. However, one individual who was indicted for fraud in connection with this and other banks, Jake Butcher, is discussed in Chapter 6.[12]

In the early 1970s, Michael Hellerman faced a long prison term for masterminding securities frauds. Instead of going to jail, he provided testimony that led to the conviction of organized crime figures in New York. Hellerman explained his links to organized crime in his 1977 book, *Wall Street Swindler*. His coauthor, Thomas C. Renner, describes Hellerman in the book as having the "characteristics of a chameleon. He could and did create new swindles while playing the secret role of informer for federal prosecutors. . . . Hellerman was driven by an almost insatiable desire for riches and luxury. . . . Hellerman was the very personification of the white-collar criminal."[13]

Under the federal witness protection program, created in 1970 by the Omnibus Crime Control Act, Hellerman's name was changed to Michael Rapp, and he moved to Florida. His eventual partner, Charles J. Bazarian, had received a four-year suspended sentence for mail fraud in 1978. Following a bankruptcy, Bazarian had gained wealth and fame from real estate investments. At the time of this case, he was under investigation by the Justice Department for real estate activities in Oklahoma and California. Bazarian was also named in a FSLIC lawsuit in connection with the failure of Consolidated Savings Bank, Irvine, California. Consolidated had made loans to Bazarian's Oklahoma-based corporation for about $9 million without appraisal or proper loan documentation.[14] Bazarian was also involved with Bloomfield Savings and Loan (Detroit, Michigan) where he allegedly borrowed $15 million when the S&L's lending limit was $3.5 million.[15]

John A. Bodziak, a third partner, was chairman of Florida Center Bank, Orlando, Florida. The bank had about $37 million in assets.

Rapp, aided and abetted by Renda and Bazarian, secretly purchased the controlling interest (51 percent) in Florida Center Bank from Bodziak and other shareholders. The bank was in poor financial condition and had been operating under a cease-and-desist order from the FDIC. The bank stock proved to be a poor investment for Bodziak, and Rapp was willing to pay him 10 times its actual value. The sale of the stock was financed by the proceeds of a bogus $30 million, 10-year loan to PaceCom Inc. to install pay telephones. According to federal investigators, Rapp secretly owned PaceCom. Rapp offered to pay Clyde Pichford (a Virginia stockbroker who needed money to replace cash he had stolen from certain accounts) and Dallas, Texas, investors a $5 million fee to arrange a loan of $20 million for PaceCom, providing that Rapp's role be kept secret.[16] The terms of the loan called for no scheduled interest payments and no payment of principal until maturity. Moreover, the loan could not be declared in default during its term. The collateral for the loan was 2,000 pay telephones and a 10-year CD, on which the bank prepaid all of the interest to PaceCom. Rapp obtained an opinion letter from a Miami lawyer stating that the loan conformed to regulations, laws, and guidelines. (Litigation is pending against that lawyer in connection with the opinion he rendered.)

At the time the loan was granted, the bank received large inflows of brokered deposits (which accounted for 40 percent of total deposits before it failed). Mario Renda met with Rapp, Pichford, a Texas investor, and Bazarian who wanted to "rent" $20 million for one day to buy a CD that could be offered as security for the loan. The funds would be loaned, provided that they never left Bazarian's possession. When the transaction was completed, Bazarian wired $100,000 to Renda's attorney for Renda's use.

Some of the funds from the loan were used to pay for the stock and to make a capital injection into the bank. Pichford never got his $5 million. About half of the loan funds had been disbursed before the regulators blocked the transaction. The bank was closed shortly thereafter.

Rapp received a 32-year prison term and a $1.75 million fine. He was also indicted for defrauding Sun Bank of Miami in a check-kiting scheme. (The Hellerman a.k.a. Michael Rapp) story is not over. We will eventually examine how Hellerman and organized crime figures contributed to the failure of The Aurora Bank, Aurora, Colorado, and his role in the failure of Flushing Federal Savings and Loan, Queens, New York.) Bodziak was sentenced to 10 years in prison and fined $50,000. Renda and Bazarian were each sentenced to two years in prison and fined $100,000, and Pichford was sentenced to 25 years in prison in Virginia for embezzlement and bank fraud in that state.

PENSION FUND SCANDAL

Martin Schwimmer was a financial consultant and agent of First United Fund. He was also an investment adviser registered with the SEC. As such, he served as an adviser and agent for the employee benefit plans of union Locals 38 and 810. Local 38 of the Sheetmetal Workers International Association of the AFL-CIO, and Local 810 of the International Brotherhood of Teamsters, Chauffeurs, Warehousemen, and Helpers of America were both from New York. As their consultant, Schwimmer advised them to invest in long-term jumbo CDs brokered by First United Funds. Renda actively engaged in the solicitation of banks and savings and loans, and in the negotiations and terms concerning the long-term jumbo CDs. First United Fund raised more than $100 million in funds from two union employee benefit plans. These funds were used to purchase long-term jumbo CDs at 18 banks and S&Ls. The failure of at least two of the S&Ls, Old Court Savings and Loan in Baltimore, Maryland, and Mainland Savings Association in Houston, Texas, was associated with fraud in those institutions.

Schwimmer and/or Renda opened six noninterest-bearing checking accounts in the name of First United Fund and First United, Inc. that were not recorded on First United's books, which is generally called the *off-the-book accounts*. These off-the-book accounts were located in banks in California, Connecticut, Iowa, New Jersey, and New York. The off-the-book accounts were concealed from First United's auditors and from the trustees of the unions' employee benefit plans. Renda also opened an account at European American Bank in Mineola, New York, which was recorded on First United's books.

Renda and his coconspirators directed the banks and savings and loans to transfer more than $14 million in commissions to the off-the-book accounts, telling them falsely that the funds would be used for the benefit of the unions' employee benefit plans. Similarly, $2 million was deposited in the European American Bank account. Eventually, Schwimmer and Renda used some of these funds for the benefit of themselves and others, including the purchase of stocks, bonds, luxury items, and the transfer of funds to companies that they controlled or in which they held an interest. Some funds were used to pay cash kickbacks to officials of Local 810 and its employee benefit plan. The commissions paid to the union officials were cash payments of about seven-eights of a percentage point of the face value of each CD.

The indictment against Schwimmer and Renda charged that they created false documents to hide the existence of their conspiracy and impeded government investigators. It also charged that Renda embezzled $4 million from Local 810's employee benefit plan and used it himself. This list of charges against Schwimmer and Renda is by no means complete, but does give some indication of the magnitude of their fraudulent dealings.

ANANT KUMAR TRIPATI: WORLD CLASS CON MAN

Anant Kumar Tripati was described by the United States Attorney for the District of Wyoming as "a world class con man."[17] Tripati, a native of India, allegedly was being investigated in Fiji for insurance fraud and in London for a scam involving letters of credit. He was president and chief executive officer of Fort Lincoln Group, Inc., Santa Monica, California, a holding company for Fort Lincoln Life Insurance Company and Fort Lincoln Life Assurance Company of Minot, North Dakota. Tripati convinced the Insurance Commissioner of North Dakota that he, Tripati, had more than $300 million in CDs in a nonexistent London bank called Credit Internationale. The Insurance Commissioner believed him and certified this as true.

Tripati's Fort Lincoln Life Insurance Company sold millions of dollars of annuities to three small banks, two of which failed.[18] The total dollar value of the annuities purchased by the banks exceeded their legal lending limits. Western National Bank of Lovell, Wyoming, had $1.4 million in capital and $16 million in annuities, and it failed. Community Bank of Hartford, South Dakota, had $3.3 million in capital and $10 million in annuities, and it failed. First National Bank & Trust Company, Wilbaux, Montana, survived but regretted its dealings with Tripati because Tripati's scheme was elaborate.

Tripati posed as a buyer of Western National Bank and First National Bank & Trust Company while he bought Community Bank of Hartford. All three banks were for sale. At First National Bank & Trust, Tripati staged a closing transaction by presenting a check for an undisclosed sum of money to one of the stockholders. Posing as the new or prospective owner gave him instant credibility at that bank and other banks, and dutiful bank officers and employees did as they were told to do. He promised Western National Bank Vice President Michael Carter and First National Bank President James Carter (no relation to Michael Carter) promotions to boost their careers, and he paid a $110,000 "finders fee" to Raymond Dana, Community Bank's president. Eventually, it was the two Carters and Dana who authorized the purchases of annuities from Tripati's insurance company.

To induce the banks to buy annuities, Tripati offered rates that exceeded current market rates of interest on annuities. Another inducement was that the annuities had short maturities that ranged from one month to three years. When the first annuities matured, the insurance company sold additional annuities to pay off the first ones. Therefore, if regulators forced Tripati to pay off the annuities at one bank, he could sell annuities to another bank and use those funds to satisfy the regulators. The scheme had considerable potential for growth if everything had worked the way Tripati had planned it.

The financial statements of Fort Lincoln Life Insurance Company shown to the banks were incomplete, since 14 of 21 pages were missing. Although the financial condition of the insurance company could not be verified, events showed that it did not have sufficient funds to pay off the annuities it sold.

The funds used to buy the annuities came from brokered deposits supplied by Mario Renda's First United Fund. At one time Renda and Tripati were partners in owning a condominium in Florida. According to one report, Tripati instructed bank employees to use First United Fund to buy brokered deposits. The three banks involved in the scheme purchased more than $37 million in brokered deposits. Almost $26 million of those funds went into accounts controlled by Tripati to buy annuities. He used some of the funds from annuity sales to buy banks, and some he intended to send off-shore where it would be safe for him to retire when he tired of the scheme and left the country.

At Western National Bank, he induced the bank to buy $15.9 million in brokered deposits from First United Fund. Western then purchased $9.6 million in annuities from Fort

Lincoln Life Insurance Company. It is alleged that Tripati embezzled $6 million from the bank funds that resulted from the sale of the annuities. Brokered deposits accounted for 64 percent of Western's total deposits. Some funds from the accounts Tripati controlled were used to purchase the bank.

The scheme began to fall apart during a routine FDIC examination of Imperial Bank in Los Angeles, where Tripati had an account. Bank examiners became suspicious of a $10 million check drawn on Community Bank of Hartford for the benefit of Fort Lincoln Life Insurance Company. Why would a small community bank write such a large check to an insurance company? The FDIC contacted banking authorities in South Dakota who began an investigation. The FDIC froze Tripati's account in Los Angeles, which made it impossible for him to cover the annuities coming due at Western National Bank, Wyoming. South Dakota bank officials closed the Community Bank of Hartford, and one week later the OCC closed Western National Bank, Wyoming. Therefore, First National Bank & Trust Company was able to back out of its deals with Tripati. Eventually, Tripati was convicted on 10 counts of bank fraud violations and was sentenced to 10 years in prison.

Gold Diggers

Dennis Nowfel, president of The Aurora Bank, Aurora, Colorado, was described as flamboyant, brusque, and hot tempered, but he was well respected in the banking community.[19] Both Nowfel and his vice president, William Vanden Eynden, had a problem. They liked to gamble. Unfortunately, they were also losers. Between drugs, prostitutes, and hotel bills, they spent up to $30,000 in a weekend at Las Vegas and they borrowed from other Denver banks to pay off their gambling debts and other debts.

Nowfel and Vanden Eynden met Faud Sam Jezzeny, a Las Vegas gambler, who proposed a deal that would make all of them rich. Part of the deal included paying Jezzeny's living expenses and gambling debts; subsequently, the bankers introduced Jezzeny to Heinrich Rupp, who had a metal recovery business in Aurora. Allegedly, Rupp had been tried for Nazi war crimes, skied on the Swiss Olympic team, was a pilot for King Faisal of Saudi Arabia, and had a large stash of gold. Rupp opened the "Swiss American account" at The Aurora Bank that channeled the fraudulent loan money. The bankers claimed that Rupp was the exclusive representative of five Swiss banks wanting to make large loans to American firms.

The cast of characters is almost complete when the bankers and Jezzeny meet Michael Rapp in Florida. Michael Rapp, also known as Michael Hellerman, caused the downfall of Florida Center Bank that was described previously. Rapp introduced them to members of various East Coast crime families who were interested in getting loans from the Aurora and Swiss banks. John Napoli, a New York career criminal who was present at that meeting, told the bankers that by putting up $2 million his mob contacts would pay them $9 million for the laundering of stolen cash called "hoist money."

Over a two-year period, the bankers made more than 100 loans for almost $10 million in the Swiss American account. The bank records falsely showed that the loans were made for use in Rupp's business, for tax shelters, and for a chain of delicatessens. Two loans to fund the stolen cash were made by Anthony DelVecchio and Jilly Rizzo, who will be discussed shortly.

According to Napoli, the bankers flew around the world, dropping off money to his friends and relatives while they waited for the elusive $9 million.[20] Some of the funds were used by Napoli and Joseph Chilli III, a reputed Bonanno mobster, to set up a delicatessen where other mobsters were invited to hang out, and the FBI was invited to film them, which they did. The FBI filmed mobsters, including Gambino capo Thomas Bilotti, who was later gunned down, while talking about murder and other crimes. Napoli helped the FBI in their deli sting operation in order to get a reduced sentence in a drug con. Napoli and Frank (Frankie Butch) Guglieimini conned a drug dealer (who had previously conned Napoli) out of $180,000, only to discover that the drug dealer was working for the Drug Enforcement Agency. Napoli was sentenced to 10 years, and while on appeal, he decided to cooperate with the FBI.

Although the bankers delivered almost $2 million to the mobsters, they never got their $9 million in stolen cash. The bankers hid the mounting overdrafts from the bank's directors by altering the books and bouncing checks between other banks. At one point, the overdraft in the Swiss American account amounted to $1.3 million. In a desperate move to cover their tracks, the bankers issued a $1.6 million note secured by drums of gold-bearing ore valued at $2 million that was buried in Rupp's backyard. The actual value turned out to be $1,200. When they could no longer hide their scheme, they reported it to the bank's directors and were fired. State banking authorities closed the bank, which by then had a negative equity capital of $2.05 million.

Nowfel pleaded guilty to bank fraud and got a two-year prison sentence, and Vanden Eynden pleaded guilty to bank fraud and tax charges and got a seven-year sentence.

Michael Hellerman (a.k.a. Michael Rapp), Anthony DelVecchio, and Jilly Rizzo were also involved in the failure of Flushing Federal Savings and Loan Association in Queens, New York. Flushing failed following two years of rapid and uncontrolled growth and risky lending practices. Hellerman and others who borrowed $8 million from Flushing were sued by the Federal Savings and Loan Insurance Corporation for violations of RICO. Hellerman, DelVecchio, and Rizzo were also named as defendants in a civil suit.

NOTES

1. President's Commission on Organized Crime, Report to the President and the Attorney General, *The Impact: Organized Crime Today*, April 1986, Washington, Government Printing Office, 29.
2. See "Money Laundering," A Special Report, *American Banker*, July 24, 1989, 7-29; Suspicious transactions can be reported by calling 1-800-BSA-CTRS at Treasury, 1-800-BE-AlERT at the U.S. Customs Service.
3. President's Commission on Organized Crime, Interim Report to the President and the Attorney General, *The Cash Connection: Organized Crime, Financial Institutions, and Money Laundering*, October 1984, Washington D.C., U.S. Government Printing Office, viii. This source contains numerous examples of laundering by crime figures as well as business concerns including Gulf Oil Corporation, Lockeed Aircraft, and McDonnell Douglas Corporation.
4. Vincent P. Cookingham, "Organized Crime: The Corporation as Victim," *Security Management*, Vol. 29, No. 7, July 1985, 28-31; "Bank Fraud and Embezzlement," *FBI Law Enforcement Bulletin*, February 1975, revised February 1978.
5. U.S. House, *Adequacy of Federal Efforts to Combat Fraud, Abuse, and Misconduct in Federally Insured Institutions*, Hearing before the Commerce, Consumer, and Monetary Affairs Subcommittee of the House Committee on Government Operations, 100th Cong., 1st, Sess., November 19, 1987, 868; Michael Violano, "The High-Tech Future of Foiling Fraud and Forgery," *Bankers Monthly*, April 1989, 37.
6. U.S. House, *Combating Fraud, Abuse, and Misconduct in the Nation's Financial Institutions: Current Federal*

Efforts are Inadequate, 72nd Report by the Committee on Government Operations, House Report 100-1088, 100th Cong., 2d Sess., October 13, 1988, 182-185.

7. Between August 1983 and March 1989, *American Banker,* published 55 articles dealing with Mario Renda and his associates. The most significant articles were written by Richard Ringer and Bart Faust. The information presented here draws heavily on those articles, but they are not cited individually. Similarly, Pete Brewton wrote a series of articles for *The Houston Post,* linking Renda to Herman K. Beebe, Sr., who is examined in Chapter 5, and to organized crime. These include the following: "Bank Fraud Investigators Looking for a National Plot," February 11, 1988; "S&L Probe Grew—and Grew Again," March 13, 1988; "Major Break Foreseen in Bank Fraud Probes," May 3, 1988; "Mafia's Involvement in S&L Failures Probed," October 8, 1988; "Bentsen Says He Has no Objections to Probe of Mob Role in S&L Failures," October 9, 1988; "Conviction Won't Stop Probe into Bank Fraud," November 9, 1988—this article deals with Schwimmer who is discussed later; "Links to Mob Figures, Suspect Offshore Companies Abound," December 8, 1988, "Brokered Deposits Case Produces Prison Term," March 1, 1989 (Schwimmer); Other sources include U.S. House, House Report 100-1088, October 13, 1988, *Ibid.,* 185-186. U.S. House, *Federal Regulation of Brokered Deposits in Problem Banks and Savings Institutions,* Committee on Government Operations, House Report 98-1112 (Committee on Government Operations Report No. 52), September 28, 1984; U.S. House, *Federal Regulation of Brokered Deposits: A Followup Report,* 38th Report by the Committee on Government Operations, 1985, House Report 99-358; U.S.

House, *Impact of Brokered Deposits on Banks and Thrifts: Risks Versus Benefits,* Hearing before the Subcommittee on General Oversight and Investigations of the Committee on Banking, Finance and Urban Affairs, 99th Cong., 1st. Sess., July 16, 1985, Serial No. 99-36; FHLBB, FDIC Joint Press Release, PR-42-89 (2-28-89);

8. 12 CFR, 330, 561, 564.

9. U.S. v. *Schwimmer* and *Renda*, 692 F. Supp 119 (E.D.N.Y. 1988). Although not discussed here, in Count 79 of Schwimmer's indictment, the government was going to introduce evidence that Schwimmer was involved with organized crime figures; *U.S.* v. *Martin Schwimmer and Mario Renda,* Eastern District of New York, CR 87-00432, Filed June 28, 1988. These were the primary sources for the discussion of the Pension Fund Scandal.

10. U.S. House, Hearing, July 16, 1985, 39.

11. Under the Financial Institutions Reform, Recovery and Enforcement Act of 1989, Sec. 910, civil money penalties can be imposed on institutions which willfully employ, without the permission of the appropriate banking agencies, persons convicted of certain crimes. This includes "persons participating in the conduct of the affairs of" an institution.

12. U.P.I., "Jake Butcher Indicted for Fraud in Florida," Sept. 1, 1989, 2; Press Release, U.S. Attorney, Middle Distrtict of Florida, August 30, 1989; Middle District of Florida. It is alleged that Butcher and others conspired to bilk $4 million from the Florida Center Bank. Butcher, who is currently in federal prison for bank fraud, is charged with 19 counts in the current indictment. According to Ricardo R. Pesquerza, Assistant U.S. Attorney, there was no link between Butcher and Hellerman (a.k.a. Rapp).

13. Michael Hellerman and Thomas C. Renner, *Wall Street Swindler,* New York: Doubleday & Company, 1977, ix.

14. Allen Pusey and Lee Hancock, "Network Fueled
$10 billion S&L Loss," *Dallas Morning News*, De-
cember 4, 1988, 31A. This article deals extensively
with Herman K. Beebe Sr. and others.
15. Stephen Pizzo, Mary Fricker, and Paul Muolo, *Inside Job: The Looting of America's Savings and Loans*,
New York: McGraw-Hill, 1989.
16. U.S. v. Rapp, 871 F.2d 957 (11th Cir. 1989).
17. U.S. House, *Adequacy of Federal Efforts to Combat
Fraud, Abuse, and Misconduct in Federally Insured
Institutions*, Hearing before the Commerce, Consumer, and Monetary Affairs Subcommittee of the
House Committee on Government Operations,
100th Cong., 1st Sess., November 19, 1987, 77-78.
Other information about Tripati was taken from the
articles cited in connection with Mario Renda. These
sources differ on whether Tripati is a native of Fiji
or India.
18. National banks may only invest in instruments for
which it has express authority (12 U.S.C., #24
(Seventh); 12 C.F.R. part 1.). That authority does not
include investing in single-premium retirement
annuity contracts as an investment.
19. Sue Lindsay, "Aurora Gold Dealer Goes on Trial,"
Rocky Mountain News, November 29, 1987, 10; Sue
Lindsay, "Final Chapter Opens in Bank's Downfall,"
Rocky Mountain News, November 29, 1987, 8, 26; Sue
Lindsay, "5 Indicted in Fraud Scheme that felled
The Aurora Bank," *Rocky Mountain News*, April 23,
1987, 9. Telephone conversation with Sue Lindsay,
5/18/89. The Aurora Bank which is described here
has no connection with The Bank of Aurora, Aurora, Colorado, which failed May 24, 1989 (FDIC
News Release, PR-108-89, 5/24/89).
20. Jerry Capeci, "He Straddled the Fence," *New York
Daily News*, date unknown.

5 CASE STUDIES OF CRIMES BY OUTSIDERS—PART 2

This chapter examines major frauds and kickback and credit card schemes that are relatively small by themselves, but collectively qualify as major frauds. It is estimated that credit card schemes cost banks more than $100 million in 1988.[1] VISA and MasterCard credit card frauds amounted to $300 million. Criminal networks of bank insiders are also involved in major frauds, kickbacks, and credit card schemes. For example, there was a secret meeting of 30 S&L executives who discussed actions to keep the regulators off their backs. These actions included evasion of loan limits to one borrower, evasion of growth limits by the sale of participations, daisy chains, and other issues.[2] According to an attorney for one former S&L executive, there was actually a "network" of S&Ls, but they were all called associations who had come together after regulators changed their rules and made their lives more difficult.[3] Finally, we will examine a Nigerian flimflam operation.

MAKE LOTS OF MONEY QUICK

Kickbacks are usually relatively small amounts of illegally received money that by themselves do not qualify as major bank fraud. However, the practice is so common that when totalled the amount of kickbacks adds up to huge sums. For example, consider the case of Larry K. Thompson and Tyrell G.

Barker.[4]

Thompson was a real estate and loan broker who agreed to buy a 366-acre tract of property in Midland, Texas. Tyrell "Terry" G. Barker was the owner and chairman of the board of State Savings and Loan Association in Lubbock, Texas. He was also the owner of Barker Development Corporation, a real estate development company in Dallas. Barker, who has dyslexia, could only read at a third-grade level according to a psychologist's report, but he was smart and learned to speculate in the real estate market. Barker, who knew little about banking, borrowed the funds to buy State Savings from Herman K. Beebe Sr., owner of a Houston S&L and chairman of the board of AMI Inc., a firm in Shreveport, Louisiana with interests in nursing homes, motels, and credit life insurance. Beebe financed the purchase of State Savings to have the S&L sell his credit life insurance. Barker was not particularly successful at selling credit life insurance, but he more than made up for it in real estate deals.[5] Barker was willing to lend money on real estate projects where he got a 50 percent interest, and where the borrowers were not required to invest any of their own money.

Thompson asked Barker to coventure the real estate deal, and Barker agreed, telling Thompson that State S&L would fund the deal, and that, in turn, Thompson would take on six new partners, all Barker associates. At Barker's direction, they formed a partnership known as Make Lots of Money Quick (MLMQ #1). Their plan was to coventure with Thompson in order to purchase and develop a tract of land known as the Northwood Venture. Barker arranged for State S&L to lend $2 million for the purchase and closing costs of Northwood Venture. From that amount, a $200,000 commission would be paid to Thompson, who would then wire $100,000 of it to the Barker Development Corporation. Several of the MLMQ #1 partners objected to the scheme and it was dropped. Instead, one of the partners, who was a real estate broker and business associate of Barker, would assume as assignee the partnership's interest in the joint venture and would close the Northwood Venture deal. Eventually, Thompson received $200,000, identified in the closing documents as a commission, and wired $100,000 of it to the Barker Development Corporation.

Both Thompson and Barker pleaded guilty to misapplication of funds, a violation of Title 18, U.S. Code section 657 that carried a maximum sentence of five years and a $5,000 fine. While Thompson received only a three-year suspended sentence, 150 hours of community service, and a $2,000 fine, Barker received the maximum five year sentence because he was also convicted of misapplication of funds at Brownfield Savings and Loan Association, where he was also the chairman.[6] In addition, he was convicted of fraud in connection with an attempt to acquire a Colorado S&L.[7]

The kickback scheme just described was not an isolated case of two hapless individuals. Thompson was involved in another scheme to defraud individuals seeking loans. He, and others, claimed to represent foreign lenders who had large sums of money to lend at below market rates. Thompson and his associates induced a prospective borrower to advance them more than $2 million in connection with loan applications, yet no foreign money was forthcoming.

Barker was also involved in various other fraudulent schemes. In one of them, State Savings loaned $4.4 million to Beebe and an unnamed partner to finance a ranch near Vernon, Texas. The ranch cost $2.8 million, and the borrowers asked for $1.05 million as "working capital." The money was wired to Beebe's bank in Bossier City, Louisiana, where he used some of the funds to retire an outstanding loan from Barker. It was also alleged that the funds were used for payments to Beebe and other parties, including Woody Lemons, president and CEO of Dallas–Texas, based Vernon Savings & Loan. Woody Lemons was eventually indicted for defrauding Vernon with the intent of enriching himself.[8] Beebe, whose criminal record was described as being "uglier than a mail-order suit," was convicted of defrauding the Small Business Administration of about $1 million.[9] He also pleaded guilty to two felony charges of wire fraud and conspiracy. In 1976, Beebe was a major figure in the scandal surrounding the failure of Citizens State Bank in Carrizo Springs, Texas. He has also been involved in the downfall of at least 15 other failed banks.[10] A Public Broadcasting television special broadcast about financial fraud in Houston, Texas, mentioned Beebe in connection with the failure of Houston's Mainland S&L. Mainland Savings was referred to as "Gangland Savings" because of its connections to organized crime. Mario Renda's First United Fund, which was the subject of the previous chapter, was a major lender of brokered deposits to Mainland, and his associates were borrowers from that S&L.[11] On the television broadcast, it was alleged that Beebe was a "front" for Carlos Marcello, the head of the New Orleans La Cosa Nostra family.[12] Because of the close connections between Barker, Beebe, and Donald Dixon, we will examine Vernon S&L next.

VERNON SAVINGS AND LOAN ASSOCIATION

Vernon S&L was owned by Donald R. Dixon and his wife Dana, who were close friends of Barker and Beebe. Beebe also helped Dixon finance the purchase of Vernon S&L in 1982. Through various complex transactions, he owned about one-third of the stock in the holding company controlling the S&L. Dixon had been a successful real estate developer in the Dallas area. When Dixon bought Vernon S&L in 1982, it had virtually no delinquent loans, but he changed that condition quickly over the next few years. Although Dixon's only official capacity at Vernon S&L was to serve on its loan committee for a short period, he received $8 million in compensation and dividends between 1983 and 1986—not bad for a part-time job.

While Barker did not excel at selling Beebe AMI credit life insurance, Dixon did. He used the hard-sell approach. Prospective real estate borrowers who wanted to buy credit life from their own insurance agents were told to try to get their mortgage loans from those insurance agents. Subsequently, AMI netted $2.5 million from the sale of credit life insurance at Vernon S&L.

After Dixon acquired Vernon S&L, the association started an aggressive growth strategy, and its assets grew 1,023 percent over the next five years, from $120 million at the end of 1982 to $1.3 billion at the end of 1986. The growth was financed through high-cost brokered deposits and jumbo CDs, which amounted to 28 percent of its total deposits. Most of these funds were used to finance speculative acquisition, development, and construction loans, which were characterized by deficient underwriting practices, including the lack of appraisals. Vernon S&L is also accused of swapping bad loans with another S&L, a practice called a *daisy chain*. Edwin T. McBirney, former chairman of Sunbelt Savings (discussed in Chapter 3), bought stock loans to help inflate Vernon's profits, and Vernon S&L made $20 million in paper profits from that deal. But when it was placed in receivership in March 1987, 96 percent of the loans were delinquent.[13]

A FSLIC lawsuit for $350 million charges that Dixon and six other officers "looted" Vernon's assets for their personal gain. Dixon and others hid real estate losses from examiners and reported profits, although Vernon S&L had a negative net worth of $350 million. Based on the fictitious profits, Dixon's holding company received $22.1 million in dividends and $15 million in bogus bonuses. There were also millions of dollars in losses from questionable loans. It seems that Dixon measured his success by the number of toys he owned. Dixon's—and consequently Vernon's—toys included:

- A fleet of seven aircraft, including a seven-passenger helicopter (to avoid crosstown traffic), a Lear Jet, a Cessna Citation, a Beechcraft King Air, and others.
- A $2 million beach house in Camino Del Mar, California, plus $800,000 operating expenses. Vernon S&L sold the house at a loss to a friend of Dixon's, and financed it 100 percent.
- $5.5 million in artwork at Vernon.
- $500,000 in furnishings at Dixon's Rancho Santa Fe home.
- A $10 million 100-foot yacht, used for political fund raisers.
- A $22,000 two-week trip to Europe that Dana Dixon called "Gastronomique Fantastique." She described

the trip as a "flying house party" of "pure unadulterated pleasure."[14] The tour was arranged, in part, by Philippe Junot, the former husband of Princess Caroline of Monaco. Don Dixon made five other trips to Europe that were billed to Vernon S&L. During these visits, Vernon S&L set up an operation in Switzerland to attract foreign funds. Vernon S&L also loaned money on the purchase of a hotel site in the "Sun Coast" of Spain and a restaurant in the Bordeaux wine region of France.[15]

Dixon had political ties to former House Majority leader Jim Wright (D. Texas), who used Vernon's Lear Jet for his political campaign. Wright interceded on Dixon's behalf to keep the FHLBB from closing Vernon S&L. The Political Action Committee of Texas S&Ls gave Wright $250,000 to block unfavorable legislation, and the funds were laundered through Vernon.[16] One check had the phrase "For Jim Wright" written on it. Pat L. Malone, former executive vice president of Vernon, admitted that he established a system that used Vernon's funds to reimburse $55,000 to the S&L's officers for political campaign contributions. Court records showed donations included unspecified contributions to Wright.[17] Wright's chief of staff claims that Wright does not know Dixon and that he was trying to help the entire S&L industry in Texas and the people they serve.[18] Nevertheless, an article in *Bankers Monthly* said that: "The story of Wright and Dixon is a story of greed and selfishness, of abuse of power and wealth, of perversion of democracy. It's another example of how Texas politicians carry the water for the state's business tycoons and how they answer the call of constituents who say that they're being persecuted by unreasonable regulatory agencies."[19]

Other congressmen used Vernon's yacht for fund-raising. This distinguished group included Senator Pete Wilson (California), former Senator Paul Laxalt (Nevada), and former House Majority Whip Tony Coelho (California). Coelho called Wright's aide and asked for Wright's help in forestalling the FHLBB's closure of Vernon.[20] Both Wright and Coelho resigned from their congressional seats. Noted politicians who flew on Vernon's jets included former President Gerald Ford, Jack Kemp, Jim Wright, and Tony Coelho.[21]

Credit Cards

Telemarketing.   Telemarketing means selling goods and services by telephone.[22] Most telemarketing firms are honest, but some are not. A telephone solicitor representing a dishonest telemarketer tells prospective customers about the goods for sale, such as water purifiers or packaged vacations. The lucky person talking to the telemarketer can pay for goods by providing the telemarketer with a credit card number. Frequently the telemarketer's calls are preceded with a letter to the prospective customer stating, "You have won one of four fabulous prizes. To obtain your prize, you must call the following number within the next 48 hours." When the customer calls, the telemarketer confirms that they have won one of the prizes, but they must pay shipping and handling charges which can be billed to their credit card.

Telemarketers frequently use a "boiler room" operation, which is a room full of telephones where telephone solicitors make cold calls hoping to sell their goods. In either case, the telemarketer's objective is to get a credit card number. The credit card number is then used to record customer-authorized sales, and in some cases unauthorized charges are made on the accounts. By using "electronic data capture," the telemarketers send account information to banks electronically, leaving no paper trail, and funds are credited to the telemarketer's account the next day. When paper credit card sales drafts are used, they can get cash within a few days, and they can be in a distant location by the time the goods, if any, are shipped to the customer.

When the sale is completed and the goods are shipped and received by the customer, the customer frequently discovers that the goods are inferior quality or that they are not what the customer expected. The fancy musical organ that the customer expected turns out to be a plastic toy. The outboard motor for a 16-foot boat is a small electric motor powered by two D-cell batteries and only suitable for powering a toy in a bathtub. A $500 water purifier turns out to be a bag of charcoal. The list of fraudulent merchandise goes on and on, and when the customer attempts to return the goods, he or she finds that the telemarketer has closed shop and has no forwarding address or phone number. Therefore, the customer refuses to pay the credit card bill, because he or she believes they were cheated, and the charge is returned to the bank that had the credit card relationship with the telemarketer. The bank absorbs the losses from the telemarketer's charge-backs, which can amount to hundreds of thousands of dollars. Charge-backs from telemarketing scams can be as high as 90 percent of the volume of credit card drafts deposited. This, however, is not necessarily bank fraud; and it may not even be consumer fraud because the consumer did receive goods, although it was not what he or she expected.

Here is another credit card ploy. A well-dressed man goes into a bank to establish a business account and credit card relationship. He explains to the banker that he is a florist and that he has recently opened BlossomTime Flowers (or some other type of business). Furthermore, he intends to expand the business with telephone orders from throughout the United States. The banker, wanting to help a new business grow, provides him with the means to grow. However, the credit card sales drafts from BlossomTime can be a subterfuge used to pay for activities, such as prostitution, gambling, and drugs—things that do not qualify for credit cards. The florist buys credit card charges for prostitution at a discount and then collects on them from the bank. The volume of credit card sales drafts from the florist may be reasonable at first, but then it grows to $200,000 or more. Then the florist withdraws all of his funds from the bank, either by wire transfer for by cash, and leaves town. It takes about 90 to 120 days before the full impact of the loss from the charge-backs is felt at the bank, and once again, the bank is the loser.

Factoring. Factoring, which is also known as laundering, is a variation of the theme just described. Factoring is when a telemarketer convinces a legitimate merchant, usually a small-to-medium size "mom and pop" operation, to handle the telemarketer's credit card sales drafts for a three to ten percent commission. Banks usually charge merchants a discount of two to four a percent, so the merchant expects to make money, depending on the volume of deposits. The telemarketer gives several thousand dollars worth of sales drafts to the merchant who sends them to the bank to be cleared.

In Denver, Colorado, credit card fraud cost three banks $4.5 million.[23] In Miami, Florida, telemarketing frauds cost the Southeast Bank $1.8 million in the last three years.[24] In the Kansas City, Missouri, credit card telemarketing and factoring may cost area banks more than $1 million.[25] First National Bank of Lees Summit, with $20 million in assets, could have $500,000 in charge-backs. Many of the charges at First National Bank involved William "Pat" Campbell (and other business associates) who sells credit card services in the area. Campbell "joint ventured" with local merchants to handle his billings. He and three associates do business under at least six different company names: Gibralter Management, KC Management, TKE Enterprises Inc., Solomon, TKC Inc., and Atlas Marketing. Factoring is not illegal in Missouri, but as previously noted can cause large losses to banks when consumers ask that the credit card charges be removed from their accounts.

Many merchants are not aware that factoring is a violation of the bankcard merchant agreement. When factoring is used, the merchant is responsible for all financial losses, and if fraud is involved, the merchant, not his bank, could face criminal prosecution.

VISA and MasterCard filed a complaint in Northern California in September 1988, against Daryl Wayne Jay, Jay Management Group Inc., and Robert Picou.[26] It is alleged that Jay and Picou accepted credit card sales drafts from middlemen in Florida, who had received them from telemarketers selling vacation travel and vitamins. Jay hired a toy store firm in St.

Paul to deposit more than $350,000 in credit card sales drafts in a local bank. Because of the time lags between receiving customer complaints, the bank was unsure at the time of the complaints about how much it had lost. Previously, Picou had factored $1 million through a hosiery shop in Seattle, and Jay had also been involved in a factoring scheme in Hong Kong where drafts were laundered through a Toronto bank. Needless to say, account numbers can be sent anywhere in the world in a few minutes by using FAX, and the dangers are inherent. Therefore, MasterCard and VISA were granted a restraining order against the defendants and are seeking restitution and $5 million in damages.

Most of credit card losses described here are preventable, if banks follow the guidelines and controls established by the major credit card companies. The message is simple: Failure to follow established guidelines and controls results in losses. Crooks find a bank or banker who is lax and exploit that weakness.

Finally, information about credit card fraud and other scams is shared between financial institutions and law enforcement officers through the International Association of Credit Card Investigators.[27] The IACCI publishes information about various types of fraud, including information about the Nigerians, who are major contributors to bank fraud.

A Nigerian Flimflam and Other Crimes. It is rumored that a government-run school in Lagos, Nigeria, trains Nigerians how to defraud U.S. banks and businesses. Nothing is done about the school because Nigeria is a major oil producer and the United States is dependent on its oil. Also, most of the individual crimes involve relatively small amounts of money. Collectively, however, this type of fraud adds up to millions of dollars. Those who commit the frauds may be connected with each other because of their ethnic heritage, or they may be part of international organized crime. According to Harold W. Evanson, vice president and manager of investigations for NCNB Texas National Bank, Dallas, Texas, there are about 30,000 to 50,000 Nigerians in the United States, and 75 to 90 percent of them participate in frauds.[28] They are especially active in New York, Texas, Washington, D.C., Oregon, Minnesota, South Dakota, Tennessee, North Carolina, and Rhode Island. Most of the perpetrators enter the country on student visas and are extensively pursuing undergraduate and graduate degrees. They also bribe officials to obtain fraudulent and legitimate INS form 120, which indicates their foreign student status. Sometimes they arrange sham marriages to U.S. citizens to obtain INS green cards that permit them to stay here. Those who are students use their correct names to register at universities and to establish credit during their freshman and sophomore years. As juniors and seniors, however, they begin to defraud the system by obtaining loans and running credit cards beyond their limits. Subsequently, a substantial amount of their crimes occur in cities with universities and in schools with foreign students. Tracking these individuals is difficult because they move and have their mail forwarded through coconspiritors. Some have even worked in financial institutions and have helped other Nigerians commit crimes.

Guaranteed Student Loans, administered by the U.S. Department of Education, are the main source of funding for Nigerian students. Most of the Nigerians applying for these loans indicate that they are U.S. citizens, and banks do not bother to check on the validity of the Nigerian applications because Guaranteed Student Loans are 100 percent guaranteed by the U.S. Government. In addition, some Nigerians claim to be from the Virgin Islands, which makes them eligible for welfare benefits and fraudulently explains their accents, and once again, the U.S. taxpayer is funding their fraud. Moreover, the funds and goods that they steal are sent back to Nigeria. In fact, one group tried to buy 80 typewriters and have them shipped to Nigeria. Other purchases include fraudulently purchased guns and automobiles.

Some say that if Nigerians are caught and returned to Nigeria, their heads are cut off. Others say that they are re-trained and returned to the United States to steal again. While these are probably rumors, there is still no doubt about their widespread crimes.[29]

According to reports from various sources, groups of well-organized Nigerians have made false applications for credit cards by using identities of individuals whose names are listed in telephone directories, college yearbooks, and other sources. Other information listed on the credit card applications is also incorrect, but enough of it is of sufficient quality to pass a point scoring approval. Once they receive their credit cards, they obtain driver's licenses by using false Nigerian birth certificates and their names imprinted on the new credit cards. In Nigeria, birth certificates are rarely used; and when Nigerians apply for student or tourist visas, all that is needed to obtain a birth certificate is a name and birthdate. South Carolina has been a frequent source for driver's licenses used in these scams. Using false identification, they obtain charge accounts at stores and open checking and savings accounts at financial institutions. In the upcoming flimflam example, the accounts are kited up, then the funds are withdrawn. Checks with insufficient funds are used to pay merchants for goods, and the charges on the credit cards are never paid.

The following case is a "typical" Nigerian flimflam operation that occurred at one bank located in Alabama. The scam was perpetrated in other Alabama banks and thrifts on or about the same time. One of a pair of roving foreign nationals, using false identification and American sounding names (that is, Scott, Williams, Cole), opened a savings account for $100 in one of an Alabama bank's many branches. Their primary interest was to establish an account of any type. Shortly thereafter, a check for $4,900 was deposited in the account at a different branch. The deposit was a check stolen from Tennessee and drawn on a nonexisting account. The timing of the deposit would allow funds to be available for withdrawal before a weekend, but the check could not be returned until the following week. The perpetrator withdrew $100, thus recovering the initial investment and testing whether the account was operational. Then $4,500 was withdrawn from the account at another branch before the weekend. Since the fraud would not be discovered until the following week, the perpetrator had ample time to move to Florida, where the scam was repeated. After doing the flimflam there, the perpetrator returned to Alabama for repeat performances. This time, however, he was caught. He was part of a team of Nigerians who were committing similar crimes at other banks. They were all caught, convicted, and are serving prison sentences.

NOTES

1. Rebecca Cox, "Con Men Turn to Phone Scams to Fleece Credit Card Banks," *American Banker*, May 18, 1989, 1, 10.
2. Pete Brewton, " 'Secret' Meeting of S&Ls Part of Probe," *The Houston Post*, February 12, 1989.
3. Allen Pusey and Lee Hancock, "Network Fueled $10 billion S&L Loss," *Dallas Morning News*, December 4, 1988, 1, 30A, 31A.
4. *U.S. v. Larry K. Thompson*, Northern District of Texas, Lubbock Division, CR-5-88-002, CR-5-88-024; *U.S. v. Tyrell G. Barker*, Northern District of Texas, Dallas Division, CR-3-88-017-D.
5. Bill Powell and Daniel Pedersen, "Loan Stars Fall in Texas," *Newsweek*, June 20, 1988, 42-45.
6. Allen Pusey, "5 Named in 1 charge of Texas S&L inquiry," *Dallas Morning News*, February 9, 1988, 1A, 7A.
7. Michael Swaicki and Ross Ramsey, "5 Charged with Banking Fraud in Probe of Texas Institutions," *Dallas Times Herald*, February 9, 1988; *U.S. v. Tyrell G. Barker*, Northern District of Texas, CR-3-88-017-D, Filed February 8, 1988; *U.S. v. Larry K. Thompson*, Northern District of Texas, CR-5-88-002, CR-5-88-024, Filed May 20, 1988; *U.S. v. Herman K. Beebe, Sr.*, Northern District of Texas, Dallas Division, CR-3-88-124-D, Filed April 29, 1988.
8. *U.S. v. Woody F. Lemons*, Northern District of Texas, Dallas Division, CR3-88-234-T, Filed November 10, 1988.
9. William M. Adler and Michael Binstein, "The Speaker and the Sleazy Banker," *Bankers Monthly*, March 1988, 84; Bill Powell and Daniel Pederson, *ibid.*, 43.
10. Allen Pusey, "Problems, Players Surfaced in '70s Scandal," *Dallas Morning News*, December 4, 1988,

31A; Allen Pusey and Lee Hancock, *ibid.*; Pete Brewton, "He Saw the S&L Crisis Coming," *Houston Post,* May 14, 1989. This article links Beebe to 23 S&Ls.

11. *U.S.* v. *Martin Schwimmer and Mario Renda,* Eastern District of New York, CR 87-00423, filed January 28, 1988. Refer to the pension funds scandal in Chapter 4, for more information. However, funds from the pension plan were only a small part of First United's involvement with Mainland.

12. Dan Gifford, Financial Fraud: A Special Report, Public Broadcasting, Houston, Texas, February 2, 1989; Conversation with Pete Brewton, Reporter, *Houston Post,* June 23, 1989; Pete Brewton wrote a series of articles for *The Houston Post,* linking Renda to Herman K. Beebe Sr and to organized crime. These articles include the following: "Bank Fraud Investigators Looking for a National Plot," February 11, 1988; "S&L Probe Grew - and Grew Again," March 13, 1988; "Major Break Foreseen in Bank Fraud Probes," May 3, 1988; "Mafia's Involvement in S&L Failures Probed," October 8, 1988; "Bentsen Says He Has No Objections to Probe of Mob Role in S&L Failures," October 9, 1988; "Links to Mob Figures, Suspect Offshore Companies Abound," December 8, 1988; Conversation with Jim James, formerly with the Texas Attorney General's Crime Strike Force, June 26, 1989; The President's Commission on Organized Crime, *The Cash Connection, ibid.,* 10;

13. Federal Home Loan Bank Board "News" (FHLBB Places Texas Thrift into Management Consignment Program), March 20, 1987; David LaGesse, " 'Daisy Chain' Loan Swapping Described by Ex-Thrift Exec," *American Banker,* August 28, 1987; LaGesse, "FSLIC Alleges Vernon's Officers Lived High at Thrift's Expense," *American Banker,* April 29, 1987; LaGesse, "Vernon S&L's Yacht Was Used for Fund-Raiser,"

American Banker, June 19, 1987; LaGesse, "FSLIC Charges Vernon Savings was "Looted," *American Banker*, April 28, 1987; June 18, 1987.

14. William M. Adler and Michael Binstein, *ibid.*, 81.
15. Byron Harris, S&L Stories 1987-1988, WFAA Television, Dallas, Texas, 1988.
16. "Wright's Troubles Seem Unrelenting," AP, Sherman, Texas, *Democrat*, May 7, 1989.
17. "Ex-VSL Officer to Plead Guilty to Fraud Charges," Vernon, Texas, *Record*, May 23, 1989.
18. "Speaking for the Speaker," *Bankers Monthly*, May 1988, 87.
19. William M. Adler and Michael Binstein, *ibid.*, 80.
20. "Wright, Coelho and the S&L Fiasco," *U.S. News and World Report*, June 12, 1989, 21-22.
21. Byron Harris, *ibid.*
22. The definition of telemarketing, as it appears in the "Telemarketing Fraud Prevention Act of 1989," 101st Cong., 1st. Sess., H.R. 1354, refers to telephone sales across state lines. It does not include transactions where there have been personal meetings between the buyer and the sellers concerning the transaction.
23. Rebecca Cox, "3 Colorado Bank Firms Report Credit Card Fraud," *American Banker*, June 15, 1989, 3, 13.
24. Rebecca Cox, "Bankers Urged to React Quickly to Card Fraud," *American Banker*, May 24, 1989, 11.
25. Carey Gillam, "Credit Card Scam Could Cost Area Banks $1 Million-Plus," *Kansas City Business Journal*, March 13, 1989; Carry Gillam, "Credit Card Operation Could Hit bank for up to $500,000," *Kansas City Business Journal*, March 20, 1989.
26. "A New Attack on Credit Card Draft Laundering," *Credit Card News*, October 15, 1988, 1-2; *MasterCard International Inc., etc. et al.* v. *Daryl Wayne Jay, etc. et al.*, United States District Court for Northern District of California, C-88-20629 RPA, Filed Septem-

27. International Association of Credit Card Investigators, 1620 Grant Ave., Novato CA 94945, phone 415-897-8800.

28. Eavenson, Harold W., Vice President and Manager of Investigations and Special Services, NCNB, Texas National Bank, Dallas, "Investigating International Fraud," Bank Adminstration Institute, Bank Security Conference, Nashville, TN., April 10, 1989. Some of the information in his presentation, and mentioned here, was prepared by several government agencies.

29. U.S. House, *Adequacy of Federal Efforts to Combat Fraud, Abuse, and Misconduct in Federally Insured Institutions*, Hearing before the Commerce, Consumer, and Monetary Affairs Subcommittee of the House Committee on Government Operations, 100th Cong., 1st, Sess., November 19, 1987, 868; Michael Violano, "The High-Tech Future of Foiling Fraud and Forgery," *Bankers Monthly*, April 1989, 37; Susan Faludi, "Credit Card Ring Charging Millions," *The Atlanta Journal*, February 1, 1984; Susan Faludi, "Calls Pour in on Nigerian Mafia's Credit Card Ring," *The Atlanta Journal*, February 1, 1984; John Brady, "Foreigners Jailed in Credit-Card Theft Ring," *The Atlanta Journal*, January 27, 1984; "Cultural Crime Ring," International Association of Credit Card Investigators (IACCI) *News*, May/June 1989, 5-6.

6 CASE STUDIES OF CRIMES BY INSIDERS

Two cases are covered in this chapter: Empire Savings and Loan, and the Butcher Brothers financial empire, in which United American Bank, Knoxville, Tennessee, played a key roll. The Empire Savings and Loan case involved massive fraud and illustrates the use of land flips, nominee loans, kickbacks, and other abuses and misconduct by both insiders and outsiders. At the time this chapter was written in 1989, more than 100 people had been convicted for their involvement in the schemes that caused Empire's failure, and the court trials were still in progress. So the mere magnitude of this case deserves attention.

The failure of the Butcher brothers' banking empire was the largest failure in U.S. banking history. Their schemes involved more than 60 interlocking corporations and partnerships that borrowed loans from Butcher-controlled banks. Needless to say, the Butchers used state-of-the-art techniques to juggle bad insider loans from bank to bank and to enhance their wealth.

EMPIRE SAVINGS AND LOAN ASSOCIATION

Empire Savings and Loan Association, Mesquite, Texas, was closed with losses of over $170 million.[1] Empire was the first federally insured S&L closed in Texas and the FSLIC's largest disbursement to depositors in its 50-year history. The cost to pay off depositors was over $279 million. The cost could have been less if the Texas Savings and Loan Department and the Federal Home Loan Bank Board would have acted more swiftly and decisively when problems were discovered at Empire. However, Empire's books were in such disarray that their auditor, Coopers & Lybrand, was unable to meet their accounting deadlines nine times in 1982. The Federal Home Loan Bank granted each extension.[2] In October 1982, federal examiners gave Empire a CAMEL rating of "3C," which is not good, for imprudent lending practices in the areas of underwriting, appraisal, and risk exposure.[3] For instance, speculative condominium construction loans accounted for 47.8 percent of total loans. Eventually, in August 1983, a special examination revealed virtual chaos at Empire and it was given a CAMEL rating of "4." By this time, construction loans accounted for over 65 percent of their total loan portfolio, and the examination report revealed that borrowers had little or no equity in 27 condominium projects. Loans in excess of the sales price were made to speculators and secured by vacant land. And there were verbal commitments for $178 million in additional condo construction loans.[4] For good reason, Empire Savings and Loan was closed in March 1984.

The principal characters in the schemes that led to Empire's demise included Spencer H. Blain, Jr.; James L. Toler; David L. "Danny" Faulkner, and Clifford L. Sinclair. Faulkner and Toler are alleged to have masterminded the schemes, and together Blain, Faulkner, Toler, and others are accused of stealing more than $100 million from Empire. To do this, Empire, and its wholly owned real estate subsidiary Statewide Service Corporation, engaged in land flips, false appraisals, and questionable lending practices, such as financing speculative land loans.

The I-30 Corridor.   About $1 billion real estate investment in the Garland–Lake Ray Hubbard area was financed by Empire and other S&Ls. The area is referred to as the Interstate Highway-30 (I-30) corridor, and it is located about 20 to 25 miles east of Dallas. After Empire failed, only about one-third of the completed 2,200 condominiums in the city of Garland were occupied, and another 2,200 or more were still under construction. Building permits were issued for more than 6,400 condos and 232 apartments, despite the fact that the average sales of condos in east Dallas County were only 68 per month. Depending on which report one reads and which geographic area was covered by those reports, the supply of condos along the I-30 corridor was enough to satisfy market needs for the next 3 to 12 years. At one point, the vacancy rate in the area was 47 percent according to a Fannie Mae survey, and it was estimated that the condos were worth only 10 percent to 35 percent of what Empire had loaned on them.

Real estate developers enticed other prospective lenders to make loans in the overbuilt I-30 corridor area by promising them high rates of interest on their loans, fees as high as eight points (8 percent of the loan), and kickbacks of $0.50 per square foot of the project. The developers also arranged for the loans to be sold to other financial institutions, leaving the originating S&L with the fee income and no I-30 real estate loans on their books. The major problem was the lack of buyers and the large number of defaults on loan payments by those who did buy the condos.

The first major player in this condo development is Spencer H. Blain, Jr., who acquired controlling interest in Empire in 1982, and became its chief executive officer and chairman of the board. Before that, Blain was president of a larger S&L in Austin, a former president of the Texas Savings and Loan League, and a director of the Federal Home Loan Bank of Little Rock, serving as vice-chairman of the board and chairman of the executive committee. Therefore, he had outstanding credentials as a savings and loan executive. Blain's annual salary at Empire was $30,000 per year. Other remuneration from Empire was $251,458, most of which was a bonus.[5]

Blain acquired controlling interest (67 percent) of Empire from Danny Faulkner, James Toler, and their associates. However, Blain failed to file a change of control notice with the bank regulators prior to making the acquisition, as is required by law.[6] When he did finally file the notification, however, they did approve it. To finance the stock purchase, he borrowed about $831,000 from Faulkner and Toler. Subsequently, he approved $40 million or more in loans on Faulkner-Toler real estate projects.

When Blain acquired Empire, his plans were to make construction loans, sell them in the secondary market without recourse, earn fees for making those loans, get larger by using jumbo deposits, be a limited partner in building condos, close the loans to buyer, and finally, sell the loans to Fannie Mae or Freddie Mac.[7] In retrospect, he achieved most of his goals.

In the year and a half that Blain was at the helm of Empire, he used brokered deposits to spur the growth of deposits from $17.3 million on June 30, 1982, to $308.9 million on January 31, 1984—a growth rate of over 1,700 percent in a year and a half! Perhaps this was because Empire often paid two percentage points higher on their brokered deposits than other banks and S&Ls. In August 1983, Empire had assets of $340 million. Mortgage loans were $276.5 million (excluding $77.5 million sold in participations), and $181.3 million outstanding in land and construction loans (excluding $61.2 million sold in loan participation).[8] In a desperate effort to survive, Empire continued to buy brokered deposits until the day before it failed, and in the end its brokered deposits of $262 million accounted for 85 percent of its total deposits. When it closed in March, 1984, Mario Renda's First United Fund had brokered most of those deposits.

After Empire was closed, Blain testified before Congress. "I have never knowingly involved myself or lent to anyone else who was involved in what has been characterized as a `land flip,' although land flips are not illegal and not uncommon."[9] When Congressman Doug Barnard, Jr. asked Blain if he had made any profits or commission on some of the properties that he financed, Blain answered, "No, sir, I did not."[10]

According to federal prosecutors, Blain made more than $112 million in bogus condominium deals. Blain also made $21 million in real estate profits during his reign at Empire. However, he gave up most of it in settlements with the Federal

Home Loan Bank Board to recover some of their insured losses. As part of the settlement, the FSLIC got part ownership, with Blain, of 132 oil and gas wells. He acknowledged no wrongdoing. According to Blain, the impatience of the bank regulators, rather than any wrongdoing, caused the failure of Empire.[11]

This second major player in the bogus condominium deal is David L. "Danny" Faulkner, who quit school in the sixth grade, worked as a painting contractor, and became a self-made multimillionaire real estate developer. Faulkner wore Italian made alligator shoes, rode in a Rolls Royce, and wore a diamond studded Rolex watch. He was widely known in the Dallas area for his philanthropic activities. He was, by many people's standards, a pillar of the community. For example, he donated $1 million to build a church sanctuary for a young girl who was dying of cancer, but, some of his gifts raise questions about potential conflicts of interest. It was the regional head of Fannie Mae who approved land purchases for Faulkner along the I-30 corridor while the official's wife was a Faulkner employee. In fact, she bought one of the condos, and Faulkner gave her a Mercedes-Benz for a surprise birthday present.[12] Clifford Sinclair also testified that Faulkner ordered him to pay Texas State Senator Ted Lyon a $10,000 fee and give him a $26,104 Lincoln car for helping to settle a zoning dispute which increased the value of Faulkner's property by several million dollars.[13] In addition, Faulkner gave real estate appraiser Larry W. Hutson's wife a $5,000 fur coat, and Hutson received $387,000 for providing bogus appraisals on real estate.[14]

In 1979, Faulkner developed a condominium project called "Faulkner Point" on Lake Ray Hubbard. By 1982, he had stopped developing his own condominiums, and he and James Toler had bought options to purchase land in the area, then sold the land at inflated prices to condominium investors. By using options (contracts to buy the land at a stated price during some specified time period), they invested little cash of their own. Faulkner and Toler and their associates handled the appraisals and development.

The third major player in the I-30 Corridor-Condo Scam is Clifford L. Sinclair, who owned Kitco Developers Inc., a mortgage banking company, and Kitco Management. Currently serving a 13-year sentence for fraud, Sinclair had a long history of illegal activities. He successfully fought extradition to Alabama where he allegedly operated a phony mortgage brokerage firm, and a similar charge was pending in Arkansas.[15] Sinclair testified that he was a real estate promoter who found buyers to purchase the property owned by Faulkner and Toler in the I-30 corridor in Garland and that he submitted false financial statements and credit applications for some buyers. He even instructed employees how to change buyers' Social Security numbers to prevent discovery in a credit check.[16]

Sinclair, in financing the "Kirby Mills" development, made 39 loans from Empire for $39 million to purchase land. Each loan had a one-year term. Almost one year after they were made, no construction had begun on the project.[17] Construction loans of $105 million were planned, part of which would be used to repay the land loans. In connection with the "Faulkner on the Greens" condo project, Empire also made land loans of $23.7 million to finance the purchase of land from Sinclair and construction loans of $46.6 million.

The fourth major player in the I-30 scheme is James L. Toler, former Mayor of Garland and a land developer, who owned Lato Inc. and Zigga Inc.. Toler was associated with Danny Faulkner and was one of the owners of Empire. In one transaction, Toler's Zigga Inc. bought land at $0.83 to $1.25 per square foot. Toler had a false appraisal made at $13 per square foot. The title to the land in such transactions would change from Toler (or his associates) to Faulkner (or his associates) at inflated prices on each exchange. This transaction is called a land flip. The same tract of land was sometimes flipped six times a day.

Consider the following example of land flips by Blain's Empire Savings and Loan and its real estate subsidiary, Statewide Service Corp. Statewide had a 25 to 50 percent limited partnership interest in many real estate development projects. Statewide purchased 36.4 acres of land from James Toler's Lato

Inc. for $280,000. That same day, Statewide swapped that tract and other land. Then Blain bought 48.9 acres from Toler for $261,948, which included the Lato tract that Statewide had sold previously. Blain also purchased 16.95 acres of adjoining property for $424,500, which included the Toler Bay Condo Joint Venture owned by Toler and Faulkner. The total 65.85 acres cost $696,448 and was sold to Clifford Sinclair for $14.9 million in cash, plus two tracts of land in Steamboat Springs, Colorado, which were valued at $1.1 million.[18]

In another transaction, Statewide purchased about 82 acres for $0.52 per square foot, or $1.86 million. That same day it sold the same acreage to Faulkner and Toler for $0.85 per square foot, or $3 million. Then Faulkner and Toler sold 18.6 acres of that property to one of their associates, who in turn subdivided it into seven plots and sold them to condominium investors for $6.95 per square foot, or $5.6 million. In one day Faulkner and Toler made a profit of about $3.74 million, and still owned 63.4 acres of land.[19]

Empire and other lenders provided the financing for the land flips and the condominium investors. The land flips were financed with short-term land loans, and the proceeds were sufficient to cover 6 to 12 point (percent) loan fees, interest, and closing costs. When the land loans matured, construction loans were granted and additional fees were generated to cover all of the costs. According to a congressional report, "Empire could speculate in real estate development while increasing its paper assets with an artificially and fraudulently inflated loan, and increasing its paper net worth with income from loan fees, interest, and closing costs that Empire itself was, in reality, paying."[20]

To illustrate the financing of flips, consider the following transactions.[21] Some land totaling 6.7 acres was sold for $392,113. On the same day the land was sold again for $1,379,469, and Empire loaned the borrower $1,414,531.

In another set of transactions, Kitco Developers (Sinclair) sold 3.6 acres for $156,816 to Ozark Service Corp. The same day, Ozark sold it again for $1,332,936 to Bob Ward Enterprises, Inc., then it flipped one more time for $1,724,976. Empire eventually loaned $1,898,250 to a Mr. Carpenter on that transaction, and the price increased from $1.00 to $12.10 per square foot on the 3.6 acres in these transactions, which occurred over about a two-and-one-half-month period.

Once a parcel of land had reached high values—as high as they were going to flip that parcel—it was divided into smaller plots and sold to a prearranged group of more than 150 condominium investors. Empire and other S&Ls loaned 110 percent of the value to the condominium investors who were then paid "bonuses" from the funds they borrowed. The bonuses were as much as $43,000 depending on the size of the loans.

Many of the investors who bought the plots grossly exaggerated their net worths to qualify for the loans and bonuses that were mentioned previously. Carl Wren told Bell County Savings that he owned over $1 million in marketable securities when he owned none.[22] Brenda Stemwede told Lancaster First Federal Savings that she had cash value life insurance worth $130,000 when she had none. Jerry Buchingham told Empire he owned two houses, which was a lie. These people and others were greedy and either did not realize the risks involved, or they were willing to take the risks to earn the bonuses. When the loans came due, and the investors at the bottom of the pyramid could not pay for them, or sell the land at the prices they had paid for it, many of them went to jail.

UNITED AMERICAN BANK (KNOXVILLE, TENNESSEE) AND THE BUTCHER BROTHERS

Jacob "Jake" Franklin Butcher was a born salesman and an unsuccessful Democratic gubernatorial candidate in Tennessee in 1978.[23] His younger brother, Cecil Hilgie "C.H." Butcher, Jr., was a gruff, hard-driving businessman, who called the hard financial shots for the two brothers. C.H. gained some banking experience working in his father's Union County Bank of Maynardville, Tennessee. In 1968, the Butcher brothers bought their first bank in Lake City. They arranged financing of the purchase through Jesse Barr, a banker at Union Planters National Bank, Memphis. By 1974, they controlled nine banks. By 1982, their assets amounted to about $180 million, and they controlled 14 financial institutions with more than $3 billion in deposits. The next year their financial empire collapsed.

Jake Butcher acquired approximately 51 percent of Hamilton National Bank of Knoxville in February 1975, and eight months later changed its name to United American Bank, N.A. (UAB Knoxville). He borrowed about $16 million to finance the purchase. Hamilton had a history of poor asset quality and above average loan losses. Hamilton's earnings had been depressed by high interest costs on time deposits that were used to fund its growth.

In 1976 the Office of Comptroller of the Currency (OCC) expressed concern to UAB's board of directors that Jake's $200,000 salary was considerably more than that paid at comparable banks, and that he had diverted $98,000 from the sale of credit life from the bank for his own use. Federal law prohibits insiders and employees at national banks from benefiting personally from the sale of credit life insurance to that bank's customers.[24] In November 1976, Jake converted the bank to a state charter to avoid that law, to avoid adding capital, to make bigger loans, and to free noninterest-bearing deposits from the Federal Reserve. He also withdrew the bank from the Federal Reserve System. The following year, Jake's income from credit life was $241,300. His gross income in 1977 was $2.3 million. His tax deductions for interest and other expenses amounted to $2 million. Butcher was reported to have said he made a lot of money fast because he owes so much.[25]

In 1980, the two brothers separated their holdings. Alleged reasons for their separation included the possibility of lending money to each other and to skirt federal regulations. Jake Butcher had controlling interests in UAB Knoxville, where he was chairman and chief executive officer. He also controlled United American Banks of Chattanooga and Memphis,

Tennessee, and Somerset, Kentucky. Citizens Union National Bank and Trust Company of Lexington, Kentucky, became part of the UAB group in early 1982.

C. H. Butcher, Jr. had controlling interest in a chain of 30 smaller rural banks in four states. However, City and County (C&C) Bank of Knox County was his flagship bank. Other Tennessee C&C banks included C&C Bank of Anderson County, C&C Bank of Hawkins County, C&C Bank of Jefferson County, C&C Bank of Monroe County, C&C Bank of McMinn County, C&C Bank of Rhea County, C&C Bank of Roane County, and C&C Bank of Washington County. There were also C&C banks in Kentucky. Other C.H. Butcher banks that were not part of the C&C group included the Bank of Commerce in Morristown, Citizens Bank of Sneedville, United Southern of Nashville, and others. Both brothers had interests in family trusts that held bank stocks, including stock in UAB Knoxville.[26]

The Butcher's strategy was to borrow money to buy a bank, pay it off, and then buy another one. However, much of the Butcher banking empire was financed with loans made from one Butcher bank to another, sometimes with loans made by a bank to purchase its own stock. For example, UAB Knoxville loaned Anderson Trust, in which C.H. Butcher was the principal beneficiary, $1.5 million to buy stock in C&C Bank of Anderson County, which C.H. controlled. Similarly, UAB Knoxville loaned funds to Hamilton Bank of Memphis Trust, where Jake was the principal beneficiary, to buy stock in Hamilton Bank in Memphis. Finally, Jake told La Follette, Tennessee, grocer Robert L. Woodson, III, that he could buy more stockholders' shares in UAB Knoxville. Moreover, Jake offered to lend him the funds from his Kentucky bank to buy the shares, and even to pay half of the interest on the loan. Woodson agreed, but he never received the shares because the other stockholder had pledged them as collateral against another loan.[27]

Jesse Alfred Barr was Jake's adviser and business associate. Barr was president of Service and Management, Inc., a Butcher related company. He was also a director of C&C Financial

Interstate Service, Inc., a data processing firm specializing in banking services, and an umbrella corporation for C.H's business interests. Barr had resigned as executive vice president from Union Planters National Bank, Memphis, Tennessee, and was later indicted and convicted for embezzlement and misapplication of that bank's funds. Union Planters claims Barr's crimes cost them $30 million, and they got a $17.6 million civil judgment against him. Because of the 1976 conviction, Barr could not work in a bank again. However, he could and did serve as a "consultant" to the Butcher brothers. Barr also acted in Jake Butcher's name to approve loans and to shift them from bank to bank to avoid regulatory scrutiny.

In connection with the Butchers, Barr was convicted of conspiring to obtain fraudulent loans for Butcher from banks he or his family controlled, among other charges. One such loan was to buy a $460,000 yacht. At the sentencing, the Judge called Barr "the key player who made possible his [Butcher's] million dollar thefts."[28]

Barr helped Jake try to acquire Union Planters Bank, but Jake shelved those plans in 1974 when he decided to run for governor. After Jake lost the campaign, he tried, but failed to get a seat on the bank's board of directors.

Barr also helped Jake put together the 1982 World's Fair in Knoxville, with the help of President Jimmy Carter, Senator Howard Baker (R. Tennessee), and former Budget Director Bert Lance. Lance was President Carter's budget director who resigned because of the banking scandal that was covered in Chapter 1. At one time, Butcher had loaned Lance money to buy a bank. Lance, his companies and relatives had borrowed $4.1 million from Butcher banks. In fact, millions of dollars in loans were made to state political figures.[29] Jake also donated to Carter's presidential campaign. It paid off to mix banking and politics. Eventually, the Butcher group persuaded federal officials to spend $295 million on the fair and related projects. Much of it was spent on construction contracts with firms that had close ties to the Butchers. According to the General Accounting Office, there was a lack of competitive bidding for these projects, and the possibility of unwarranted private gains. Barr was a partner in a trust controlling at least one of the projects. Many of the loans to fair-related ventures defaulted in 1982, a year that was characterized by falling market rates of interest and a deep recession. One such defaulted UAB loan for $701,000 was to Barr's secretary who organized a company to provide linen service to the fair.

Under Jake Butcher's reign, UAB Knoxville's assets grew rapidly, financed largely by interest rate-sensitive borrowed funds, such as large CDs, that were then commonly called "purchase money" or "hot money." The financial innovation of brokered deposits seemingly emerged in the late 1970s and grew rapidly in the early 1980s.

Over the six-year period the Butchers controlled the bank, it engaged in a pattern of unsafe, unsound, and unlawful banking practices such as forged notes, loans in the names of nominees, and misrepresentation of collateral values. According to William M. Isaac, former chairman of the FDIC, UAB Knoxville "eschewed caution in favor of leverage, reasonable conservatism in favor of aggressiveness, and diversification in favor of real estate concentration and loans to insiders or quasi-insiders and their interests. . . UAB was a bank bordering on being out of control."[30] In one case involving limited partnerships, a $15,000 investment by the partners in a project resulted in a $4 million loan loss by the bank. In another case, UAB loaned $300,000 to CC (Buddy) Pack, a resort developer. The bank took a second mortgage on Pack's property, which already had a $497,000 lien against it. Pack's company had reported losses of $690,000 for that year, and Pack had filed a paupers oath in court several months before he received the loan. Finally, he didn't own all of the real estate he put up as collateral.[31]

The pattern of insider lending was a long-standing practice at the UAB Knoxville. Press reports in 1978 observed that Butcher's bank had a high percentage of insider loans that exceeded the bank's equity capital.[32] Frequently the borrowers were close personal friends or associates of those making the lending decisions at the bank. Borrowers sometimes dictated the terms of their loans to the bank officers. Although friends, associates, and families of insiders are not insiders in the legal sense of the term, their loans amounted to $211.5 million, or 506 percent of total equity capital and reserve in 1982. All of these loans were adversely classified: $27.5 million was considered a loss, $62.3 million was classified as doubtful, and $121.7 million was classified substandard. Loans to insiders (officers, directors, and their interests) amounted to $38.1 million, or 62 percent of equity capital and reserves. Of this amount, $25 million was adversely classified. The bank's five largest borrowers, including their various interests, owed the bank $251 million. Such policies were reflected in the bank's low returns. In 1981, the return on assets was 0.50 percent, about half of what peer banks earned.[33]

The Butchers' chain and financial dealings involved about 40 loosely affiliated banks and five savings and loans that fell under the authority of seven different federal and state regulatory agencies. It also included more than 60 interlocking corporations and partnerships that borrowed millions from their banks. Some of the loans were legal, some were forged. For example, Franklin Haney, a real estate developer who was involved with Jake Butcher on several projects, claimed that a $2.7 million loan from UAB Knoxville was forged. Milton Turner, another real estate developer, claimed to know nothing about $2.4 million in loans made by UAB in Memphis and UAB in Somerset to one of his real estate companies in Texas. One note was signed by Gene Cook as an officer of that company. No Gene Cook was employed by that company. However Jake's farm manager was named Gene Cook, and he said he did not sign the note.[34]

Lack of Regulatory Effectiveness. Lack of cooperation between government agencies seriously compromised the regulator's effectiveness, but made it easier for the Butchers' and their associates to subvert the system. The following example of check kiting $16 million illustrates the point. Because the FDIC and the Tennessee Department of Insurance did not communicate with each other, it was improbable that they would have detected the check-kiting scheme involving UAB Knoxville, Southern Industrial Banking Corporation (SIBC), Knoxville, and City and County Bank of Hawkensville County, although both banks were supervised by the FDIC. SIBC was chartered in 1929, and because of a "grandfather" clause in the law was permitted to use the term "bank" in its name. It was founded by Cecil H. Butcher, Sr., the brothers' father, and associates, to finance furniture, automobiles, and farm equipment. C.H. Butcher, Jr. gradually took control of it. SIBC was a thrift—a finance company that made consumer and commercial loans funded by the sale of uninsured "investment certificates" to retail customers. It was supervised by the Tennessee Department Insurance. The supervision consisted of checking to determine if SIBC met minimum capital standards. The Tennessee Department of Insurance does not classify loans.[35] Edward C. Browder was a director of both SIBC and UAB Knoxville. C.H. Butcher was the chairman of SIBC and controlled City and County Bank of Hawkensville County. Cecil H. Butcher, Sr. served on SIBC's board of directors.

On October 8, 1982, UAB Knoxville sold, without recourse, $16 million in loan participations to SIBC. SIBC paid for the participations with a check drawn on its account at City and County Bank of Hawkensville County. However, SIBC only had $10 million in its account at City and County Bank at the time the check was drawn. On October 12, 1982, SIBC drew a $16 million check on its account at UAB Knoxville, when its balance was only $1.7 million, payable to City and County Bank. On October 14th and 15th, UAB Knoxville loaned SIBC a total of $13 million to cover the check that SIBC had drawn on October 12th.

SIBC was used as a "dumping ground" in the shell game of moving at least $25 million worth of bad loans from one Butcher controlled bank to another in order to avoid being discovered by bank examiners. Subsequently, bad loans were exchanged for collectible consumer loans made by SIBC.[36] Jesse Barr engineered the movement of loans between banks, and between November 11th and December 23rd, UAB Knoxville repurchased for its own account the entire $16 million in loan participations, even though it had no written commitment to do so. Some of the loans sold in these transactions were of such poor credit quality that they were adversely classified by FDIC examiners. While the FDIC was concerned about UAB Knoxville's repurchase of bad loans before the bank was closed, it may not have been aware of the check kiting scheme until a later date.

C.H. Butcher's SIBC borrowed funds from UAB Knoxville to help finance Jake's failed gubernatorial race. To help payoff $900,000 of those debts, SIBC loaned Financial Services Leasing $870,000. Financial Services Leasing was a shell company and was not even listed in the telephone book. The same day as the loan was made, SIBC sold all of its furniture and equipment to Financial Services Leasing, and then leased them back at a cost of $12,500 per month for five years. SIBC transferred the $870,000 promissory note, without recourse, from Financial Services and $30,000 cash to pay off SIBC's loan from UAB Knoxville. Now Financial Services, rather than SIBC, owed UAB Knoxville $870,000. Then SIBC paid $12,358 per month to UAB Knoxville to reduce Financial Services' debt.

Financial Leasing was also used by SIBC to dump $500,000 of its bad debts and for other purposes. For instance, Financial Leasing made a $2.8 million loan to C.H. Butcher for undetermined purposes. It bought 74 houseboats from Jake Butcher's wife and leased them to Jesse Barr for $2.8 million. (They were to be used as floating hotels during the world's fair.) When it filed for bankruptcy, Financial Leasing was $25 million in debt. Most of it was owed to Butcher-controlled banks. Unfortunately, Financial Leasing had no credit files and no collection system, so most of the debt will go uncollected.[37]

SIBC also engaged heavily in loans to insiders. Eight Butcher associates, including C.H. Butcher, had borrowed $28.5 million in loans, almost half of SIBC's loan portfolio.

In another set of transactions unrelated to SIBC, loans were used to pay off or increase other loans. On August 31, 1982, an unnamed S&L (supervised by the Federal Home Loan Bank

Board) made a $2.5 million loan to a Butcher-related person. On September 1, a $901,402 loan at UAB Knoxville was repaid. Then UAB Knoxville purchased a $1,235,000 participation in the $2.5 million S&L loan. Therefore, rather than the loan at UAB Knoxville being repaid, it was increased by $333,598 ($1,235,000 − $901,402 = $333,598).[38]

Those in control of the S&Ls had close financial links to the Butchers. For example, one majority stockholder of an S&L borrowed the money to buy the stock from the Butchers. Others were business associates. The complex nature of these transactions made them difficult to uncover; and the fact that many regulatory agencies were involved frustrated the ability of some regulators to deal with the situation. Nevertheless, the U.S. House Committee on Government Operations concluded that UAB Knoxville, Penn Square, and Franklin National Banks failed, in part, because of indecisive actions by banking regulators.[39]

The House Committee also examined the role of Ernst & Whinney (Ernst & Young), a major independent public accounting firm which had audited UAB Knoxville's books since 1975. Net income (unaudited) for the first nine months of 1982 was $1.05 per share of common stock, compared to $0.80 per share in the previous year. The profit picture changed in the fourth quarter. The net income for the entire year was a loss of $0.76 per share of common stock, compared to $1.17 per share earned in the previous year. E&W signed an unqualified audit report and certified that the financial statements fairly represented the financial position of the bank and conformed with generally accepted accounting principles applied on a consistent basis. The statements were released by the bank on January 28, 1983, and the bank was closed 10 days later. According to the FDIC, the financial statements were materially false and misleading.

This was not the first time that these accountants had deficiencies in their auditing of banks. The FDIC sued Ernst & Ernst in connection with their auditing of Franklin National Bank, which failed.[40] However, Ernst & Ernst, now Ernst &

Young, was not alone in their failure to find and report problems at banks. Peat, Marwick Mitchell & Co. gave an unqualified report for Penn Square Bank, Oklahoma City, Oklahoma, before it failed.[41] More will be said about auditing in Chapter 8.

On November 1, 1982, the day after the World's Fair closed, 180 FDIC examiners (10 percent of their audit force) closed in on the Butchers' banks simultaneously so that they could not pass bad loans from bank to bank. The FDIC would have moved in sooner, but all of the hotel rooms in Knoxville were filled with tourists from the World's Fair. On February 14, 1983, UAB Knoxville was declared insolvent. It had deposits of $838 million and $794 million. It was the third largest commercial bank to fail in U.S. banking history, following the Franklin National Bank (deposits of $1.4 billion) and the United States National Bank of San Diego (deposits of $932 million). Within the next six months, eight other banks owned or controlled by the Butchers failed. Collectively, their deposits amounted to $1.7 billion, making the Butcher-related failures the largest in U.S. history. Eleven other Butcher-related banks in Kentucky and Tennessee were sold or merged. On February 15, 1983, the FDIC announced that it had sold UAB Knoxville's deposit liabilities and assets to First Tennessee Bank, Knoxville, Tennessee.[42]

NOTES

1. U.S. House, *Adequacy of Federal Home Loan Bank Board Supervision of Empire Savings and Loan Association*, Hearing before the Commerce, Consumer, and Monetary Affairs Subcommittee of the Committee on Government Operations, 98th Cong., 2nd Sess., April 25, 1984, numerous press clippings appear in the hearings. pp.550-587 and other pages; U.S. House, *Federal Home Loan Bank Board Supervision and Failure of Empire Savings and Loan of Mesquite Tex.*, 44th Report by the Committee on Government Operations, House Report 98-953, 98th Cong., 2d Sess., August 6, 1984; Other published reports dating from the early 1980s to the present include: Allen Pusey, "The Fall of Empire," Austin, Texas, *American-Statesman*, April 23, 1989; Bill Lodge, "Garland Man Recounts Land Sale in I-30 Trial," Dallas, Texas, *Dallas Morning News*, May 13, 1989; "Key Testimony Opens in Condo Fraud Trial," Sherman, Texas *Democrat*, April 18, 1989; "Witness' Past Probed in I-35 Condo Trial," Sherman, Texas, *Democrat*, April 25, 1989; "FSLIC Gets Oil Well Interest in Empire Savings Settlement," *American Banker*, April 27, 1987; Andrew Albert and Richard Ringer, "Questions Raised by `Penn Square of Thrifts' Get Scrutiny At Congressional Hearing Today," *American Banker*, April 25, 1984; Andrew Alber and Richard Ringer, "Regulators Evaluating Empire's Cost," *American Banker*, March 20, 1984; "In Empire's Wake, A Dynasty Shakes," *American Banker*, March 27, 1984; Rick Atkinson and David Maraniss, "Turning Anger into Action on Thrifts," *The Washington Post*, June 13, 1989, A1, claim FSLIC's loss on Empire is $165 million.

2. Rick Atkinson and David Maraniss, "Only Ambition Limited S&L Growth," *The Washington Post*, A18.

3. U.S. House, House Report 98-953, 6-27; U.S. House, Hearing, April 25, 1984, Report of Examination, 191.
4. U.S. House, Hearing, April 25, 1984, 254.
5. U.S. House, Hearing, April 25, 1984, 276.
6. National Housing Act, Section 407(Q).
7. U.S. House, Hearing, April 25, 1984, 155.
8. U.S. House, Hearing, April 25, 1984, 257.
9. U.S. House, Hearing, April 25, 1984, 152.
10. U.S. House, Hearing, April 25, 1984, 162.
11. "Failed Texas Thrift's Former Head Blames Agency's Impatience," *Wall Street Journal*, April 27, 1984.
12. U.S. House, Hearing, April 25, 1984, 297.
13. "Witness Says Senator Got Cash and Car for Help," Bonham, Texas, *Favorite*, April 20, 1989.
14. Bill Lodge, "Witness Says I-30 Figures Got Bogus Appraisals," *Morning News*, Dallas Texas, June 26, 1989; Bill Lodge, "I-30 Defendants Prepare Case; Toler Set to Testify," *Morning News* Dallas, TX, July 3, 1989.
15. U.S. House, Hearing, April 25, 1984, 554-557.
16. Debbie Howell, "Defense Questions Sinclair," Garland, Texas, *News*, April 22, 1989.
17. U.S. House, Hearing, April 25, 1984, 401.
18. "Ex-Chief of Empire Savings Sued By FSLIC over Texas Land Deals," *American Banker*, August 30, 1984; U.S. House, House Report 98-953, 14-15; U.S. House, Hearing, April 25, 1984, 271, 357, 430, 553, 562.
19. op. cit., Allen Pusey.
20. U.S. House Report, 98-953, 24.
21. U.S. House, Hearing, April 25, 1984, 262, 430.
22. Robert Bork, Jr., "Never Give a Sucker an Even Break," *Forbes*, July 15, 1985, 72, 77.
23. This section draws on the following sources: *Borrowed Money, Borrowed Time: The Fall of the House of Butcher*, A collection of 27 articles by *The Tennessean*

and *The Knoxville Journal,* November 18, 1983; U.S. House, *Federal Supervision and Failure of United American Bank of Knoxville, Tenn., and Affiliated Banks,* 23rd Report by the Committee on Government Operations, House Report No. 98-573, 89th Cong., 1st. Sess., November 18, 1983; U.S. House, *Federal Supervision and Failure of United American Bank (Knoxville, Tenn.),* Hearing before the Commerce, Consumer, and Monetary Affairs Subcommittee of the Committee on Government Operations, 98th Cong., 1st. Sess., March 15 and 16, 1983.

24. 12 CFR Part 2, Section 22.
25. U.S. House, Hearings, March 15 and 16, 1983, 571.
26. U.S. House, Hearings, March 15 and 16, 1983, 572-573.
27. *Borrowed Time, Borrowed Money,* ibid. 9, 10.
28. Michael J. Stedman, "Doing Time: Advice from a Jailed Banker," *Bankers Monthly,* November 1988, 18.
29. *Borrowed Money, Borrowed Time,* ibid., 37-38.
30. U.S. House, Report No. 98-573, 4, 36; U.S. House, Hearings, March 15 and 16, 1983, 39.
31. U.S. House, Hearing, March 15 and 16, 1983, 616.
32. U.S. House, Hearings, March 15 and 16, 1983, 569.
33. U.S. House, Hearings, March 15 and 16, 1983, 21, 41, 170-172.
34. *Borrowed Money, Borrowed Time,* ibid., 23, 28.
35. U.S. House, Hearings, March 15 and 16, 1983, 606. Also see *Borrowed Money, Borrowed Time,* 14-16.
36. U.S. House, Report No. 98-573, 11; Hearings, March 15 and 16, 1983, 143; 592-593; Stedman, *ibid.* 20; *Borrowed Money, Borrowed Time, ibid.,* 10, 33.
37. *Borrowed Money, Borrowed Time, ibid.,* 29.
38. U.S. House, Report No. 98-573, 47.
39. U.S. House, Report No. 98-573, 50-57.
40. Re: Franklin National Bank Securities Litigation, 445 F.Supp. 723 (1978).

41. U.S. House, Report No. 98-593, 43; U.S. Hearing, March 15 and 16, 1983, 120, 162-163; 258, 272-274, 287-288; 609.
42. For the terms of the Purchase and Assumption Agreement, and the Indemnity Agreement, see U.S. House, Hearing, March 15 and 16, 1983, 175-198.

7 THE ROLE OF BANK DIRECTORS

The Office of the Comptroller of the Currency (OCC) found that deficiencies within boards of directors contributed to insider abuse and fraud, to bank failures, and to problem banks.[1] The boards of such banks were frequently weak (lacking oversight responsibilities and controls) overly aggressive, or some combination of the two. In contrast, none of the continuously healthy banks that the OCC examined had such deficiencies with their boards. The OCC concluded that one of the major differences between failed banks and healthy banks was the caliber of management that reflected the policies of an active and involved board of directors.

A study of 205 failed S&Ls came to a similar conclusion—the directors of virtually all of them failed to act prudently.[2] In another study of failed S&Ls, the boards were passive. One director said the thrift's board did not question business decisions of the former chairman because he owned the thrift. They thought that he could do as he pleased.[3] With that in mind, this chapter presents an overview of what bank boards should and should not do. By carrying out their duties correctly, bank directors can go a long way toward eliminating the conditions in which insider abuse and fraud can flourish.

Unfortunately, weak and ineffective boards of directors are not uncommon according to management expert Peter

Drucker. He wrote, "But there is one thing all boards have in common, regardless of their legal position. *They do not function.* The decline of the board is a universal phenomenon of this century. Perhaps nothing shows it as clearly as when the board, which, by law, is the governing organ of a corporation, was always the last group to hear the trouble in the great business catastrophes of this century. Whenever a financial scandal breaks, the board's failure to act is blamed on stupidity, negligence, or on the failure of management to keep the board informed. But when such malfunction occurs with unfailing regularity, one must concede that it is the institution that fails to perform rather than the individuals."[4] The massive failures of banks and S&Ls in recent years is strong evidence that there is a structural problem with our institutions. Drucker goes on to say that boards have become a legal fiction. While that may be so *de facto, de jure* they are charged with certain responsibilities for which they are held liable. Not only can banking regulators sue directors of failed institutions, but shareholders can institute class action suits too. In a class action suit pending in Los Angeles against certain officers and directors of the parent company of Lincoln Savings & Loan, the shareholders are charging securities frauds and racketeering arising from the sale of bonds that are virtually worthless that caused their stock to decline in value.[5]

THE RESPONSIBILITIES OF A BANK'S BOARD OF DIRECTORS

The bank's stockholders elect a board of directors to oversee its affairs and to ensure competent management, thereby giving the board the ultimate responsibility for the success or failure of that bank. This applies whether the bank is independently owned or part of a holding company.

Statutes and regulations provide boards of directors with general guidelines with respect to their structure and duties. Federal banking regulations establish the minimum and maximum number of board members for national banks. They must have at least five, but no more than 25 board members. Similarly, S&Ls have requirements concerning the composition of their boards. For example, no more than two directors can be from the same family, nor more than two lawyers from the same law firm. Moreover, participation by independent directors is essential to provide perspective and objectivity to board decisions. The intent here is to eliminate conflicts of interest and promote independent judgment.

In addition to a regular board of directors, banks may have advisory directors who bring particular expertise to the board. Advisory directors usually play a limited role in board activities and can not be held liable for board decisions.

The legal duties of directors are dictated by laws and regulations. Under common law, directors are expected to carry out their functions with "duty of care" and "duty of loyalty." These legal terms mean that directors are required to be diligent and honest in managing the affairs of the bank, and they authorize bank management to do only those things that the bank is permitted to do by law and regulations. The duty of care holds directors to a standard of care equal to that which a prudent man would use in similar circumstances.[6] In this regard, directors are expected to know what is going on at their banks. They have a "duty to investigate" existing problems or ones that may develop and to make sure that steps are taken to correct them. Failure to comply with the duty-of-care standard may be considered "negligence" in the eyes of the court that said: "Directors who willingly allow others to make major decisions affecting the future of the corporation wholly without supervision or oversight may not defend their lack of knowledge, for that ignorance itself is a breach of fiduciary duty."[7]

The duty-of-care standard does not expect directors to guarantee the conduct of a bank's officers, its profitability, or hold them accountable for errors in business judgment. It does, however, expect them to act in good faith and carry out their duties diligently.

The duty of loyalty prohibits directors from putting their personal or business interests, or those of others, above the interests of the bank. Directors may not take advantage of business opportunities that they learn of as a result of their position, without first offering them to the bank. Stated otherwise, directors cannot make inappropriate gains because of their connection with the bank. They can, however, do business with the bank provided that the relationships are fully disclosed to the board, which must determine the fairness of those transactions to the bank, and if there are any conflicts of interest. For example, the president of a thrift formed a separate corporation to receive loan referral fees for identifying borrowers to that thrift. The FHLBB informed the thrift that its president was an affiliated person who could not properly accept such fees.[8] The board's guiding principle is that the bank comes first. In addition, directors cannot disclose confidential information about the bank or its customers that they acquired as a result of their position on the board.

National banks and other types of financial institutions are also subject to federal and state statutes. In determining liability under certain statutory provisions, Congress has required that directors can be liable for "knowing" violations of law. This means that the director knew, or should have known, the facts concerning the violations. Therefore, the courts presume that directors know the laws.

Finally, banks and their directors are subject to regulations from bank regulators and other government agencies. Bank regulators, such as the OCC, can take administrative actions against banks and directors who engage in unsafe or unsound practices. (These practices will be explained shortly.) The administrative actions include cease and desist orders, civil money penalties, and removal of individuals from office.

In summary, the board of directors is responsible for the welfare of a bank. The attitude of the directors towards ethics and internal controls is a major factor in preventing and detecting frauds. Laws and regulations set broad limits on what bank boards can or cannot do. However, the laws and regulations do not tell us much about how boards operate.

TYPICAL COMMITTEES

The board of directors elects its own officers, which usually consist of a chairman, vice chairman, and a secretary. Equally important, it elects the officers of the bank who are expected to carry out the plans, policies, and controls established by or approved by the board. Oversight then becomes the board's primary responsibility.

The oversight functions are carried out by various committees composed of board members. It is more efficient for large boards of directors to have a few committee members deal with specific areas of concern than to encumber the entire board. Moreover, certain committees are limited to particular members of the board. Committees can make decisions on the board's behalf, or they can report back to the full board for further consideration. In either case the full board of directors is responsible for all committee decisions.

To avoid misunderstandings, the purposes, responsibilities, authority, and duration of all committees should be set forth clearly in writing. In addition, these committees should be given the resources and authority to discharge their responsibilities. And last, but not least, they should be informed and vigilant.

The structure of committees varies from bank to bank, depending on the bank's size and need. The typical committees found in banks and their general duties are presented here. In addition to their general duties, each committee must ensure that applicable laws and regulations are followed.

Executive Committee.   The executive committee is usually authorized to act on behalf of the full board of directors between its regular meetings. It may review and coordinate information from other committees as well as oversee bank operations.

Audit Committee.   This is a "watch dog" committee. Its primary responsibility is overseeing that the bank complies with applicable laws and regulations. This committee should be composed exclusively of independent directors, the minimum number should be no fewer than three independent directors, and the committee size should be small enough so that each member can be an active participant. The functions of the audit committee are (1) to select independent auditors and to work with internal auditors, (2) to review auditor's and bank examiner's reports and to consider their recommendations, and (3) to report to the board the committee's recommendations for the issues raised by the auditors. The audit committee may also consider the bank's internal controls concerning fraud and other risks. In addition, it should follow up the changes that are recommended to ensure that they are carried out.[9]

This overview of the audit committee does not cover the details of their activities. However, they should meet at least quarterly with the internal and external auditors, they should evaluate the internal audit staff and programs, and they should review management actions to correct the weaknesses and problems outlined in internal and external audit reports and examinations. This listing is not complete, but it is sufficient to indicate the key roles played by this committee.

Asset/Liability Committee. The mandate of this committee is to oversee the bank's entire balance sheet—capital, funding, and asset allocation. The major concerns of this committee include capital adequacy, interest rate sensitivity, and the quality of credits. Specific issues dealing with investments and lending are handled by other committees.

Investment Committee. The scope of the investment committee is narrower than the asset/liability committee. The investment committee establishes investment strategies and objectives. To provide guidelines for management, the committee must approve an investment policy that takes into account liquidity, pledging requirements, size, risk, and diversification of the portfolio.

Loan Committee. This committee establishes and revises lending policies to meet the changing needs of the bank. It must set standards for valid appraisals of real estate and other collateral. In some banks the loan committee participates in credit decisions. Therefore, the committee must have knowledge concerning the economy in the market area and have a clear understanding of financial statements. Above all, it should not be a "rubber stamp" for loan officers.

The committee may also be in charge of loan review, which may be external and internal, depending on the size and needs of the bank. Loan policies and loan review will be discussed shortly.

Trust Committee. Banks with trust activities have special fiduciary responsibilities to safeguard the interest of the trust customers. An important part of this is the establishment of a so-called Chinese wall to separate trust activities from other activities of the bank and to avoid conflicts of interest between the trust department, the bank, and insiders. Like the other committees, it establishes policies, fees, and deals with other aspects of trust operations. A separate *trust audit committee* oversees an annual audit of trust activities. Banking regulations require that the trust audit committee consist of directors who are not bank officers. Moreover, the directors should not serve simultaneously on the trust audit committee and the trust committee.

Personnel Committee. Quality personnel is the key to success. Thus, the board must establish policies to attract and maintain such persons. At the same time, personnel policies should be instituted that minimize the possibility of white-collar crime.[10] These should include periodic reviews of personnel policies, making sure that employees who handle money are adequately compensated so they do not embezzle funds to supplement their incomes. In addition, it should establish a written policy that adverse personal financial situations will not affect job security or promotion. This alerts the employer to potential problems and provides some measure of security to the employee. Along this line, employee education concerning white-collar crime and free and confidential financial counseling should be considered. All employees should be required to take regular vacations, which makes it difficult for them to cover up crimes on a continuing basis. Key financial personnel should be rotated for the same reason.

LENDING POLICIES

The *Comptroller's Handbook for National Bank Examiners* describes what the OCC believes to be essential elements of a bank's formal written policy statements. The board writes the statements and management is expected to implement, administer, and amplify upon them. The focus is on lending to illustrate the OCC's elements of sound policies. Lending generates most of a bank's income and is where most, but not all, of the major frauds occurred.

Loans must be made with the following objectives in mind:

1. Loans must be made on a sound and collectible basis.
2. Funds must be invested profitably for the benefit of shareholders and the protection of depositors.
3. The bank should serve the legitimate credit needs of the community in which it is located.

The handbook gives the following overview of lending policies that apply to banks in general.[11]

The lending policy should contain a general outline of the scope and allocation of the bank's credit facilities and the manner in which loans are made, serviced, and collected. The policy should be broad in nature and not overly restrictive. The formulation and enforcement of inflexible rules, not only stifles initiative, but also may, in fact, hamper probability and prevent the bank from serving the community's changing needs. A good lending policy will provide for the presentation, to the board or a committee thereof, of loans that officers believe are worthy of consideration but which are not within the purview of written guidelines. Flexibility must exist to allow for fast reaction and early adaptation to changing conditions in the bank's earning asset mix and within its service area.

In developing the lending policy, consideration must be given to the individual bank's available financial resources, personnel, facilities and future growth potential. Such guidelines must be void of any discriminatory practices. A determination of who will receive credit, and of what type and at what price, must be made. Other internal factors to be considered include who will grant the credit, in what amount, and what organizational structure will be used to ensure compliance with the bank's guidelines and procedures. As authority is spread throughout the organization, the bank must have efficient systems for monitoring adherence to established guidelines. That can best be accomplished by an internal review and reporting system which adequately informs the directorate and senior management of how policies are carried out and provides them with information sufficient to evaluate the performance of lower echelon officers and the condition of the loan portfolio.

The handbook also lists components that form the basis of a sound lending policies for banks: (Not every component is applicable for every bank.)

Geographic Limits. A bank should have geographic limits for its lending activities that reflect its trade area. The policy should state the restrictions and exceptions. New banks located in Iowa, for example, should not finance Texas real estate developments.

Distribution by Category. Limitations should be placed on the aggregate distribution of total loans in various categories of loans such as commercial, real estate, consumer, agriculture, and so on. However, some flexibility is required to meet the changing needs of the bank and the community it serves.

Types of Loans. Guidelines should be established in making specific types of loans (that is, energy, out-of-area real estate development loans), depending on the expertise of the lending officers and other factors. Particular attention should be paid to loans secured by collateral that require more than the normal policing and to types of loans where there have been abnormal losses.

Maximum Maturities. Loans should be structured with realistic repayment plans that take into account the value of collateral. Making a 15-year loan on equipment that has an economic life of five years is asking for trouble.

Loan Pricing. Loan pricing must reflect all relevant costs (cost of funds, overhead, compensating balances, fees, and so forth) and provide for a reasonable return. The rates established on loans should take risk into account, thereby attracting certain types of borrowers and discouraging others.

Maximum Ratio of Loan Amount to Appraised Value and Acquisition Costs. Many bank fraud cases involve loans in excess of appraised values and appraised values in excess of real values. Guidelines must be established concerning appraisal procedures and the amounts that will be loaned relative to appraised values.

Maximum Ratio of Loan Amount to Market Value and Pledged Securities. Banks can go beyond the restrictions on these loans imposed by Regulation U and establish additional policies for other types of marketable securities that are acceptable as collateral for loans.

Financial Information. Current, complete, and accurate information concerning a borrower's credit standing is essential before credit is granted and during the term of the loan. The loan policy should explain the types of information required from businesses and individual borrowers, such as audited quarterly financial statements and so on.

Limits and Guidelines on Purchasing Loans. Loan sales and participations are a common ingredient in bank fraud. Accordingly, policy should be established concerning the aggregate limits of such loans, contingent liabilities, and the manner in which they are evaluated, handled, and serviced.

Limitations on Aggregate Outstanding Loans. Policy should limit the amount of loans outstanding relative to other balance sheet items.

Concentrations of Credit. Diversification is considered an essential element of sound lending policy in order to balance out expected returns and risk. The problem with loan concentration is that when the repayment of those loans depends on one or more key factors that go bad, the entire concentrated part of the portfolio is affected.

Loan Authority. Lending limits should be established and enforced for all loan officers, or groups of officers, based on their lending experience. The policy should also cover the loan approval process, especially for large loans.

Collections and Charge-Offs. The policy should define delinquent loans and explain how to deal with them, including appropriate reports to the board.

Two examples of loan policies containing these and other elements of sound lending are presented in Appendixes B and C at the end of this book. As a general rule, the length of a loan policy is directly related to the size of the bank where it is used. That is, small banks have short policy statements and large banks have large policy statements. Those shown at the end of the book are for medium-size banks. Keep in mind that most major frauds that have caused bank failures were at small- and medium-size banks.

Lending Authority

Policy statements vary from bank to bank. Nevertheless, it may be useful to examine differences in procedures for loan approval at a small-, medium-, and large-size bank. The procedures are presented only for purposes of illustration. They are not being endorsed as being appropriate for other banks.

First City Bank (FCB) has $29 million in assets, with the main office and two branches serving a city with a population of 70,000. As shown in Figure 7-1, FCB divides loans into four categories: secured, unsecured and overdrafts, loans to insiders, and loans to employees. FCB has four loan officers. Their lending authority ranges from $1,500 for unsecured loans, $7,500 for secured loans for the most inexperienced loan officer, and $25,000 unsecured/$50,000 secured for the most experienced one. The president has the authority to approve unsecured and secured loans up to $100,000. Secured and unsecured loans above $100,000 must be approved by the officers' loan committee, which consists of the chairman, president, and vice president of the bank. This committee can approve loans up to $200,000. Above that amount, loans must be approved by the executive committee. The executive committee and the board of directors must approve all loans to insiders. The executive committee must also approve all loans to employees.

Southwest Bank has $150 million in assets and is part of a holding company. Southwest places significant emphasis on commercial lending as opposed to loans to individuals. The bank has 10 loan officers. New officers' limits are $25,000 and are reviewed annually by the board of directors. With favorable

Figure 7-1   First City Bank ($29 million assets)

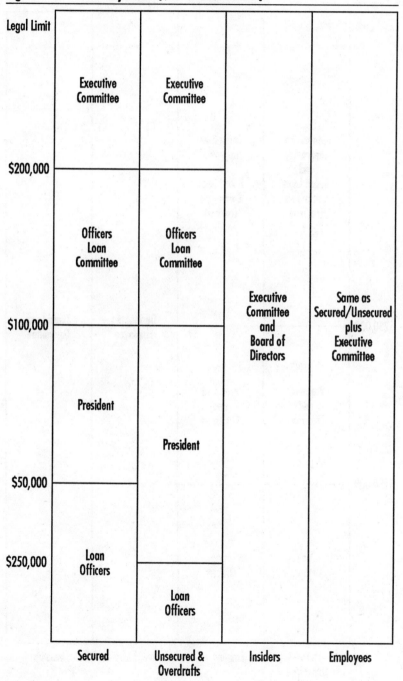

Figure 7-2 Southwest Bank ($150 million assets)

	Secured & Unsecured	Employees	Overdrafts	Insiders
Legal Limit	Loan Committee (approval) and Board Loan Committee (review)	Loan Committee (approval) and Board Loan Committee (review)		
$250,000			Designated Employee	Board Loan Committee
	President and Chairman	President and Chairman		
$150,000				
	Loan Officers	Loan Officers		

reviews, lending limits might be raised to $100,000 within two years. Southwest's two most experienced officers have limits of $150,000. The president and chairman can approve secured and unsecured loans and loans to employees up to $250,000. Loans above that amount must be approved by the loan committee (bank's executive officers and loan officers) and must be reviewed by the board's loan committee (chairman, president, vice president, and three rotating directors). Overdrafts must be approved by a designated employee with advice from a loan officer. The board's loan committee must approve all loans to insiders (see Figure 7-2).

Western Bankshares is a $4.8 billion holding company, with its banks divided into five regional areas. Each region has a regional loan committee that includes regional bank officers and directors. The lending authority in this bank is shown in Figure 7-3. Individual lending authorities range from zero for trainees to $500,000 secured/$250 unsecured for each of the regional presidents. The regional loan committee may approve loans up to $2 million. Loans between $2 million to $5 million requires approval from the regional loan committee and two regional presidents. Loans above that amount require approval from the holding company loan committee.

In Western Bank, a customer's total lending relationship is considered when a request for a new loan is made. If a customer has an outstanding loan for $100,000 and requests an additional $10,000, the request is considered a $110,000 loan in the approval process.

Loans to insiders must be approved by the board of directors, and employee loans by an officers executive committee. This committee includes a regional president and senior vice-presidents.

In reviewing the approval processes for the three banks, it is clear that large loans for all the banks are approved by higher authorities within the bank. Since most major fraud involves large loans, checks and balances must be established by the board. One check is the loan review process.

Figure 7-3   Western Bankshares ($4.8 billion assets)

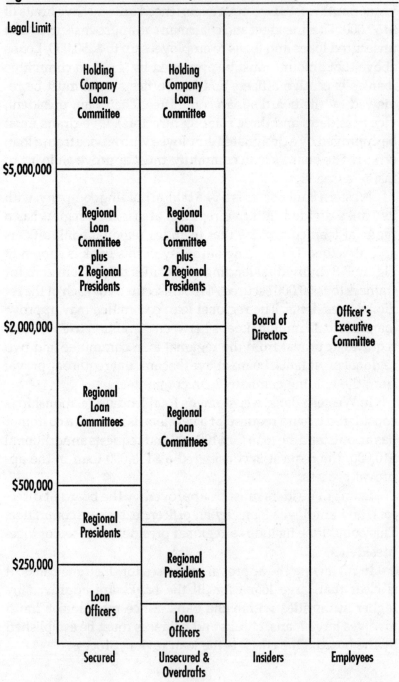

LOAN REVIEW

The primary purpose of loan review is to audit the lending function of the bank on a regular basis. Loan reviews should be used to determine if a bank's lending policies are being followed by its loan officers and credit analysts, and if there are potential loan losses or problem loans that have not been recognized. Early detection of potential problems permits the bank to take corrective actions before they become major problems.

The loan reviewers may be internal or external, depending on the size of the bank. Large banks are better able to afford an internal review system than small ones. Some of the factors that must be considered in establishing an internal review are:

1. Structure of the loan review function. Will loan review be centralized in the main bank or decentralized at the branches? Will each branch have its own loan review staff, or will there be only one loan review department?
2. Reporting. Who will be in charge of the loan review, and to whom does this person report? Are there potential conflicts of interest?
3. Staffing. How many employees will loan review need to support its function?
4. Functions. What will loan review do? Exactly what should the reviewer look for—documentation, credit analysis, external problems, or fraud?
5. Scope. Will all loans above or below a certain dollar amount be reviewed, or will a sample be taken?

Here is how a $3 billion bank holding company does its loan review. Its organization is based on functional lines where the main divisions are the corporate group, general banking, and investments. Loan review is operated at the holding company level, and it reports to the corporate group division manager, who reports to the vice-chairman of the board. It has a staff of ten loan review officers and support personnel. The loan review officers are experienced in all areas of lending and knowledgeable in documentation.

The loan review department reviews, on an annual basis, all loans over $50,000, and they sample loans below that benchmark for consumer loans. Reports are written on each loan review stating whether it showed any signs of repayment problems or documentation problems. Problem loans are reviewed three or four times each year until the problems are resolved.

External reviews have certain advantages for small-size banks. According to a recent study, the costs of a permanent loan review staff may be too high for almost 60 percent of the banks—those with assets of $50 million or less.[12] Because of their small size, one advantage of an external review is an independent assessment of the loan review function. Another advantage is the ability to control the costs of the review. Finally, the directors of new banks may have little experience in the area of loan review. External reviews provide that experience. Along this line, it may be noted that there are a large number of failures among new (de novo) banks and savings and loan associations. The directors of de novos need all of the help they can get at a reasonable price.

PRACTICES DEEMED UNSAFE OR UNSOUND[13]

The board of directors of a bank is responsible for establishing the bank's operating practices. We have examined what banks are expected to do in the lending area to illustrate operating practices. Now lets look at the other side of the coin and learn what they should not do. According to the FDIC, certain practices are considered "unsafe or unsound." *Unsafe or unsound* refers to practices that are contrary to the generally accepted standards of prudent operation and, if continued, could result in the abnormal risk of loss to the bank, to its shareholders, or to the federal insurance fund. The following examples, based on the FDIC's *Manual of Examination Policies*, illustrate such practices. However, two caveats are in order. First, the examples do not cover every type of unsafe or unsound activity. Second, not every instance of these activities is unsafe or unsound. Therefore, each situation must be considered on its own merits.

Lack of management actions deemed unsafe or unsound:

1. Failure to provide adequate supervision and direction over the bank's officers in order to prevent unsafe or unsound practices and the violation of laws and regulations.
2. Failure to make provision for sufficient reserves to cover possible loan losses.
3. Failure to make prompt postings to the general ledger.
4. Failure to account properly for transactions and to keep accurate books and records.
5. Failure to enforce loan repayment policies.
6. Failure to have proper documentation on the priority of liens on loans secured by real estate.

Management actions deemed unsafe or unsound:

1. Operating with inadequate capital to support the quality of assets held.
2. Engaging in hazardous lending and lax collection practices. Such practices include making loans with inadequate security, extending credit without first obtaining current and complete financial information about the borrower, extending credit in the form of overdrafts without proper controls, and inadequate diversification of loan portfolio.
3. Operating with inadequate liquidity or sources of funding.
4. Operating with inadequate internal controls on official checks and unissued CDs, failure to segre-

gate duties of bank personnel, and the failure to reconcile differences in correspondent bank accounts.

5. Engaging in speculative investment policies.
6. Paying excessive dividends taking the banks financial condition into account.
7. Paying excessive bonuses, salaries, fees, and commissions to insiders and their related interests.

Condition of a bank deemed unsafe or unsound:

1. Maintaining very low net interest margins (interest income less interest expense divided by average earning assets).
2. Excessive overhead expenses.
3. Excessive volume of loans classified by the examiners.
4. Excessive net loan and lease losses.
5. Excessive volume of past-due loans.
6. Excessive volume of nonearning assets.
7. Excessive dependence on large denomination liabilities.

THE SERVE PRINCIPLE

The activities of directors are summarized in the SERVE principle:[14]

- *Select* qualified management.
- *Establish* business goals, policies, standards, and procedures.
- *Review* business performance.
- *Voice* opinions and questions.
- *Enforce* compliance.

Ethical behavior is the final consideration. In this context, it refers to a director's choice for courses of action that benefit the bank, its stockholders, and customers. The director's choices do not benefit his or her own interests, and they do not harm others. If directors cannot comply with the SERVE principles, or if they have significant disagreements with other directors or management that cannot be resolved to their satisfaction, they should resign. The power of resignation is less costly for independent directors than for inside directors. Nevertheless, it is an option that should not be ignored.

Finally, directors should establish a code of ethics for all directors, officers, and employees of the organization. The code of ethics sends a strong message from the top of the organization down to all other levels as to how business is to be conducted. A code of ethics is discussed in Chapter 9.

Notes

1. *Bank Failure: An Evaluation of the Factors Contributing to the Failure of National Banks, Washington, D.C.: Office of the Comptroller of the Currency,* June 1988, 5-7, 15-16.

2. Philip F. Bartholomew, Financial Economist, Federal Home Loan Bank Board, Statement before the United States Sentencing Commission, April 7, 1989; Also see U.S. General Accounting Office, *Failed Thrifts: Internal Control Weaknesses Create an Environment Conducive to Fraud, Insider Abuse, and Related Unsafe Practices,* Statement of Frederick D. Wolf before the Subcommittee on Criminal Justice Committee on the Judiciary, House of Representatives, GAO/T-AFMD-89-4, March 22, 1989, 13.

3. U.S. Government Accounting Office, *Thrift Failures: Costly Failures Resulted from Regulatory Violations and Unsafe Practices,* GAO/AFMD-89-62, June 1989, 18.

4. Peter F. Drucker, *Management: Tasks, Responsibilities, Practices,* New York: Harper & Row, Publishers, 1974, 628.

5. "A Seat on the Board Is Getting Hotter," *Business Week,* July 3, 1989, 73.

6. *The Director's Book: The Role of a National Bank Director,* Washington, D.C., Office of the Comptroller of the Currency, August 1987, 56-57; Alan E. Grunewald and Richard B. Foster, Jr., "Bank Directors' Liability for Negligence and the Business Judgment Rule," *Journal of the Midwest Finance Association,* Vol. 12, 1983, 109-127; Michael Patriarca, The Role and Responsibility of a Savings Institution Director," *Perspectives,* Federal Home Loan Bank of San Francisco, Fall 1988, 2-6.

7. *Joy v. North,* 692 F.2d 880, 896, (2d Cir. 1982), cited in Federal Home Loan Bank Board Memoranda #R-62, Directors' Responsibilities: FHLBB Guidelines;

Procedures for Obtaining Information to Support Directors' Decisions," November 1988, 2689.

8. U.S. General Accounting Office, *Failed Thrifts:*, March 22, 1989, ibid. 16-17.

9. See "Good Practice Guidelines for the Audit Committee," *Report of the National Commission on Fraudulent Financial Reporting*, National Commission on Fraudulent Financial Reporting, October 1987 (no city listed), 179-182.

10. Joseph T. Wells, "White-Collar Crime: Myths and Strategies," *The Practical Accountant*, August 1985, 43-45.

11. *Comptroller's Handbook for National Bank Examiners*, Washington, D.C.: Office of the Comptroller of the Currency, Section 205.1, September 1977.

12. Fred H. Hays, Daniel L. Enterline, and Probir Roy, "Community Bank Directors: Should Your Bank Have an External Review?" *Journal of Commercial Bank Lending*, April 1989, 21-29.

13. This section is based on the FDIC *Manual of Examination Policies*, parts of which appear in: U.S. House, *Federal Response to Criminal Misconduct by Bank Officers, Directors, and Insiders, Part 2*, Hearings before the Commerce, Consumer, and Monetary Affairs Subcommittee of the Committee on Government Operations, 98th Cong., 2d Sess., May 2 and 3, 1984, 1383-1384.

14. *The Director's Guide: The Role and Responsibilities of a Savings Institution Director*, Federal Home Loan Bank of San Francisco, 1988, 26.

8

INTERNAL CONTROLS AND AUDITING

Reasons for Using Internal Controls

A substantial amount of fraud can be prevented using strong internal controls as illustrated by the following case.[1] According to Bob Serino, deputy chief counsel of the operations section of the OCC, this situation was the best example of the worst controls. The installment loan department of a community bank in Colorado was under the control of one individual. The loan officer's responsibilities included accepting applications, making credit decisions, and granting extensions and renewals. The bank's directors were pleased with the loan officer's performance. The installment loan portfolio increased and generated needed income. The portfolio had a low level of loan losses, and the volume of past-due accounts was manageable. New customers were brought into the bank.

Over a three-year period, OCC examiners and external auditors criticized the bank for poor internal controls in all departments. Recognizing that smaller banks have a limited number of personnel and have logistical problems in segregating duties, the importance of close supervision and review was continually stressed for areas where proper controls could not be applied realistically. Also, management reporting systems were weak, and the board of directors was not receiving accurate information to exercise its duties and responsibilities fully. The reports often reviewed by the board were erroneous, and problems in the management information systems were repeatedly brought to the board's attention, but the problems continued.

A result of the identified deficiencies was an expanded examination and audit. Subsequently, additional reporting errors were disclosed. Consistent reprimands for internal control deficiencies and reporting errors contributed to the dismissal of the installment loan officer.

The problem then multiplied. The quality of the installment loan portfolio deteriorated, and the volume of past-due loans increased. Loans were found to be undercollateralized, and the volume of extensions was extremely high. It was then discovered that the installment loan officer had made fraudulent loans and had embezzled the proceeds. Loans were made under fictitious names, either unsecured or secured, with the same collateral held for true loans. With complete control of the installment loan department, it was not difficult for the installment loan officer to extend payments on fraudulent loans, maintaining a current status. Consequently, new loans were created to pay maturing loans, and a legal lending limit violation was concealed to prevent scrutiny of the loan portfolio. Management reports were generated manually; therefore, they were easily manipulated to reflect a high-quality loan portfolio.

Research by external auditors and an enlightened board of directors disclosed that the defalcation amounted to more than $1 million. The bank's capital could not sustain a loss of that size, and shortly thereafter, the bank failed.

Management is responsible for devising and maintaining internal controls. *Internal controls* can be defined as the plan of organization, methods, and measures used to safeguard assets, to ensure the accuracy and reliability of data, to ensure compliance with policies and applicable laws and regulations, and to promote management efficiency.[2] Stated otherwise, internal controls are procedures for prevention and detection within the context of accounting and administrative systems. They are intended to prevent individuals from taking unwanted actions, such as altering financial records, and they help to detect errors and irregularities. *Errors* are unintentional mistakes or omissions. *Irregularities* are intentional mistakes or omissions and include fraudulent financial reporting. A loan that does not conform to an institution's loan policy may be an error. Making a fictitious loan is an irregularity. The existence of strong internal controls may be sufficient to deter some fraudulent acts. According to the Comptroller of the Currency, good internal controls exist when no one person is in a position to make significant errors or perpetrate significant irregularities without timely detection. Internal controls also allow managers and auditors to verify the accuracy of the accounting for transactions. Thus, internal controls are an essential element of good management. However, even the best control systems will not work if they are not used properly. Someone, or a group of individuals, intent on circumventing controls can probably do so.

There are additional reasons for using internal controls. First, the Foreign Corrupt Practices Act of 1977 has accounting provisions that apply to all publicly held companies having securities registered with the Securities and Exchange Commission.[3] The act requires such firms to keep reasonably detailed financial records reflecting their financial activities and disposition of assets. The Act also requires them to devise and maintain a system of internal controls sufficient to provide reasonable assurances that transactions are executed in accordance with management's authorization; that transactions are recorded to permit the preparation of financial statements in conformity with generally accepted accounting standards, and maintain accountability for assets; and that access to assets is permitted only with management's authorization.

Second, the board of directors of a financial institution has a fiduciary responsibility to its depositors and shareholders to provide an adequate internal control structure and to ensure that the controls are operating effectively.

The final reasons for using internal controls are that strong internal controls serve as a buffer against adverse economic conditions. They can also help deter insider abuse and fraud.

Weaknesses in internal controls are a significant factor in bank failures. These are findings from a U.S. General Accounting Office (GAO) study.[4] The study covered external factors over which management had no control, such as adverse economic conditions and restrictions on branch banking. These factors affected all banks in Texas and other parts of the country. Controls must change to adapt to changing business environments and external factors. Some changes in the business environment that may weaken existing controls are the acquisition of new types of businesses where the existing accounting systems are left in place, the introduction of new products or technologies that may affect reserves for loan losses, and rapid growth which causes problems because control procedures rely on individuals who become overloaded.[5] The GAO found severe internal control weaknesses were pervasive in all of the banks that failed, while they were present to a lesser extent in healthy banks.

In a separate study of thrifts that failed, the GAO found internal control deficiencies, violations of laws and regulations, and unsafe practices existed at all of the institutions that failed.[6] According to GAO Director Frederick D. Wolf:

> Some people within the financial institutions industry have expressed the view that the unprecedented problems and re-sultant failures are largely due to economic downturns in certain regions. However, both of our reviews led to a different conclusion. Well-managed institutions with strong internal controls appeared able to remain viable institutions despite downturns in local economies. Conversely, existing problems at poorly run institutions were exacerbated by adverse economic conditions, often leading to failure.[7]

The key points are that well-managed institutions survived and that having strong internal controls is one aspect of good management. Conversely, lack of strong internal controls raises questions about the quality of management.

ESTABLISHING INTERNAL CONTROLS

In the past, accounting controls were considered separate from administrative controls. In April 1988, the American Institute of Certified Public Accountants, (AICPA) considered the two together, describing them as the "internal control structure." The AICPA defines *internal control structure* as "The policies and procedures established to provide reasonable assurance that specific entity objectives will be achieved." The AICPA Statement on Auditing Standards Number 55, *Consideration of the Internal Control Structure in a Financial Statement Audit*, describes the three elements of an internal control structure. The first element, control environment, concerns the environment in which the controls are used. In short, the effectiveness of the controls depends on the collective effect of various factors, including management philosophy, organizational structure, the role of the board of directors and its committees, the communication of authority and responsibility, management control methods, the internal audit function, personnel policies and procedures, and environmental factors. The second element, accounting system, deals with the methods and records used to report transactions and maintain accountability for assets and liabilities. The control procedures, the final element, deals with the policies and control procedures established to assure that management's objectives are carried out.

Auditing standard number 55 provides guidance for independent auditors who must evaluate the internal control structure of an organization and for planning and performing an audit. Federal and state bank examiners have somewhat different but overlapping concerns in evaluating a bank's internal controls.

The *Comptroller's Handbook for National Bank Examiners* explains the Comptroller of the Currency's view of internal controls and provides detailed "Internal Control Questionnaires" for areas of concern to national bank examiners.[8] The OCC states that while procedures are an important element of internal controls, actual practices must be taken into account. In addition, the procedures must be performed by competent individuals. Equally important is independent performance. Independent performance refers to the effective segregation of duties or "positions." For example, a cashier is the sole check signer and an assistant prepares the monthly reconcilement. Although both may be competent individuals, the assistant is under the direct supervision of the cashier. Therefore, the assistant's duties should be viewed as if they were performed by the cashier.

The Internal Control Questionnaires are a starting point for examiners to determine a bank's control procedures. The questionnaires are general because the OCC recognizes that what applies to one bank may not apply to another. Accordingly, the questionnaires provide some insights into what the OCC considers good controls and into problem areas that might undermine the controls. Figure 8-1 is the Internal Control Questionnaire for Commercial Loans, and it is used to illustrate a typical questionnaire. The asterisks by certain questions indicate that they are critical areas of concern that require substantiation by examiner observation or testing. Question number three is the first question so marked. It deals with the preparation and posting of subsidiary commercial loan records. The second critical question deals with the reconciliation of those records.

AUDITING: CLOSING THE EXPECTATION GAP

The Securities and Exchange Commission (SEC) is the principal federal agency involved in accounting and auditing standards for publicly traded companies. It establishes rules and regulations for public disclosure and independent audits. The SEC has accepted the Generally Accepted Accounting Principles (GAAP) promulgated by the Financial Accounting Standards Board, and the Generally Accepted Auditing Standards (GAAS) promulgated by the AICPA as the standards for meeting its disclosure requirements. Federal banking regulators also impose

Figure 8-1   Commercial Loans Internal Control Questionnaire Section 206.4

Review the bank's internal controls, policies, practices and procedures for making and servicing commercial loans. The bank's system should be documented in a complete and concise manner and should include, where appropriate, narrative descriptions, flowcharts, copies of forms used and other pertinent information. Items marked with asterisks require substantiation by observation or testing.

Commercial Loan Policies

1. Has the board of directors, consistent with its duties and responsibilities, adopted written commercial loan policies that:
    a. Establish procedures for reviewing commercial loan applications?
    b. Define qualified borrowers?
    c. Establish minimum standards for documentation?
2. Are commercial loan policies reviewed at least annually to determine if they are compatible with changing market conditions?

COMMERCIAL LOAN RECORDS

*3. Is the preparation and posting of subsidiary commercial loan records performed or reviewed by persons who do not also:
     a. Issue official checks or drafts singly?
     b. Handle cash?
*4. Are the subsidiary commercial loan records reconciled daily with the appropriate general ledger accounts, and are reconciling items investigated by persons who do not also handle cash?
5. Are delinquent account collection requests and past due notices checked to the trial balances that are used in reconciling commercial loan subsidiary records with general ledger accounts, and are they handled only by persons who do not also handle cash?
6. Are inquiries about loan balances received and investigated by persons who do not also handle cash?
*7. Are documents supporting recorded credit adjustments checked or tested subsequently by persons who do not also handle cash (if so, explain briefly)?
8. Is a daily record maintained summarizing note transaction details, *i.e.*, loans made, payments received and interest collected, to support applicable general ledger account entries?

Figure 8-1   Continued

9. Are frequent note and liability ledger trial balances prepared and reconciled with controlling accounts by employees who do not process or record loan transactions?

10. Is an overdue account report generated frequently (if so, how often _____)?

11. Are subsidiary payment records and files pertaining to serviced loans segregated and identifiable?

LOAN INTEREST

*12. Is the preparation and posting of interest records performed or reviewed by persons who do not also:
    a. Issue official checks or drafts singly?
    b. Handle cash?

13. Are any independent interest computations made and compared or tested to initial interest record by persons who do not also:
    a. Issue official checks or drafts singly?
    b. Handle cash?

COLLATERAL

14. Are multicopy, prenumbered records maintained that:
    a. Detail the complete description of collateral pledged?
    b. Are typed or completed in ink?
    c. Are signed by the customer?
    d. Are designed so that a copy goes to the customer?

15. Are the functions of receiving and releasing collateral to borrowers and of making entries in the collateral register performed by different employees?

16. Is negotiable collateral held under joint custody?

17. Are receipts obtained and filed for released collateral?

18. Are securities and commodities valued and margin requirements reviewed at least monthly?

19. When the support rests on the cash surrender value of insurance policies, is a periodic accounting received from the insurance company and maintained with the policy?

20. Is a record maintained of entry to the collateral vault?

Figure 8-1   Continued

21. Are stock powers filed separately to bar negotiability and to deter abstraction of both the security and the negotiating instrument?

22. Are securities out for transfer, exchange, etc., controlled by prenumbered temporary vault-out tickets?

23. Has the bank instituted a system which:
  a. Insures that security agreements are filed?
  b. Insures that collateral mortgages are properly recorded?
  c. Insures that title searches and property appraisals are performed in connection with collateral mortgages?
  d. Insures that insurance coverage (including loss payee clause) is in effect on property covered by collateral mortgages?

24. Are coupon tickler cards set up covering all coupon bonds held as collateral?

25. Are written instructions obtained and held on file covering the cutting of coupons?

26. Are coupon cards under the control of persons other than those assigned to coupon cutting?

27. Are pledged deposit accounts properly coded to negate unauthorized withdrawal of funds?

28. Are acknowledgments received for pledged deposits held at other banks?

29. Is an officer's approval necessary before collateral can be released or substituted?

OTHER

30. Are notes safeguarded during banking hours and locked in the vault overnight?

31. Are all loan rebates approved by an officer and made only by official check?

32. Does the bank have an internal review system that:
  a. Re-examines collateral items for negotiability and proper assignment?
  b. Test checks values assigned to collateral when the loan is made and at frequent intervals thereafter?
  c. Determines that items out on temporary vault-out tickets are authorized and have not been outstanding for an unreasonable length of time?
  d. Determines that loan payments are promptly posted?
  e. Insures compliance with the requirements of governmental agencies insuring or guaranteeing loans?

Figure 8-1 Continued

33. Are all notes recorded on a note register or similar record and assigned consecutive numbers?

34. Are collection notices handled by someone not connected with loan processing?

35. Are payment notices prepared and mailed by someone other than the loan teller?

36. Does the bank prohibit the holding of debtor's checks for payment of loans at maturity?

37. Concerning livestock loans:
   a. Are inspections made at the inception of credit?
   b. Are inspections properly dated and signed?
   c. Is there a breakdown by sex, breed, and number of animals in each category?
   d. Is the condition of the animals noted?
   e. Are inspections required at least annually?

38. Concerning crop loans:
   a. Are inspections of growing crops made as loans are advanced?
   b. Are disbursements closely monitored to assure that the proceeds are properly channeled into the farmer's operation?
   c. Is crop insurance encouraged?

39. In mortgage warehouse financing, does the bank hold the original mortgage note, trust deed or other critical document, releasing only against payment?

40. Concerning commodity lending:
   a. Is control for the collateral satisfactory, *i.e.*, stored in the bank's vault, another bank, or a bonded warehouse?
   b. If collateral is not stored within the bank, are procedures in effect to ascertain the authenticity of the collateral?
   c. Does the bank have a documented security interest in the proceeds of the future sale or disposition of the commodity as well as the existing collateral position?
   d. Do credit files document that the financed positions are and remain fully hedged?

41. Concerning loans to commodity brokers and dealers:
   a. Does the bank maintain a list of the major customer accounts on the brokers or dealers to whom it lends? If so, is the list updated on a periodic basis?

Figure 8-1   Continued

b. Is the bank aware of the broker/dealer's policy on margin requirements and the basis for valuing contracts for margin purposes (*i.e.*, pricing spot vs. future)?

c. Does the bank attempt to ascertain whether the positions of the broker/dealer's clients that are indirectly financed by bank loans remain fully hedged?

CONCLUSION

42.   Is the foregoing information an adequate basis for evaluating internal control in that there are no significant additional internal auditing procedures, accounting controls, administrative controls, or other circumstances that impair any controls or mitigate any weaknesses indicated above (explain negative answers briefly, and indicate conclusions as to their effect on specific examination or verification procedures)?

24.   Based on a composite evaluation, as evidenced by answers to the foregoing questions, internal control is considered _____ (good, medium, or bad).

Source: Comptroller's Handbook for National Bank Examiners August 1982

reporting requirements for the institutions they regulate. Independent audits are an important part of the disclosure process.

> Full, fair, and accurate disclosure of financial results is a cornerstone of our system of public securities markets... The public accountant's audit is an important element in the financial reporting process because the audit subjects financial statements, which are management's responsibility, to scrutiny on behalf of shareholders and creditors to whom management is responsible.[9]

Against this background, our primary concerns are with bank fraud and the ongoing operations of banks. We know that the existence and effective operation of internal controls reduces the chance for fraud and enhances the ability of a bank to survive. Nevertheless, fraud exists and banks fail for a variety of reasons. Therefore, the issues are: (1) to what extent can auditors detect fraud, (2) if they do discover it, what should they do about it? Also, to what extent do auditors detect and report financial difficulties that may affect the survival of a bank? One difficulty in examining these issues involves the so-called expectation gap, which is the difference between the public's expectation and the accounting profession's expectations of auditors. The public expects auditors to be able to detect fraud or irregularities and to do something about it, such as reporting fraud to bank regulators or law enforcement officials. The public expects auditors to have some insight into the ability of firms to survive. The public confidence in auditors was shaken in the mid-1970s for reasons that will be explained shortly. This lack of confidence was expressed in the following accountant's report that appeared on the cover of *Forbes* (March 15, 1977).

> To the directors and stockholders:
>
> We have examined the Consolidated Balance Sheet of the company and Consolidated subsidiaries as of December 31, 1976 and 1975. In our opinion, these financial statements present fairly the financial position of the companies, in conformity with generally accepted accounting principles consistently applied.
>
> On the other hand, there is a growing body of opinion that holds that our opinion is not worth a damn.

As part of an effort to alter this opinion, Congress introduced legislation (House Bill 5439) in 1986 requiring auditors to detect and report material fraud directly to the SEC. The accounting profession has a different set of expectations. What is an audit and the auditor's point of view?

According to the American Accounting Association,

> Auditing is a systematic process of objectively obtaining and evaluating evidence regarding assertions about economic actions and events to ascertain the degree of correspondence between those assertions and established criteria and communicating the results to interested users.[10]

This comprehensive definition suggests that auditors seek to determine if management's full and fair disclosures about their financial condition are represented fairly within the context of generally accepted accounting standards. To make this determination, auditors take into the account audit objectives for various components of the financial statements. Selected objectives for auditing a bank's assets are presented to illustrate one aspect of the audit process.[11] These audit objectives are:

1. Existence or occurrence—Determine if the assets presented in the balance sheet exist.
2. Completeness—Determine if the quantities of particular assets, such as securities, include all items on hand, held by others, or in transit. In addition, all amounts that should be recorded are, in fact, recorded.
3. Rights and obligations—Determine if the bank has legal title to the assets, excluding collateral owned by others or pledged on loans.
4. Valuation or allocations—Determine that assets are properly valued at cost, market value, or fair value.
5. Presentation and disclosure—Determine that the assets are properly categorized in the balance sheet and that their basis for valuation, pledging, or assignment is adequately disclosed in the financial statements.

All of this is done to determine if management is fair in its assertions about its assets. Different audit objectives are applied to other parts of the financial statements to determine "fairness." Unfortunately, the concept of "fair" in fraud is by its very nature covert and difficult for auditors and investigators to uncover. This is especially true when a complex fraud involves numerous seemingly unrelated banks and firms. Thus, the discovery of fraud is infrequently a by-product of the audit process. Therefore, it is not surprising that auditors' track records for discovering fraud are not good. Moreover, if they do discover fraud, they do not disclose it to the public or regulatory authorities. There is a long history of controversy regarding auditors' reporting responsibilities.[12] They are guided by conflicting demands (the Code of Professional Ethics, SASs, laws, and so on) and are pulled by the interests of various stakeholder groups—shareholders, creditors, SEC, bank regulators, and others. Each of these groups expects the auditors to act on their behalf; consequently, auditors have compartmentalized their responsibilities. Their primary reporting responsibility is to the client for illegal acts, to the SEC for filings, to the IRS for tax returns, and to shareholders and creditors for their opinion on financial statements taken as a whole.

In the early 1970s several large companies were cited for making illegal or questionable payments to foreign officials as bribes to get contracts and for other purposes. In a 1976 program of voluntary disclosure to the SEC, some 250 companies admitted to such payments. In 1977, Congress enacted the Foreign Corrupt Practices Act requiring SEC registrants to maintain the accounting standards that were explained previously. The following year, the Commission on Auditor's Responsibilities (the Cohen Commission) recommended that auditors have a duty to search for fraud. In 1987, the National Commission on Fraudulent Financial Reporting (the Treadway Commission) made 49 recommendations to detect and deter fraudulent financial reporting.[13] Furthermore, the Treadway Commission examined 119 enforcement actions against public companies or individuals and 42 enforcement actions against public accountants or their firms brought by the SEC from 1981 to 1986. Their study revealed that fraudulent financial reporting was usually the result of environmental, institutional, or individual forces or opportunities. A frequent incentive for engaging in fraudulent reporting was to improve a company's financial appearance or to postpone dealing with financial difficulties.

In 1988, the AICPA's Auditing Standards Board issued new Statements of Auditing Standards (SAS) that addressed some of these issues, but it did not resolve them to everyone's satisfaction. Traditionally, auditing standards have recognized the auditor-client relationship, and the auditor's primary responsibility for reporting illegal acts was to the client. This reporting relationship is changing. It is demonstrated by the following auditing standards. Although auditors report to their clients, the U.S. Supreme Court in *United States* v. *Arthur Young & Co.* emphasized that "The independent public accountant... owes ultimate allegiance to the corporation's creditors and stockholders, as well as to the investing public."[14]

SAS No. 53, *The Auditor's Responsibility to Detect and Report Errors and Irregularities* states that auditors should exercise due care in auditing and the proper degree of professional skepticism to "achieve reasonable assurance that material errors or irregularities will be detected."[15] If irregularities are detected, the auditor must assess the risk. Will they have a direct and material effect on the determination of financial statement amounts? If such a condition exists, the auditor should insist that the statements be revised; and if they are not, give a qualified or adverse opinion and disclose the reasons for doing so. The auditor should communicate the findings to the audit committee or the board of directors. Under certain conditions, a duty may exist to make disclosures to parties other than the client. Those conditions are:

- When the organization reports an auditor change to the SEC on Form 8-K.
- To a successor auditor when inquiries are made in accordance with SAS No. 7, *Communications Between Predecessor and Successor Auditors.*
- In response to a subpoena.
- To a funding agency, or government agency requiring audits of organizations receiving their financial support.

Unfortunately, such cooperation from auditors is not always forthcoming. Arthur Young & Company audited Lincoln

Savings and Loan Association, the nation's largest thrift failure, which is expected to cost taxpayers $2.5 billion. Richard Breeden, chairman of the Securities and Exchange Commission said Arthur Young auditors were "very unhelpful, very unforthcoming and very uncooperative in any shape, way or form" during an SEC investigation of securities violations at Lincoln Savings and Loan.[16]

SAS No. 53 goes on to say that because of ethical and legal considerations, the auditor may wish to get legal counsel before discussing the results with outside parties except their client. It also states that the subsequent discovery of material misstatement in financial statements does not, in and of itself, mean that the audit was inadequate.

SAS No. 54, *Illegal Acts by Clients* defines illegal acts as violations of laws or government regulations. Illegal acts by clients are acts attributable to the entity whose financial statements are under audit, or acts by management or employees on behalf of the client. They do not include personal misconduct by the entity's personnel unrelated to their business activities.

The final determination of legality is normally beyond the scope of an auditor's professional competence. Keeping this in mind, auditors should consider laws and regulations from the perspective of their known relation to the audit objectives and report and/or disclose irregularities accordingly. The Financial Institutions Reform, Recovery and Enforcement Act of 1989 (Title XII) requires the FDIC (or other federal insurance corporations) to designate the applicable laws and regulations relating to safety and soundness that managements of financial institutions must consider. It also requires independent public accountants to review and report on management's assertions concerning their internal controls and compliance with applicable laws and regulations.

If the illegal act does not have a direct and material impact on the financial statements, and the audit was conducted in accordance with generally accepted auditing standards, there is no assurance that the illegal act will be detected or that any contingent liability that may result from that act will be disclosed. However, as in SAS No. 53, the auditor may have a duty to notify outside parties of the illegal acts.

SAS No. 58, *Reports on Audited Financial Statements* clarifies the auditor's role with new statements in the auditor's reports. The statements say the financial reports are the responsibility of the entities management, and the auditor's responsibility is to express an opinion on those statements. The auditor's report goes on to elaborate on the procedures performed and auditor assurance.

SAS No. 59, *The Auditor's Consideration of an Entity's Ability to Continue as a Going Concern* deals with the potential failure of a firm. The auditor has the responsibility in all audits to evaluate whether there is substantial doubt about the entity's ability to continue as a going concern for the next year. If there is substantial doubt, the auditor should consider the adequacy of disclosure and include an explanatory paragraph in the audit report to reflect that conclusion. If the firm's disclosures are not adequate in this regard, the auditor can give a qualified or adverse opinion. One member of the Auditing Standards Board dissented on voting on this SAS. He argued that without new auditing procedures to fulfill this new responsibility, the result widened, rather than narrowed, the expectation gap.

SAS No. 60, *Communications of Internal Control Structure Related Matters Noted in an Audit* concerns significant deficiencies or "reportable conditions" in the design or operation of the internal control structure. Auditors finding conditions that could adversely affect the organization's ability to produce reliable financial disclosures are required to report them to the audit committee or its equivalent.

SAS No. 61, *Communications with Audit Committees* requires auditors to ensure that the audit committee or its equivalent receive information regarding the audit that may assist them in overseeing the financial reporting and disclosure process for which management is responsible. The statement does not require such communications with management.

Auditor's ability to detect and report the financial difficulties of banks leaves a lot to be desired. For example, the GAO studied the most recent audit reports performed by certified public accountants (CPAs) on 11 failed S&Ls.[17] The study found that in six cases, the CPAs did not adequately audit and/or report the S&L's financial or internal control problems in accordance with professional standards. The latest audit reports for the 11 S&Ls showed a combined net worth of about $44 million before failure. At the time the S&Ls failed, which ranged from 5 to 17 months after the audit reports, they had a combined *negative* net worth of about $1.5 billion. No doubt some of these failures occurred immediately after the audits were made. Nevertheless, that does not explain the following examples of CPA audits and disclosures:

- Lack of sufficient evidence in working papers that the CPA firm performed an analysis of the collectibility of acquisition, development, and construction (ADC) loans because the loans were new and the CPA firm assumed them to be collectible. In their defense, the *AICPA Audit and Accounting Guide for Savings and Loan Associations* contained little discussion of the risks associated with land and ADC loans.

- Lacked sufficient evidence in working papers that the CPA firm identified and evaluated the effect of restructured loans. Federal examiners found that the S&L did not report that it had restructured about $625 million in loans during the period covered by the audit. In that same audit, the CPAs did not evaluate the collectibility of $30 million past-due loans guaranteed by two principal shareholders.

- A CPA firm did not properly disclose in its audit report that an S&L incorrectly reported $12 million in expected recoveries from law suits that were pending. The S&L used the expected recoveries to offset reported losses. Accounting principles prohibit the reporting recoveries from lawsuits until the cases are resolved. Also, the CPA firm did not disclose its own findings that the S&Ls losses would probably be greater than reported.

- A CPA firm failed to disclose that an S&L had several hundred million dollars of loans secured by property in a limited geographic area. Most of the loans were made to principal shareholders of that association.
- Two CPA firms reported that their clients had no material weaknesses in internal controls despite the fact that the S&Ls were under formal regulatory enforcement actions for severe internal control weaknesses.

The expectation gap is narrower than it was before; however, we still have a long way to go before it is closed. In fact, some issues will never be resolved. For example, the author of a recent article stated that " . . . companies search for accounting methods that best suit the game plan. This results in a patchwork of accounting methodology that adheres to particular, and often conflicting, viewpoints while objectivity falls by the wayside."[18]

Another factor that inhibits the gap from closing is that auditors are not trained criminal investigators. Auditing methodology is directed toward objectivity and away from criminal investigation.[19] To illustrate one difference, consider the concepts of materiality and evidence. Auditors must determine if there is a "reasonable assurance" that important information about financial transactions is presented fairly. They set the desired level of assurance to fit the existing circumstance and acquire the information or evidence to achieve the desired level of assurance. Under the rules of law, matter offered in evidence in a case must be relevant to the issues and either tend to establish or disprove them. What is relevant and material, admissible and unadmissible is clearly delineated, and there is little room for "reasonable assurance."

Internal Auditors

The previous discussion centered on independent audits. However, the first line of defense against fraud is the internal auditor. The objective of the internal audit function is to assist the audit committee and management by providing them with an objective evaluation of the accuracy, adequacy, and effectiveness of various aspects of going operations. These include internal controls, audit trails, operational procedures, compliance, and so on.

The Institute of Internal Auditors is a professional association that is dedicated to the professional development of internal auditors. The IIA conducts seminars and conferences on control, deterrence, and investigation of fraud, as well as publishing the *Internal Auditor*, which contains articles dealing with fraud, internal controls, and other subjects.[20] The IIA bookstore provides books, videos, software, and other items for professional development of internal auditors.

The Role of Bank Examiners

Some readers may confuse bank examiners with auditors. Bank examiners are not auditors. Bank examiners perform two types of examinations: one for safety and soundness, and the other for compliance. Safety and soundness examinations are based on the CAMEL system. CAMEL is the Uniform Interagency Bank Rating System acronym for *C*apital adequacy, *A*sset quality, *M*anagement, *E*arnings, and *L*iquidity. In some states, such as Alabama, bank examiners review the adequacy of the audits. Compliance examinations determine whether banks are complying with existing laws and regulations, such as the Truth in Lending Act (Federal Reserve Regulation Z).

Bank examiners report their findings to the bank and can share their information with other regulatory and government agencies. When they find problems, they can take a series of actions in an attempt to correct the situation. The most extreme action is the closing of a bank.

Detection of fraud is an infrequent by-product of bank examinations. For example, a trainee examiner working in the First National Bank of Jacksonville, Alabama, discovered that three people who had loans with the bank used the same address. Further examination revealed more than 25 fictitious loans using the same address, and the bank failed.

NOTES

1. This case was written by Sara L. Strait, National Bank Examiner.

2. This discussion drew on the following sources: Committee on Auditing Procedure, American Institute of Certified Public Accountants, *Internal Control*, New York, AICPA, 1949, 6; U.S. General Accounting Office, *Bank Failures, Independent Audits Needed to Strengthen Internal Control and Bank Management*, GAO/AFMD-89-25, May 1989, 15; Jack C. Robertson, and Frederick G. Davis, *Auditing*, 3rd ed., Plano, Texas, Business Publications, Inc., 1982, 204-206; American Institute of Certified Public Accountants' Statement on Auditing Standards Number 55, "Consideration of the Internal Control Structure in a Financial Statement Audit"; *Comptroller's Handbook for National Bank Examiners*, Comptroller of the Currency, Section 001.1.

3. The Foreign Corrupt Practices Act amends the Securities Exchange Act of 1934, 15 U.S.C. 78q(b1); The affected companies must have $3 million or more in assets and have 500 or more shareholders.

4. U.S. General Accounting Office, *Bank Failures, ibid.,* 3, 25, 39.

5. Kenneth A. Merchant, *Fraudulent and Questionable Financial Reporting: A Corporate Perspective*, Morristown, N.J.: Financial Executives Research Foundation, 1987, 14.

6. U.S. General Accounting Office, *Thrift Failures: Costly Failures Resulted From Regulatory Violations and Unsafe Practices*, GAO/AFMD-89-62, June 1989; 62.

7. U.S. General Accounting Office, *Failed Financial Institutions: Reasons, Costs, Remedies and Unresolved Issues*, Statement of Frederick D. Wolf before the Committee on Banking, Finance, and Urban Af-

fairs, House of Representatives, GAO/T-AFMD-89-1, January 13, 1989, 11.

8. The *Comptroller's Handbook for National Bank Examiners* is distributed to national banks. Others may purchase a copy from the Comptroller of the Currency, 490 L'Enfant Plaza E., S.W., Washington, D.C., 20219 (phone 202-447-1800). The publication is loose-leaf, and is updated periodically.

9. U.S. General Accounting Office, *CPA Audit Quality: Status of Actions Taken to Improve Auditing and Financial Reporting of Public Companies*, GAO/AFMD-89-38, March 1989, 8-9.

10. Robertson and Davis, *Auditing, ibid.*, 4. The text also presents other, but narrower definitions of auditing.

11. *Audits of Banks*, New York: American Institute of Certified Public Accountants, 1983, 35-36.

12. R. K. Mautz and Hussein A. Sharaf, *The Philosophy of Auditing*, Sarasota, Florida: American Accounting Association, Monograph No. 6, 1961.

13. *Report of the National Commission on Fraudulent Financial Reporting*, National Commission on Fraudulent Financial Reporting, October 1987 (No city shown); U.S. General Accounting Office, *CPA Audit Quality: Status of Actions*, ibid., 11, 13.

14. *U.S.* v. *Arthur Young & Co.*, 465 U.S. 805, 8-7-818 (1984).

15. Statement on Auditing Standards No. 53, *The Auditor's Responsibility to Detect and Report Errors and Irregularities*, AICPA, April 1988, 3.

16. Paulette Thomas, "Over Half of Lincoln S&L Reported Net since '84 Said to Be from Sham' Deals," *The Wall Street Journal*, November 15, 1989, A3.

17. U.S. Government Accounting Office, *CPA Audit Quality: Failures of CPA Audits to Identify and Report Significant Savings and Loan Problems*, GAO/AFMD-

89-45, February 1989; U.S. General Accounting Office, *The Need to Improve Auditing in the Savings and Loan Industry*, Statement of Frederick D. Wolf before the Committee on Banking, Finance and Urban Affairs, House of Representatives, GAO/T-AFMD-89-2, February 21, 1989.

18. James R. Davis, "Ambiguity, Ethics, and the Bottom Line," *Business Horizons*, May-June 1989, 67.

19. David L. Nich and Robert D. Miller, "White-Collar Crime," *The Internal Auditor*, December 1984., 24-27.

20. The Institute of Internal Auditors, 249 Maitland Ave., Altamonte Springs, FL 32701, phone 407-830-7600.

9 POINT OF VIEW

Each of the contributors to this chapter expresses his or her own point of view on some particular aspect of the general topic of bank fraud. The contributors include William J. Crawford, California Savings and Loan Commissioner; Joseph T. Wells, chairman of the National Association of Certified Fraud Examiners; Charles A. Worsham, executive vice president of the Louisiana Bankers Association; James E. Horner, Special Supervision Division of the OCC; and Susan G. James, an attorney who specializes in criminal law and post conviction sentencing.

WILLIAM J. CRAWFORD, CALIFORNIA SAVINGS AND LOAN COMMISSIONER

Mr. Crawford expressed a concern about audits. Twenty-nine of the first 30 failed California S&Ls had clean audit opinions for the last fiscal year preceding their takeovers. As the financial conditions of some California S&Ls deteriorated, auditors frequently delayed reporting their findings. To encourage timely disclosures, the state law was changed and the penalty for late audits was implemented at $1,000 per day after 60 days. It was also announced that granting extensions for S&L audits would be very limited. Thirty-four qualified audit opinions were received the following year.

One problem with the audit process is that the partners of audit firms are salesman. They must bring in and retain clients.

Real estate appraisers are salesmen too. Every major real estate fraud starts with an appraisal. If you accept the appraiser's premises and disclaimers on the first seven pages of their reports, you must accept their conclusions on page 107. In one S&L, a special management audit was obtained at a cost of $1 million. The audit stated, "The association's appraisals appear to meet MAI standards," when that was clearly not the case. Its portfolio was loaded with real estate loans secured by over-valued properties. The S&L had $977 million in assets when it failed about 15 months after the audit. The total loss to FSLIC was $800 million.

The auditors, who are third-party validators, have an obligation not to be fooled. Their professional insights are extended to creditors and shareholders when reviewing management's financial statements. Their opinions validate that management's financial statements are fair and that the values are reasonable. However, many GAAP financial statements contain huge amounts of goodwill in assets and net worth even though the associations are economically insolvent.

JOSEPH T. WELLS, CFE, CPA

Joseph T. Wells is chairman of the National Association of Certified Fraud Examiners, and a former FBI agent.[1]

You have asked me for my perspective on the financial institution fraud failure situation. Let me predicate my comments by saying that my perspective is biased by my experience. Mostly, I have been in the trenches investigating these frauds; only recently have I begun to look at the larger forces that might control these problems. Having said that, I think three comments may sum up my attitudes and experiences.

1. It is much easier to prevent fraud than it is to detect, investigate, or prosecute.
2. Most bank criminals do not see themselves as criminals at all.
3. More vigorous prosecution and/or incarceration

has no significant effect on the rate of banking frauds.

Taking one point at a time, approximately one fraud out of five is detected by audit or management review. This certainly includes the bank examination process and explains why many of these bank frauds— committed by trusted officers, shareholders, and other insiders—are so difficult to detect.

Investigation of fraud is difficult because of the enormous amount of resources that must be dedicated to it. Both private and public sector policy lacks the capability to deal effectively with fraud investigation and prosecution. Prosecution, like the entire criminal justice system, is loaded beyond capacity with traditional property and violent crimes, not to mention the drug problem.

And prosecution does not seem to be an answer, anyhow. There does not seem to be any statistical correlation between prosecution and the rate of recidivism. That is certainly not to say that criminals should not be prosecuted, but most criminologists believe that deterrence comes from the swiftness and sureness of the punishment, not its severity.

What has a greater deterrent value? Sending one criminal to jail for 10 years, while the other nine get probation; or sentencing 10 criminals to jail for one year each? I would vote for the latter.

In investigating two thousand or so frauds over my career, I have yet to meet one who initially felt like he or she had violated the law. Dr. Donald Cressey (1919-1987) first studied this phenomenon in the late 1940s when he interviewed 300 or so embezzlers in prison. He noted that they all had three things in common: an immediate "unsharable" financial need, the perceived opportunity to commit and conceal their crimes, and the ability to rationalize their behavior as something other than criminal. (The vast majority claim that they are only "borrowing" the money temporarily.)

The great majority of financial criminals commit these offenses because of excessive indebtedness. It used to be that the criminal was typically a mid-level employee who simply was living beyond his or her means. Later, as our society became bent toward acquiring more and more, the level of the criminal grew to top management, insiders, officers, and directors. But the reasons still remain the same: excessive personal leverage. That explains why with the current savings and loan debacle (estimated to eventually reach over $150 billion) that there is little money to recover: it was spent before it was stolen—not after.

What is the eventual answer? It is not simple, and I am not sure I know. Maybe with the current emphasis on the basics of morality will help. Secondly, the accounting and audit community, in my view, must pull its head out of the sand and look around. Books and records do not commit crime; people do. Finally, and perhaps most importantly, more education needs to be done on the causes of these frauds.

Charles A. Worsham

Charles A. Worsham is the executive vice president of the Louisiana Bankers Association; he focuses on a code of ethics for the financial industry.[2]

The state of Louisiana has experienced some 46 bank and a myriad number of S&L failures since 1984. A good portion of these failures directly or indirectly involved mismanagement and abuse. A significant portion of this could have been avoided by the bank or financial institution having, maintaining, and living by a code of lender conduct.

The regulators, FDIC and FSLIC, could attest to the magnitude of this problem. The term mismanagement is a broad one and perhaps in this case it is too broad. With the ability of hindsight, we could have foreseen that lending on property values exclusively was totally insufficient in a climate where land values could decrease so dramatically and quickly. However, to categorize this as mismanagement would be incorrect. Good management should consider this event as a possibility, and this should have been a part of the lending decision.

The abusive situation is totally different. Perhaps much of it could have been swept under the carpet if the economy had not turned sour. Much of this abuse dealt with self-dealing and dealing with insiders. Insiders could be directors, officers, or appraisers who were used in determining property values. Federal authorities have dealt severely with some of these abusive cases, and in more than one case financial lenders are now serving time for their arrant ways.

Several banks in Louisiana saw the wisdom years ago of installing and instilling in their officers a very high code of ethics. This code of ethics precluded them from getting involved in projects where the bank was lending money. The policy stated that the personal interest of the individual lenders could not conflict with the duties and responsibilities they owed to the institution.

The trade association representing banks and S&L's can be an instrumental part in formulating such a code of ethics. Many of the state associations in conjunction with their counterparts in Washington have developed a sample code of ethics to be used by financial institutions. These sample codes can be augmented with key points brought out by the board of directors in an open discussion and in the development of a code of ethics. The real solution begins at the top with a board of directors, whose behavior typifies and exemplifies the code of conduct that it adopts. If the leadership at the top doesn't portray the correct image, then one can assume that those down the ladder will find just as many opportunities to deviate from the norm.

The state associations in conjunction with the committees of the association can be a great help. For instance, within the Louisiana Bankers Association the Human Resources Committee has been a tremendous asset for human resource managers throughout the state. If a bank wants a code of ethics, the association has the ability to pull together and merge and decipher various codes of ethics of conduct. With greater information, the banker can then make a wiser and more prudent decision on which one to adopt.

Once the board adopts a stringent but workable code of ethics, then the information must be disseminated to all officers and nonofficers within the bank. Small group meetings can be held within the institution to allow the mid-level managers to explain why such a policy has been adopted and the importance of everyone adhering to the new policy. As mentioned earlier, all leadership really develops at the top and is filtered down.

By adopting a code of ethics, a financial institution does not preclude itself from having situations where employees deviate from the policy. However, it is important that a policy is in place and that an ethical example be made by top management. When an individual chooses not to follow policy guidelines, then he or she must be dealt with firmly and positively so that the rest of the banking family knows that such deviations will be dealt with fairly but sternly.

I truly believe that if our financial institutions here in Louisiana had adhered to a stricter policy, then perhaps some of the problems that we have experienced would have corrected themselves. An ounce of prevention is worth a pound of cure. Prevention also needs to be strengthened by an adequate audit program that's designed to intercept any embezzlement, fraud, or other misapplication of bank funds.

JAMES E. HORNER

James E. Horner is a member of the Special Supervision Division of the Office of the Comptroller of the Currency. He gives bank examiners perspective and points out that it is impossible to eliminate the risk of fraud, but it can be deterred. The views expressed in this article are those of the author and do not necessarily represent those of the Office of the Comptroller of the Currency.

Fraud prevention, although a catchy title and worthy goal, is truly more of an ideal than a reality. A better description would be "fraud deterence." It is impossible to eliminate the risk fraud; however, it can be deterred by promoting conditions that make unauthorized transactions or concealment difficult.

Internal Fraud. The responsibility for creating an environment which lessens the risk of internal management fraud rests with a bank's board of directors. Although a directorate can depend on operating management's technical, industry, and general management expertise in running day-to-day operations, the responsibility for ensuring that those operations are properly controlled remains with the board. The board must assure that its own policies, as well as the laws and regulations which the bank operates under, are indeed followed. One important ingredient is management's attitude and philosophy about banking. Positive attributes, such as integrity and a sincere interest and desire to be successful bankers, will usually result in an atmosphere unreceptive to risk of internal fraud. This translates into an operating environment composed of skilled and satisfied employees and a management team that supports the concept of audits, controls, and systems. In fact, a fundamental key to ensuring policy and legal compliance is the implementation of a sound system of internal control and audit function.

In theory, internal controls are designed to safeguard assets, ensure accuracy and reliability of data, promote compliance with policies and law, and advance overall management efficiency. They include basic precautions such as ensuring that duties are properly separated. For example, basic precautions might include controls to prevent individuals responsible for the physical custody of an asset from also being responsible for accounting for that asset (and further, verifying the accounting).

A comprehensive audit program provides ongoing focus of control issues and a periodic review of all major aspects of a bank's operations. The OCC strongly encourages a full independent financial audit on an annual basis; and based on size and complexity, it also encourages the use of an internal audit function. Areas that present the greatest inherent risks, or that have demonstrated weaknesses in past reviews, should be targeted by auditors.

As stated in the *Comptroller's Handbook for National Bank Examiners*, "good" internal control exists when no one person is in a position to make significant errors or to perpetrate significant irregularities without timely detection. Therefore, a system of internal control should include procedures necessary to assure timely detection of accountability failure. Such procedures should be performed by individuals who have no incompatible duties. If an employee, who is accountable for certain assets or who performs duties significant in the internal control system, is permitted to avoid established controls because of other assigned tasks, the individual has incompatible duties and the control has been weakened. The mere existence of internal control procedures does not by itself deter unauthorized actions. To be effective they must actually be performed and enforced.

Deviations by bank personnel from established policies, practices, and procedures should always be a concern of management and the board. Specific examples include situations where instructions and directives are not revised to reflect current practices, employees using "short cuts" to perform their tasks, or changes in organization and activities that influence operating procedures in unexpected ways. Sometimes the simplest of controls can make a difference. For example, requiring employees in sensitive positions to take two consecutive weeks of vacation time away from the bank each year may be the best way to uncover an irregularity.

Another key element of effective internal control is the selection and retention of competent employees. Fraud prevention is highly dependent on the ability and integrity of personnel. Not only are quality employees less likely to commit fraud, they are also the most likely source of fraud detection and prevention through the fulfillment of their job responsibilities.

An effective way for management and the board of directors to test their system of internal control is to review the key functions in the bank. For each function or position identified certain issues should be considered:

- Is the position critical? Is there a possibility that a significant error or material irregularity could occur?
- In the event of error or irregularity, what is the probability that normal routines/controls would uncover the exception?
- What are the chances of concealment of irregularities and are controls in place to reduce the opportunity to conceal?

In many cases, one of the first steps an individual who desires to commit bank fraud considers is which controls can be avoided or where the effect can be the least noticed. Thus, effective prevention of fraud is based on the assumption that the "unthinkable" is likely to happen and the understanding that, if it does, systems of control within the organization cannot necessarily be relied upon to ensure that unauthorized transactions are reported and that appropriate action is taken.

External Fraud. Although the likelihood of internal fraud is greater, considerable damage can be done through the actions of external third parties. Again controls are the key line of defense. But other factors are important as well. Management knowledge of risks related to different types of transactions. Familiarity with the character of the individuals involved is a good example. The old adage, "if it sounds too good to be true, it probably is" certainly applies. In retrospect, many of the external frauds investigated by OCC have dealt with involved transactions portrayed to involve financial gain with little or no risk to the institution. This promised gain often transpired into certain loss.

Bankers should never invest money in something that is not fully understood or when certain details are missing. The notion of getting another opinion or two on complicated proposals is certainly a good idea. OCC has witnessed many schemes that before being accepted by one bank had been rejected by a number of others; therefore, there is safety in the wisdom of numbers.

SUSAN G. JAMES

Susan G. James is an attorney whose primary practice is in the area of criminal law, sentencing and post conviction in federal court with federal offenders.[3] She has represented some of the individuals mentioned in cases discussed in earlier chapters. She gives one defense lawyer's perspective on the savings and loan crisis.

Certainly, my clients involved in the savings and loan industry, as well as numerous other defendants identified and prosecuted as a result of banking and savings and loan transactions throughout the country, have explanations for their conduct, which has been determined criminal by the United States Government. The consensus explanation seems to be that they never intentionally set out to defraud any lending institution. However, after identification and explanation by the government, many of them have accepted the fact that their conduct has been labelled "criminal" by the United States Government and many have been tried, plead guilty, been convicted, and incarcerated as a result of their conduct. This does not, however, erase any of the facts and circumstances that possibly led to their individual problems and those that are so obvious throughout the country as evidenced in the downfall of many federally-insured institutions.

Possibly, the simplest explanation given by these individuals, and given to me in casual conversation, is that certain regulation changes in the savings and loan industry made the institutions havens for creative financing and tax shelters. Many real estate developers participated in creative financing with the owners of savings and loan institutions, and most of the creative financing had previously been precluded prior to deregulation of the industry in 1982. I was told that, as a result, nonrecourse loans were increasingly used and became commonplace in land and development syndications. It was indicated that probably from 1976, at the time the Tax Reform Act was passed, until probably 1987, there were no real estate syndications on income-producing property that were recourse loans. Very possibly, the government did not think that lenders would participate in the risky business of lending money on nonrecourse loans. However, the investment markets were good and inflation was actually covering the financial lenders on the property involved in the transactions, as long as things went well in the economy.

Unfortunately, as we all know, the economic crisis that evolved in the early 1980s created havoc that was not anticipated by lenders, borrowers, the savings and loan industry, the regulators, or the United States Government.

William F. Weld, former assistant attorney general, Criminal Division, Department of Justice, testified before the House of Representatives Committee on Government Operations, Subcommittee on Commerce, Consumer and Monetary Affairs, on November 19, 1987. During the course of his testimony, Mr. Weld indicated that the number of bank failures had risen from 10 in 1981 to 138 in 1986. Additionally, Mr. Weld testified that the former president of the Home Loan Bank of Dallas, Texas, in the spring of 1987, estimated that the Dallas region alone had between 26 to 28 hopelessly insolvent thrifts. The estimated loss to the Federal Savings and Loan Insurance Corporation was possibly between $8 to 10 billion.

Jeffery J. Jamar, chief, White Collar Crimes Section, Criminal Investigative Division, Federal Bureau of Investigation, testified before the House of Representatives, Committee on Government Operations, Sub-Committee on Commerce, Consumer and Monetary Affairs, on June 13, 1987. At that time, Mr. Jamar indicated that in 1984, the FBI had completed 7,390 bank fraud investigations wherein losses were estimated at $382 million. He further indicated that by 1986, the FBI had completed 10,416 cases with an estimated loss in excess of $1 billion.

William Seidman, Chairman of the Federal Deposit Insurance Corporation, testified before the House Committee on Government Operations on November 19, 1987. Mr. Seidman indicated that during 1985, 1986, and the first half of 1987, 98 of the 354 banks that failed had at least some element of fraud. The FDIC, in a response questionnaire to the United States Sentencing Commission, indicated that it estimated criminal activity to be a factor in nearly 15 percent of recent bank failures.

These statistics are provided for two reasons. One is to convey that the violations are significant. I am fully cognizant of the fact that the combination of activities in the federal savings and loan industry contributed to the overall problem. Clearly the FDIC and the FSLIC face substantial problems as a result of these failing institutions. Secondly, however, I also cite these statistics to suggest that none of the individuals *individually* corrupted the savings and loan industry. No individual created this problem. My clients who were prosecuted *did not conspire with all* others in this industry to develop a plan or scheme to defraud *nor were they involved with all* of the institutions referenced as part of the statistical data provided herein.

These statistics clearly suggest to me, and should to other objective reviewers, that the industry itself must have been ripe for general corruption and deviation from the regulations. This does not totally excuse the conduct of my savings and loan clients, nor does it indicate that they failed to recognize the seriousness of their offenses. It does, instead, provide an explanation for many of the problems in the industry.

NOTES

1. National Association of Certified Fraud Examiners, 716 West Avenue, Austin, TX 78701.
2. For information about a code of ethics for lenders, see Paul M. Dorfman and Steven K. Buster, "Drafting a Code Lender Conduct: Guidelines and Suggestions" *The Journal of Commercial Bank Lending*, July 1989, 4-12.
3. Susan G. James, Attorney at Law, P.O. Box 198, 600 S. McDonough St., Montgomery, AL 36101.

APPENDIX A   RED FLAGS

This appendix contains the red flags published in the FDIC's *Manual of Examination Policies (Appendix A)*, 1987, except for linked financing and brokered transactions that are shown in Chapter 3. The subject areas covered by the red flags in this appendix include:

- Loan participations.
- Secured lending—real estate and other types of collateral.
- Insider transactions.
- Credit card and electronic funds transfer.
- Wire transfers.
- Offshore transactions.
- Third-party obligations.
- Lending to buy tax shelter investments.
- Money laundering.
- Corporate culture ethics.
- Miscellaneous.

LOAN PARTICIPATIONS

Red flags:

1. Excessive participation of loans among closely related banks, correspondent banks, and branches or departments of the lending bank.
2. Absence of a formal participation agreement.
3. Poor or incomplete loan documentation.

4. Investing in out-of-territory participation.
5. Reliance on third-party guaranties.
6. Large paydown or payoff of previously classified loans.
7. Some indication that there may be informal repurchase agreements on some participations.
8. Lack of independent credit analysis.
9. Volume of loan participations sold is high in relation to the size of the bank's own loan portfolio.
10. Evidence of lapping of loan participations. For example, the sale of a loan participation in an amount equal to or greater than, and at or about the same time as, a participation that has matured or is about to mature.
11. Disputes between participating banks over documentation, payments, or any other aspect of the loan participation agreement.

SECURED LENDING—REAL ESTATE AND OTHER TYPE OF COLLATERAL

Red flags:

1. Lack of independent appraisals.
2. Out-of-territory loans.
3. Evidence of land flips. A land flip is a process in which individuals or businesses buy and sell properties among themselves, each time inflating the sales price to give the appearance of rapidly increasing property values. The mortgage amounts increase with each purchase until, in many cases, the amounts of the mortgages greatly exceed the actual values of the mortgaged property.
4. Loans with unusual terms and conditions.
5. Poor or incomplete documentation.
6. Loans that are unusual considering the size of the bank and the level of expertise of its lending officers.

7. Heavy concentration of loans to a single project or to individuals related to the project.
8. Concentrations of loans to local borrowers with the same or similar collateral that is located outside the bank's trade area.
9. Asset Swaps—Sale of other real estate or other distressed assets to a broker at an inflated price in return for favorable terms and conditions on a new loan to a borrower introduced to the bank by the broker. The new loan is usually secured by property of questionable value and the borrower is in a weak financial condition. Borrower and collateral are often outside the bank's normal trade area.
10. Failure to consider the risk of decline in collateral value.

INSIDER TRANSACTIONS

Red flags:

1. Financing the sale of insider assets to third parties.
2. From a review of personal financial statements, evidence that an insider is lending his own funds to others.
3. Improper fees to major shareholders.
4. Frequent changes of auditors or legal counsel.
5. Unusual or unjustified fluctuations in insiders' or officers' personal financial statements or statements of their interests.
6. Frequent appearances of suspense items relating to accounts of insiders, officers, and employees.
7. An insider borrowing money from someone who borrows from the bank.
8. Purchase of bank assets by an insider.
9. A review of the bank's fixed assets or other asset accounts reveals that the bank owns expensive artworks, expensive automobiles, yachts, airplanes,

or other unusual items that are out of character for a bank of its size and location.

10. A review of the bank's expense accounts reveals expenditures for attorneys' fees, accountants' fees, brokers' fees, and so forth, that do not appear to correspond to services rendered to the bank or that appear unusually high for services rendered.

11. Heavy lending to the bank's shareholders, particularly in conjunction with recent capital injections.

12. A large portion of the insider's bank stock has been pledged to secure debts to other financial institutions.

13. An insider has past due obligations at other financial institutions.

14. An insider is receiving all or part of the proceeds of loans granted to others.

15. An insider is receiving special consideration or "favors" from bank customers. For example, an insider may receive favorable lease terms or favorable purchase terms on an automobile obtained from a bank customer.

CREDIT CARD AND ELECTRONIC FUNDS TRANSFER

Red flags:

1. Lack of separation of duties between the card-issuing function and the issuance of a personal identification number ("PIN").

2. Poor control of unissued cards and PINs.

3. Poor control of returned mail.

4. Customer complaints.

5. Poor control of credit limit increases.

6. Poor control of name and address changes.

7. Frequent malfunction of payment authorization system.

8. Unusual delays in receipt of cards and PINs by customers.

9. Bank does not limit amount of cash that a customer can extract from an ATM in a given day.
10. Evidence that customer credit card purchases have been intentionally structured by a merchant to keep individual amounts below the "floor limit" to avoid the need for transaction approval.

WIRE TRANSFERS

Red flags:

1. Indications of frequent overrides of established approval authority and other internal controls.
2. Intentional circumvention of approval authority by splitting transactions.
3. Wire transfer to and from bank secrecy haven countries.
4. Frequent large wire transfers to persons who do not have an account relationship with the bank.
5. In a linked financing situation, a borrower's request for immediate wire transfer of loan proceeds to one or more banks where the funds for brokered deposits originated.
6. Large or frequent wire transfers against uncollected funds.
7. Wire transfers involving cash where the amount exceeds $10,000.
8. Inadequate control of password access.
9. Customer complaints and frequent error conditions.

OFFSHORE TRANSACTIONS

Red flags:

1. Loans made on the strength of a borrower's financial statement when the statement reflects major investments and income from businesses

incorporated in bank secrecy and are located in countries such as Panama and the Netherlands Antilles.

2. Loans to offshore companies.

3. Loans secured by obligations of offshore banks.

4. Transactions involving an offshore "shell" bank whose name may be very similar to the name of a major legitimate institution.

5. Frequent wire transfers of funds to and from bank secrecy countries such as Panama, the Cayman Islands, the Netherlands Antilles, etc.

6. Offers of multimillion dollar deposits at below market rates from a confidential source to be sent from an offshore bank or somehow guaranteed by an offshore bank through a letter, telex, or other "official" communication.

7. Presence of telex or facsimile equipment in a bank where the usual and customary business activity would not appear to justify the need for such equipment.

THIRD-PARTY OBLIGATIONS

Red flags:

1. Incomplete documentation.

2. Loans secured by obligations of offshore banks.

3. Lack of credit information on third party obligor.

4. Financial statements reflect concentrations of closely held companies or businesses that lack audited financial statements to support their value.

LENDING TO BUY TAX SHELTER INVESTMENTS

Red flags:

1. Block loans to individuals to buy tax shelters arranged by a tax shelter promoter.

2. Shelters that promise tax deductions that would not appear to withstand the scrutiny of the IRS.
3. Specific use of the invested funds cannot be ascertained.
4. Loan payments are to be made by a servicing company.
5. Investments reflect no economic purpose except to generate tax write-offs.
6. Financial "no cash" deals where transactions are structured to avoid any actual cash flow. For example, a long-term CD is matched against a loan payable from the proceeds of the CD at its maturity. Interest accumulates on the CD in an amount equal to or greater than the compounded interest owed on the corresponding loan. The depositor borrower never provides or receives any cash but still gets the tax write-off.

MONEY LAUNDERING

Red flags:

1. Increase in cash shipments that is not accompanied by a corresponding increase in the number of accounts.
2. Cash on hand frequently exceeds limits established in the security program or blanket bond coverage.
3. Large volume of cashier's checks and or money orders sold for cash to noncustomers. Amounts may range from $1,000 to just under $10,000 each.
4. Large volume of wire transfers to and from offshore banks.
5. Large volume of wire transfers for noncustomers.
6. Accounts that have a large number of small deposits and a small number of large checks, with the balance of the account remaining relatively low and constant. The account has many of the same

characteristics as an account used for check kiting.

7. A large volume of deposits to several different accounts with frequent transfer of major portions of the balances to a single account at the same bank or at another bank.
8. Loans to offshore companies.
9. A large volume of cashier's checks or money orders deposited to an account when the account holder's business does not appear to justify such business.
10. Large volume of cash deposits from a business that is not normally cash intensive such as a wholesaler.
11. Cash deposits to a correspondent bank account by any means other than through an armored carrier.
12. Large turnover in large bills that would appear uncharacteristic for the bank's location.
13. Cash shipments that appear large in comparison to the dollar volume of currency transaction reports filed.
14. Dollar limits on the list of bank customers exempt from currency transaction reporting requirements that appear unreasonably high considering the type and location of the businesses. No information is in the bank's files to support the limits.
15. Currency Transaction Reports when filed are often incorrect or lack important information.
16. List of exempted customers appears unusually long.

CORPORATE CULTURE ETHICS

Red flags:

1. Absence of a code of ethics.
2. Absence of a clear policy on conflicts of interest.
3. Lack of oversight by the bank's board of directors, particularly outside directors.

4. Absence of planning, training, hiring, and organizational policies.
5. Absence of clearly defined authorities and lack of
   definition of the responsibilities that go along with
   authorities.
6. Lack of independence of management in acting on
   recommend corrections.

MISCELLANEOUS

Red flags:

1. Indications of frequent overrides of internal controls or intentional circumvention of bank policy.
2. Unresolved exceptions of frequently recurring
   exceptions on exception reports.
3. Out-of-balance conditions.
4. Purpose of loan is not recorded.
5. Proceeds of loan are used for a purpose other than
   purpose recorded.
6. A review of checks paid against uncollected funds
   indicates that a customer is offsetting checks with
   deposits of the same or similar amount and main-
   tains a relatively constant account balance, usually
   small in relation to the amount of activity and the
   size of the transactions.

APPENDIX B LAKESIDE BANK—LOAN POLICY

Chapter 7 addressed the issue of loan policies. Appendices B and C examine the loan policies of two banks. They are presented to illustrate different approaches to loan policies. They are not being held out as "ideal" loan policies because each bank's needs are different.

****

Lakeside Bank shall have a standing executive committee elected by the board that will also serve as the directors' loan committee. It shall consists of the chairman of the board, president, and senior loan officer as permanent members, and not less than two other directors to serve at the pleasure of the board.

The executive committee shall review and approve all loans $15,000 and over, and approve all loans over $500,000 prior to the loan being made. In case of an emergency, loans over $500,000 may be approved by the president, executive vice president, and one member of the executive committee. These emergency loans must be ratified by the entire committee at their next meeting. The committee shall keep minutes of its meetings and report its actions in writing at each regular meeting of the board. Nonsalaried directors shall be paid a fee as set by the board.

There shall be an officers' loan committee which shall consist of the president and vice presidents in charge of commercial and installment loans. This committee shall meet daily to review all loans made the preceding day and approve or disapprove all applications requiring their approval as set out in the loan policy.

I. *GENERAL POLICY* - It is the general policy of the board that all loans should have a plan of liquidation at the time they are granted. This is considered the keystone of sound credit administration, and all loan and discount committees and lending officers are requested to observe this basic principle when approving loans. It is recognized that exceptions to this policy will occur on rare occasions. The board believes these exceptions should be held to conditions where loans are fully collateralized by cash surrender value of life insurance policies, savings accounts, certificates of deposit, and government bonds with adequate margin. The lending officer should state the plan of liquidation in writing on the note or make it a part of the credit file. This is a requirement on all loans made, whether submitted to the committee for approval or not.

All new loans to customers having a total indebtedness in excess of $15,000 must be supported by a completed loan memorandum. This memorandum should contain the name, date, amount, and rate of the loan. Also, it should state the purpose, repayment plan, and source of those funds. If there is no arrangement made other than a set maturity, it is assumed that the loan will be paid off on that date. This memorandum should be made a part of the credit file and any subsequent changes to the original terms should be reflected as a change in the original memo.

II. *TRADE AREA* - This board believes that sound local loans are one of the most satisfactory and profitable means of employing the bank's funds. Therefore, it is the intent of the board that with few exceptions the bank's lending area be limited to Lake County and the adjoining counties covering the northern part of the state. It is recognized that there will be occasions when exceptions to this policy are desirable. These exceptions should be rare. Also, reasons for exception to the policy should be clearly set forth in the minutes of the appropriate committee meeting. This policy does not prohibit participation with other banks of substantial and recognized standing when we have funds available for lending that cannot be readily invested in our local trade area.

III.   *DESIRED LOANS* - It will be the policy of the board of directors of this bank not to be content with accepting and consummating all sound loans *offered* to the bank. The bank will be aggressive in seeking desirable loans of the type described hereinafter.

Loans of the following types will be considered desirable provided each loan meets the test of a sound, prudent loan:

(a)   Loans to business concerns on a short-term basis, against a satisfactory balance sheet and earnings statement, usually for not more than 180 days.

(b)   Loans to business concerns secured by a chattel mortgage on marketable business equipment, such loans to be amortized over a period of not more than 60 months, or 72 months, when approved by the Officer's Loan and Discount Committee. The amortization terms are to be such that the residual value of the business equipment will at all times be equal to or greater than the unpaid balance of the loan. Proof of insurance and a UCC-1 filed with the Secretary of State are required.

(c)   Loans to business concerns secured by accounts receivable and inventory. Because accounts receivable may be proceeds of inventory, a security interest in both is necessary and should be perfected by filing a UCC-1. It is also recommended that regular aging reports be requested and verified periodically.

It is recognized that there will be exceptions where it is not practical for our customer to make an assignment of his accounts receivable on a notification basis. It is accepted by the board that such loans will be limited to a few of the bank's best customers. Also, the loan will have additional proper collateral, as herein provided, or a satisfactory balance sheet and earnings statement, in which case the loan should be approved additionally by the officers loan and discount committee. The board regards accounts receivable financing as somewhat more hazardous than the normal type of lending conducted by the bank. All committees and lending officers are required to give such loans careful scrutiny and greater than average surveillance at all times, with strict requirements as to liquidation or substitution of additional collateral of other accounts receivable at any time the accounts receivable are not liquidated in accordance with terms.

In addition, proper precautions and due diligence is to be exercised to avoid the commingling of funds on such accounts. In no instance shall accounts receivable be accepted when they are more than 60 days beyond the date of invoice.

(d) (1) Loans secured by negotiable U.S. Government bonds or state, county or municipal bonds properly supported by credit information. Such loans to be not more than 90 percent of the market value of the bonds.

(2) Loans secured by securities listed on a recognized exchange or over the counter market; such loans to be not more than 80 percent of the market value of the collateral and to comply in all respects with Regulation U of the Federal Reserve System. The banks will *not* make loans to carry securities where Regulation U margin requirements apply. All stock certificates or registered bonds must have the proper stock power attached.

(3) Although loans secured by the listed market securities depend on the collateral, it also is

prudent to obtain a personal financial statement of the borrower and to know his credit background. This information should be part of the credit file on the loan and be presented to the appropriate committee at the time of loan approval.

(4) Loans with securities as collateral should be checked at each renewal as to value and marginal requirements and each officer notified when the margin becomes lower than previously stated on a loan for which he is responsible.

(5) The customer should be notified at the time of borrowing of his responsibility to provide additional collateral and that the occasion might arise when the bank would be required to sell collateral to protect its loan.

(6) All security loans should have a definite repayment program agreed to by the customer. Such repayment should be from sources other than the sale of securities to eliminate tax problems and to avoid misunderstandings with the customers.

NOTE: It is recognized by the board that there will be situations where individual circumstances may vary. It is our desire to consider each customer's particular problem and to serve the needs of the customer. However, such variations from the foregoing securities policy must be approved by the officers' loan and discount committee and a memorandum clearly stating the reasons for deviating from the policy and the conditions under which the loan is being made must be submitted.

(e) Loans against the cash surrender value of life insurance policies should not exceed the cash surrender value if the loan is to be considered a fully secured loan, and must be accompanied by the proper assignment form and questionnaire to the insurance company.

(f) Loans secured by the assignment of savings accounts and certificates of deposit in this bank must have an interest rate 1 percent greater than that paid on the security. We recommend that the loan officer try to charge 3 percent more than the rate on the security.

(g) Loans secured by the assignment of savings accounts and certificates of deposit in other lending institutions. These assignments must be acknowledged in writing by the issuing institution. Knowledge of the financial strength and abilities of the issuing institution is essential.

(h) Real estate loans, secured by first liens on improved real estate, including improved farm land, and improved business and residential properties. A loan secured by real estate shall be in the form of an obligation or obligations secured by mortgages. The amount of such loan shall not exceed 66 2/3 percent of the appraised value of the real estate offered as security when made on a non-amortized basis. No such loan shall be made for a term longer than one year, except that . . .

(1) Any such loan may be made in an amount not to exceed 80 percent of the appraised value of the real estate offered as security, and for a term of not longer than 10 years, if the loan is secured by an installment amortized mortgage. The amortized term may be for a period up to 15 years with the prior approval of the officers' loan and discount committee. Real estate mortgages taken as additional collateral do not have to meet the percent of appraised value requirement.

(2) Real estate appraisals on which mortgage loans are based shall be made by appraisers approved by the officers loan and discount committee. Appraisals up to $150,000 in value may be made by two loan officers of this bank. Exceptions to this must be initialed by the president or the executive vice president.

(3) Hazard insurance is required in amounts and with companies acceptable to the bank on all real estate. This also includes flood insurance where necessary.

(4) Title insurance is required on all real estate loans in excess of $15,000. For loans less than $15,000 we can accept a title opinion at the option of the loan officer.

(5) Regardless of the value of the security, real estate mortgage loans shall not be made to borrowers who do not have a satisfactory credit record, nor in cases where it appears likely that the property may have to be liquidated to satisfy the debt.

(i) Unsecured consumer installment personal loans and loans secured by appliances to persons of good character with an assured income and satisfactory credit records, when the purpose of the loan will be of ultimate benefit to the borrower; such loans to be payable in monthly installments not to exceed 36 months or in a single payment of 90 days or less, and perfected by the proper UCC-1 recording.

(j) Personal loans secured by new or used automobiles, pick-up trucks, boats, motors, trailers. Terms should not exceed the following:

Current year new cars	60 Months
Previous year new cars	42 Months
One- and two-year models	36 Months

Three-year models	30 Months
Four- and five-year models	24 Months
Older models	12 Months

(1)   All such loans must have current titles showing Lakeside Bank as lienholder, inspection report or bill of sale, and proof of insurance coverage showing Lakeside Bank as lienholder.

(k)   Loans secured by a chattel mortgage on livestock. The herd securing any such loan shall be registered livestock and be approved by the officers loan and discount committee. Such loans shall not exceed 70 percent of the appraised value of the livestock securing the loan, and shall be for a term of not more than 12 months.

(l)   Personal loans secured by second mortgages on personal homes. Such loans to be repayable in monthly installments not to exceed 120 months. These loans must have the same documentation required for first mortgages in (h) above. In addition, there should be notification to and acknowledgment by the first mortgagee of our second mortgage.

(m)   Personal loans secured by new mobile homes, with adequate down payment, shall be repayable within 120 months. All mobile homes must be properly insured and our lien prefected by title or UCC-1 recording as appropriate.

(n)   Loans to business concerns and/or individuals for the purpose of financing insurance premiums, policy to be assigned to bank with insurance company's acknowledgment of assignment and agreement to rebate premium directly to bank in case of cancellation. Each such loan will have a recourse endorsement by the agent guaranteeing payment. Two months' premium must be paid down so that rebate amount always exceeds amount of loan and repayment to be made in equal monthly install- ments of no more than 10 months.

(o) Construction mortgage loans, where the amount advanced does not exceed the permanent loan commitment and where the loan matures prior to the expiration of the permanent loan commitment. A checkoff list of needed items is available in the collateral department.

(p) Officers are encouraged to put as many loans as possible on variable interest rates.

IV. *UNDESIRABLE LOANS* - Loans of the following type are considered undesirable loans for this bank and ordi- narily will be declined unless specifically approved by the officers' loan and discount committee for reasons that appear to justify an exception to the bank's general policy:

(a) Accommodation loans will not be made to poor credit risks on the strength of a good endorser. If the loan will not "stand on its own feet," the loan should be made to the endorser and the endorser should make a loan to the person whom he wishes to accommodate.

(b) Capital loans to a business enterprise where the loan cannot be repaid within a reasonable period, except by borrowing elsewhere or by liquidating the business.

(c) Loans to a new enterprise if the repayment of the loan is solely dependent upon the profitable opera- tion of the enterprise.

(d) Loans to persons whose integrity or honesty is ques- tionable.

(e) Real estate mortgage loan secured by property lo- cated outside the bank's recognized trade area.

(f) Loans secured by an assignment against undistrib- uted estate.

(g) Loans secured by stock in a closed corporation that has no ready market. This type of stock may be taken as additional collateral for loans.

(h) Loans for the purpose of enabling the borrower to speculate on the futures market of securities or commodities, unless the loan is properly collateralized and liquidation is not dependent on a rise in the market.

(i) Loans for the purpose of financing speculative transactions.

V. *LOANS TO EMPLOYEES, DIRECTORS, OFFICERS, AND RELATIVES OF LENDING OFFICER*

(a) Lending officers will not make loans to their personal relatives, but should refer them to another lending officer to avoid any conflict of interest.

(b) All loans to directors, whose total debt exceeds $25,000, must have prior approval of the entire board of directors.

(c) Officers' indebtedness to any bank or other financial institution will be reported to the president in writing within 10 days of the indebtedness. The president shall report this to the board at its next regular meeting. Each officer shall submit a financial statement and a list of his indebtedness by February 20th of each calendar year to the president, who, in turn, shall submit this information to the executive committee.

(d) Officer and employee loan policy attached hereto as Addendum "A." (The addendum is not included in the Appendix.)

VI. *FINANCIAL INFORMATION*

(a) A financial statement not over 15 months old is required for the following:

(1) All unsecured loans over $2,500

(2) All secured loans over $15,000 unless fully secured by cash surrender value of life insurance, savings accounts, certificates of deposit,

or listed marketable stocks with a 20 percent margin.

(b) Prior year operating statements are required on all business loans requiring a financial statement. In some cases the tax return is acceptable.

(c) Business financial statement submitted by CPA's should be a review or audit report.

(d) Unsecured loans to business firms involving $100,000 or more should have a certified public accountant's unqualified audit report as to the financial condition of the company within the current 12-month period. Where individuals are involved and if required the loan officer shall verify assets and liabilities and submit a written summary of action taken with respect to his recommendations.

(e) A current credit application is required for any loan to an individual when a personal financial statement is not required. A report from consumer reporting agency is required for the following:

(1) Individual debtors and cosigners;

(2) Endorsers and guarantors;

(3) Principal officers of a closely held corporate borrower;

(4) Owners or partners of an unincorporated business.

(f) A current trade report should be obtained on loans to businesses. In addition, loans to contractors should also be supported by direct checks of suppliers on a periodic basis.

VII. *INTEREST RATES*

(a) It is the policy of the board of directors that a loan should be turned down rather than made at an unprofitable interest rate.

(b) We wish to compete for all good loans; but do not believe that unprofitable interest rate loans should be made, regardless of competition.

(c) It is the desire of the board of directors that there

should be a uniformity of interest rates based on the quality of credit risk, and it is the belief of the board that where the risk is greater, the interest rate should be commensurate with the risk. In addition, consideration should be given to deposit relations and other factors contributing to total yield.

VIII. *PAST-DUE POLICY* - Officers will receive a list of all past-due installment loans and all past-due commercial loans every seven days. All lending officers will meet periodically to review past-due loans. A list of all commercial loans with appropriate comments which have been past due since the 25th of the preceding month will be presented to board of directors and all lending officers monthly.

IX. *COLLECTION POLICY* - The basic policy of the board of directors is that bank officers use all means available to them for the collection of indebtedness properly due the bank, including all legal action available by law. It is recognized that on some past-due loans, there will be mitigating circumstances that require careful consideration as to collection tactics that will be employed. In some cases, the president is charged with the responsibility of reviewing all facts with the bank's general counsel, and a course of action determined. Should the circumstances indicate the need for further consideration, a special meeting of the executive committee shall be called and a decision made as to proper action. The controlling action should, in all cases, be to take every step open to us to collect money due or to protect the bank from any loss.

X. *CHARGE-OFF POLICY* - The board recognizes that the lending of money is a business and necessarily includes some risks. The management is willing to undertake such reasonable risks. Some losses are to be expected, and it is the intention of the board that adequate reserves for losses be maintained at all times. It will be a policy of this bank to charge-off known losses at the end of each calendar quarter. These charge-offs shall be approved by the executive committee and reported to the board at its next regular meeting. Also it is the firm intention of the board to administrate the lending operations so that it will not be necessary for the examining authorities to recommend actions for charge-offs.

XI. *OVERDRAFT POLICY*

    (a) It is the policy of the board of directors that employees' overdrafts will not be tolerated. (See separate overdraft policy in personnel manual.)

    (b) Overdrafts by bank customers will be honored where an associated account exists which covers the overdraft, and on which the bank has the legal right of offset. (See FIRA of 1978 for overdrafts on directors.)

    (c) Overdrafts where there are no associated accounts on which the bank has the legal right of offset will not be honored except in specific circumstances where officers feel it is important to do so. Customer's accounts that repeatedly have overdrafts and returned checks will be reviewed for the purpose of closing the account.

XII. *LOAN AUTHORITY* - Loan Limits - The executive committee may approve loans up to the limits authorized by Lakeside Holding Company Loan Administration Policy. Loan limits will be delegated to the various lending officers based on the officer's lending experience. A loan limit will be set up for each of the following types of loans:

    (a) Fully secured by one of the following:

        (1) Savings accounts.

        (2) Certificated of deposit.

        (3) Cash surrender value of life insurance.

    (b) Fully secured by marketable collateral such as: chattel mortgages, various types of assignment, etc.

    (c) Unsecured.

XIII. *LAKESIDE HOLDING COMPANY LOAN POLICY* - The loan policy adopted by the Holding Company Board and amended from time to time is considered as additional loan policy for the bank. The policies set out by the

Holding Company Board are hereby considered as a part of this loan policy.

XIV. *COMPLIANCE* - The board insists that all laws and regulations of all governmental authorities be strictly adhered to by all officers and employees. Compliance with the following is a must requirement:

(a) Regulation Z - Truth in Lending and Fair Credit Billing Act.

(b) Regulation B - Equal Credit Opportunity Act.

(c) Regulation C - Home Mortgage Disclosure Act.

(d) Regulation U.

(e) Regulation X - Real Estate Settlement Procedures Act.

(f) All usury laws.

(g) The Community Reinvestment Act.

(h) Financial Institutions Regulatory and Interest Rate Control Act of 1978.

XV. *LOANS TO FEDERAL, STATE, COUNTY AND MUNICIPAL OFFICE HOLDERS* - All lending officers should be sensitive to any loans that are made to federal, state, county, and municipal office holders. At the same time, it is understood that there is a need in most cases to make such loans, and we want to accommodate all reasonable requests that fall within our normal loan policy from these officeholders. All lending officers, being aware of the present climate in which we operate, should submit to the officers' executive committee on an annual basis a report of all loans made and then outstanding to any federal, state, county and municipal officeholders. In addition, it will be the responsibility of each lending officer to make certain that all such loans are completely documented and memoranda detailing amounts, interest rates, repayment schedules, purpose, financial data, and credit reports.

XVI. *CONCENTRATIONS OF CREDIT*

(a) The board requires that all excess funds be invested daily through the sale of federal funds to other banks. Sales should only be made to holding company and approved banks and sales to any *one* bank should not exceed 25 percent of our stockholders equity.

(b) The Executive Committee is charged with the responsibility of preventing excessive concentrations of credit to any industry or related group of individuals.

XVII. *LOAN REVIEW* - A continuing loan review program is essential. The program should emphasize the following:

    (1) Credit evaluation and rating.

    (2) Loan officer evaluation and training.

    (3) Documentation.

    (4) Compliance with loan policy.

    (5) Compliance with all federal and state laws.

XVIII. *TAX FREE LOANS* - A request for tax exempt financing should be considered on the following basis:

(a) The borrower should meet all the lending criteria required in the granting of commercial loans.

(b) The granting of the request should provide an economic benefit for the community (jobs) and the bank (deposits and related banking business).

(c) The terms are not to exceed 15 years.

(d) Rates shall float with holding company base rate.

(e) The Senior Corporate Loan Officer or Senior Corporate Investment Officer should be consulted before committing to any tax exempt funding over $100,000 and quoting a rate.

(f) In the event that the holding company is required to restrict tax-free income, the letter of credit guaranty may be used to facilitate financing. For a fee our bank would issue a letter of credit to back the bonds and they would be sold to someone else. All other requirements of tax exempt loans would also apply to these guarantees.

XIX. *RELEASING COLLATERAL* - The release of collateral from any active loan requires the signature of two loan officers and a documenting memorandum in the credit and collateral file. The exception to this policy is where a specific lot release was negotiated at the inception of the loan.

XX.   *EXTENSIONS POLICY* - Extensions - It is the policy of the bank to grant an extension of an installment loan payment(s) only in special or unusual situations, where it can be clearly exhibited by the customer that his or her problems are of a short-term nature. Below is a more definitive description of the bank policy:

(a)   No free extension will be granted.

(b)   No more than one extension in a 12-month period without prior approval from the head of the Installment Loan Department.

(c)   A customer with a note two or more installments past due will not be granted a 30-day extension unless the other delinquent payments are collected.

Renewals - It will be the policy to allow a customer, to renew a loan that is past due when it can be documented that such renewal will help the customer and the bank is in a stronger position as a result of the renewal.

Before approving the renewal of a past-due loan, the lending officer should develop full information as to the reason for the request. The documentation in the file will be:

(a) Memorandum giving reasons for the renewal, what it did for customer and the bank.

XXI.   *CHARGE-OFF POLICY* - All loans (accounts) will be charged off when it is determined they are uncollectible but not later than when the loan is 90 days past due. Delinquencies are to be determined on a contractual basis and not on a recency of payment basis. For example, payment due on 4-20-89 is 30 days delinquent 5-20-89 and would be 90 days delinquent 7-20-89, at which time the loan is to be charged off. If the 3-20-89 payment was made on 7-20-89, the account is still 90 days past due and subject to immediate charge-off, unless it can be ascertained recovery will be received within the next 45 days:

(a) From collection of a physical damage insurance policy, or

(b) From collection on sale of marketable collateral, or

(c) From other collateral such as cash value life insurance or savings accounts, or

(d) Other unspecified reason that are approved by the head of the installment loan department.

A list of all loans not charged off after 90 days by reasons of the above exceptions or for any other reason should be reported to the president at the end of each quarter.

XXII. *STUDENT LOANS* - The board encourages participation in the guaranteed student loan program. It shall be the duty of the officers executive committee to set the requirements and limits for this program.

XXIII. *LETTERS OF CREDIT* - All letters of credit issued by this bank must be signed by the president or executive vice president. The loan officer should submit all credit information, collateral documentation, and final draft of the letter to obtain approval. Collateral documentation required is the same as for a loan made under the same conditions.

All letters of credit involving international companies or anything other than simple domestic letters will be issued through the International Department. Check guarantee letters to the Alcohol Beverage Control Board of the state are not considered letters of credit for requirements of this section. However, they can only be signed by the president or executive vice president.

XXIV. *MASTERCARD AND VISA* - We encourage the issuance of these cards to build the base of receivables for this bank. The president is authorized to enter into an agreement with the holding company to issue cards and service these accounts for this bank.

APPENDIX C METROPOLITAN BANK— LOAN POLICY

This document contains the official loan policy of Metropolitan Bank. Its purpose is to set forth in writing the concepts by which the loan function shall be governed within the bank.

In keeping with the general requirements of the loan policy, all loan personnel are required to apply the appropriate, existing banking regulations to carry out the loan program in a manner consistent with the directives of the board of directors and the bank's executive management. This policy is supported by the bank's interest rate and Maturity Manual, which contains significant information used in the lending process. Adherence to the general guidelines contained in this policy is required at all times; significant variations shall be deemed unacceptable. This policy shall apply to all members of the bank's staff who exercise loan authority and shall remain in effect until it is amended or rescinded.

GENERAL STATEMENT

The lending policy of Metropolitan Bank shall at all times be flexible enough to meet the needs of our trade area. In addition, strong emphasis is given to providing good service and prompt decisions; and all loan personnel are required to apply their knowledge and skills in lending in a competent and efficient manner. It is the intent of senior management to place sufficient authority in the hands of loan officers and loan committees to serve our present customer base effectively and to assist in the securing of loan relationships from the bank's prospective customers. Loan decisions made independently within the assigned loan limits are encouraged.

In all cases the loan portfolio with recognition of the mix and the loan-to-deposit ratio required by senior management should:

1. Satisfy demand.
2. Provide a reasonable diversification.
3. Obtain a reasonable balance of maturity distribution.
4. Acknowledge the requirements of the bank's high credit standards and indicate the generally conservative nature of its lending posture.
5. Carry proper and profitable interest rate differentials.

When considering a loan request of any kind, proper consideration shall always be given to the applicant's overall banking relationship. This approach to credit will provide assistance in pricing the loan, as well as in providing the opportunity to develop additional bank business.

As a commercial bank, we are entrusted with the ability to create money through the extension of credit. We should all be aware of the fact that acceptable growth and profitability depend, to a large degree, upon a consistent and workable loan policy.

Geographical Lending Area

It is the opinion of executive management that the primary lending area for the bank is constituted within the corporate boundaries of Sierra, Highland, and Boulder Counties. The majority of our loans are generated within these counties and the immediate surrounding area. Loans extended outside our immediate trade area should be restricted to national line accounts and purchased loan participations.

TYPES OF LOAN SOUGHT

Wholesale—Primarily lines of credit issued to national concerns that are not necessarily located within the bank's immediate trade area.

Commercial—Loans made to business interest that may be secured or unsecured. The loans are balance related and extended to provide the credit requirements of the business community.

Real Estate—Loans that are made on a basis consistent with the bank's policy, which may be amended from time to time. The loans may be secured by residential or commercial real estate and may or may not be balance related.

Consumer—Personal and consumer loans made for various purposes secured and unsecured and not necessarily balance related.

Broadly, the make-up of our loan portfolio on a percentage basis shall be:

1. Wholesale   5 percent

2. Commercial   40 percent

3. Real Estate   20 percent

4. Consumer   35 percent

Concentration in any one area of service or industry should not exceed 10 percent of the total loan portfolio. Wholesale loans shall be generally limited to "prime rate" accounts. The installment loan portfolio shall not contain a concentration in any one consumer category that would exceed 25 percent of the total installment loan portfolio, except for motor vehicles. It should be noted that outstandings on VISA are considered an installment credit within the loan policy.

Our basic maturities shall be as follows:

Single Payment Loans—Naturally mature within 90 days.

Extended maturities on single payment loans can adversely affect the bank's average lending rate.

Term—Term loans made to businesses shall normally mature in no more than 5 years and be payable monthly. All term loans extended shall be repaid on at least a quarterly basis and be fully secured.

Real Estate Loans—Residential and commercial mortgage loans may be made with maturity and repayment schedules which will vary with the marketplace as determined by executive management. This category includes construction loans for residential or commercial purposes.

Installment—Certain types of loans are exempted such as second mortgage or real estate, 10 years, and loans on new mobile homes, 10 years.

Repayment Provision—An understanding of the repayment provision shall be reached with the borrower at the inception of the loans. If the note itself does not specify the terms of repayment, then the repayment provision should be incorporated into an appropriate credit file memorandum. Rolling stock of any type, machinery, or other forms of depreciable equipment that is in use shall have a specific repayment plan. Preferably repayment will be in the form of monthly or quarterly payments which will retire the debit within the useful life of the collateral. It is highly desirable that a plan of repayment be an integral part of all loans made by the bank's lending officers.

PERCENTAGE OF LOANS TO APPROPRIATE BALANCE SHEET ITEMS

It is the policy of Metropolitan Bank to meet the credit demands generated within its trade area. A loan to deposit ratio of sixty-five to seventy-five percent (65% to 75%) is desirable and appears to be sufficient to meet the needs of our borrowers. Other factors that will have significant bearing upon an acceptable loan-to-deposit ratio are liquidity, types of loans, concentration, and general economic conditions that directly relate to the bank's performance. The upper limits of a desirable loan-to-deposit ratio may be changed from time to time at the discretion of executive management.

INTEREST RATE STRUCTURES

Interest on loans is the single source of bank income and traditionally represents the major portion of total earnings. The basis of this important source of income is directly influenced by the factors of supply and demand in the money market. The effects of economic conditions that weigh heavily on the strength or weakness of loan demand usually dictate the general level of interest rates throughout the country and in our immediate trade area. Therefore, the setting of loan interest rates for the various types of credit extended will reflect the existing market conditions and will bear a relationship to the prime lending rate. The setting of interest rates shall be within the legal contract rate structures provided for by federal and state regulatory agencies.

The following factors should be considered when setting an interest rate on a given loan:

1. Supply and demand in the money market.

2. The cost of money within the bank.

3. The prevailing market levels of rates for the type of loan being considered.

4. Borrowers overall relationship with the bank.

Taking into consideration the fundamentals contained above, interest rates on loans should always represent a fair value both to the bank and to the borrower.

GENERAL POLICIES ON COLLATERAL AND DOCUMENTATION

1. *Stocks and Bonds*—On closely held stocks we should not normally accept the shares for collateral unless

there is a known market usually represented by a repurchase letter from a responsible, prospective buyer. Normal advance should not exceed 33 1/3 percent of book value. Over the counter stocks with known markets should be held in the range of 60 to 65 percent. Listed stocks may be taken up to 75 percent of value depending on the market and the stocks' recent trading history. Corporate and municipal bonds may be taken with advance equal to 80 percent of the current market value. Recent developments have indicated a severe deterioration in this category of collateral. United States Government bonds may be taken as collateral with advances up to 90 percent of the current market value. Consideration should be given to maturity, interest rates, and current prices in the government bond market.

2. *Savings Accounts or Certificates of Deposit*—100 percent of available balance may be advanced, with the passbook or instrument in hand with the proper assignment and acknowledgement.

3. *Cash Value Life Insurance*—Loans may be made up to the net cash value indicated for the year prior to the loan request. Close attention should be given to the possibility of automatic premium loan provisions in lending against cash value of life insurance.

4. *Real Estate*—Advances may be made on improved residential property up to 90 percent of appraised value or cost, whichever is less. Improved commercial real estate loans may be made up to 80 percent of appraised value or cost, whichever is less. "Cost" may be waived due to the circumstances of the loan request. Accurate appraisals are desirable in all types of real estate lending.

5. *Automotive*—Loans may be advanced to 80 percent of cost for new and to the average loan value for

used autos and small trucks with a physical appraisal of the vehicle. The Black Book shall be used as a source to determine the average loan values for used vehicles. Large trucks, buses, and specialty type vehicles shall be financed on the basis of 66 2/3 percent of cost for new purchases and 50 percent for used. The advance can be adjusted upwards to consider the strong type commercial borrower and type of dealer recourse.

6. *Construction, Farm, and other special types of machinery and equipment*—Loans may be made equal to 66 2/3 percent of cost. Special emphasis should be given to U.C.C. filing on untitled equipment.

7. *Inventory and Accounts Receivable*—Loans made purely against inventory should not exceed 50 percent of stated value with consideration being given to salability and perishability. Loans secured by accounts receivable should not exceed 80 percent of the accounts acknowledged as current within 60 days. Based upon the strength of the borrower, receivables financing may be made with or without notification of the assignment and with or without direct payment being made to the bank through the use of a collateral account. Approval of the senior loan committee required.

8. *Other Forms*—Of collateral may be taken at the option of the bank. When dealing with collateral other than the normal types of bank collateral, use your common sense and, if you are in doubt, discuss it with your department head or senior loan officer.

All loan personnel shall be expected to be familiar with the various forms of documentation used in the bank in order to establish the debt and to secure proper lien positions in collateral taken. Loan personnel shall be expected to maintain at their desk or have immediate access to the *Comptrollers' Manual for National Banks, the Federal Reserve Bank Regulations, and De-*

partmental Operating Procedures. It is the bank's intention to comply with all laws, regulations, and interpretations issued by regulatory authorities pertaining to the extension of credit.

In cases where written commitments are desirable, the commitment letter shall be carefully reviewed to be certain the bank is fully protected in the matters of commitment. All written commitments must have an expiration date that normally should not exceed one (1) year. It is desirable for the senior loan officer or the members of the senior loan committee to review all letters of commitment before they are mailed from the bank. Formal lines of credit may only be granted with the concurrence of one (1) executive officer. It shall be the bank's policy to require audited statements when total loans of a business interest exceed $250,000 regardless of the basis of the credit. This requirement may be exempted based upon the type of collateral pledged and the basis of repayment. Waivers shall be granted by action of the bank's senior loan committee. When in doubt concerning documentation or matters of commitment, advice of bank counsel should be sought.

The requirements contained in this section of the loan policy represent normal and desirable conditions. It should be recognized by all persons exercising loan authority that *reasonable* variations will be allowed based upon the unique circumstances of a loan request. Exceptions or variations, which in the loan officer's judgment are justified, shall be detailed in an appropriate memorandum directed to the credit file of the borrower.

AUTHORIZED APPRAISERS

All collateral pledged to the bank to secure loans shall be properly appraised in order to determine the appropriate percentage of advance against value. The bank recognizes the sources of appraisal for commodities, stocks and bonds, and automobiles, et cetera as provided for by various financial media and publishing houses. Items of collateral which do not have a readily available and dependable source of valuation shall be appraised by at least two (2) bank lending officers. When possible, those officers making the appraisal should not be involved in the process of the loan applications. A statement of value signed by those persons making the appraisal shall be placed in the appropriate collateral file.

Real estate appraisals shall be made by two (2) lending officers prior to the granting of commitment. Following the determination of a fair market value, the maximum loan amount will be calculated within the bank's current policy. All real estate loans made by the bank shall comply without exception to the appropriate federal and state statutes and meet the requirements of RESPA Revised, Federal Flood Insurance, and the disclosure of real estate loan location as required by Census Tract Coding.

Annual appraisals are required on all real estate loans when the principal balance exceeds $250,000. This requirement specifically addresses commercial real estate loans which may, in part, be secured by machinery and equipment in addition to real estate.

The executive vice president or the senior loan officer of the bank shall from time to time designate those loan officers who are authorized to provide the appraisals as required above.

LOANS TO DIRECTORS AND THEIR INTERESTS

Metropolitan Bank recognizes its responsibility to provide for the normal borrowing requirements of the members of its board of directors and their various interests. In the extension of credit to directors and their interests, all lending personnel shall be expected to apply the requirements placed on all other credit applicants. Compromises such as low rates, high advance, and extended maturities shall be deemed unacceptable in every case. We should normally require the submission of any information necessary to render good credit judgment on all loans granted to directors and their interests. Loans to directors, or influenced by a director, which may be classed as accommodations, are discouraged.

All loans within this category shall be made on an "arm's-length" basis. Situations in the loan officer's opinion that deserve special consideration should be deferred to the president, executive vice president, or senior loan officer.

INAPPROPRIATE CREDIT PRACTICES

It is the intention of the bank to meet the credit requirements of its customers with a full range of loan services; however, our loans should be for constructive purposes. It is in this light that the following types of credit would be deemed inappropriate:

1. Loan requests that represent high-risk speculative ventures should be avoided.
2. We should not necessarily encourage unwarranted expenditures through the extension of credit that might appropriately be deferred.
3. Loans to businesses only for the purpose of acquiring their own capital stock should be avoided.
4. Unsecured "front side" or "downpayment" loans should be avoided at all times. Unsecured equity financing usually represents an extremely weak credit.
5. Loan requests should always be handled at "arm's-length." All persons with loan authority shall refrain from taking applications for credit in which they have a personal interest in the transaction. Loans of this type shall be referred to a disinterested loan officer for processing.
6. Loans for purely speculative purposes with respect to the various commodity and stock markets.
7. Loans for obvious land speculation transactions in which there is not a well-defined plan of development with a source of permanent financing.

Undesirable loans, such as those mentioned above, can easily be avoided through the application of good lending techniques, compliance with regulations and, of equal importance, the use of common sense.

Recommended Loan Authority Structure

All loans shall be extended on a secured or unsecured basis with specific limits assigned in each lending category to officers who have been granted loan authority. Loan authorities are assigned on the basis of the borrower's total debt relationship, including all names in which he may borrow, and, should not be applied on the basis of single transactions. No officer shall commit to any loan, or combination of loans, that would create a total liability in excess of his secured limit. The loan officer may request another with greater lending authority to join in the making of loans that exceed his limits. In this regard, the officers shall be required to initial all loan documentation.

Within the context of loan authority, secured loans are usually those collateralized by liquid, self-evident, and fully negotiable collateral. This type of preferred collateral is, in most cases, held by the bank with proper assignments, which allows the collateral to be sold and the loan balance liquidated without action on the part of the borrower. Loans may be secured by other types of collateral as previously described in the loan policy. These loans are subject to proper documentation and should be made within the limits of recommended advances and maturities. All other loans will be considered unsecured for loan authority purposes. Formal lines of credit and letters of commitment that exceed a loan officer's authority may only be granted and issued by the senior loan committee, the executive committee or an executive officer. Lending limits for individual loan officers and the various committees shall be established or amended from time to time by executive management.

Specific Lending Procedures

In order to set forth in a specific manner, procedures of the bank for certain types of loans and operating procedures have been established by the loan departments. Necessary additions or deletions will be made based upon recommendations of executive management.

Nondiscriminatory Practices

The lending division will make credit available to all credit-worthy persons without regard to race, color, religion, national origin, sex, marital status, age; because all or part of the applicant's income derives from any public assistance program; or because the applicant has in good faith exercised any right under the Consumer Credit Protection Act.

It will continue to be the policy of the lending division to extend credit to present and future customers who qualify under our standards. It will also be the continued policy of the lending division to extend credit to our customers without discriminating against them on a prohibited basis with respect to any aspect of a credit transaction.

The lending division does not deny mortgage or home improvement loans to anyone for reasons of race, color, religion, sex, or national origin. The division does not discriminate in the fixing of the amount, interest rate, duration, or other terms, such as application and collection procedures.

Synopsis

While this loan policy is not all inclusive, it does give a clear indication as to the bank's position in the lending process. It is the opinion of bank management that if you are adhering to the guidelines contained in the loan policy, you will be performing your duties within acceptable parameters.

The loan policy is subject to annual review by the bank's executive officers, and interim additions or deletions may be made as deemed necessary.

SELECTED SOURCES OF INFORMATION

This listing of sources includes some that were not cited in the book. Page numbers were not available for some articles and other sources because they were obtained from clippings and publications, such as U.S. House hearings, which did not list them.

"A New Attack on Credit Card Draft Laundering," *Credit Card News*, October 15, 1988, 1-2.

"A Seat on the Board Is Getting Hotter," *Business Week*, July 3, 1989, 73.

Adler, William M., and Michael Binstein, "The Speaker and the Sleazy Banker," *Bankers Monthly*, March 1988, 79-84.

Albracht, Steve W., and David W. Schmoldt, "Employee Fraud," *Business Horizons*, July/August 1988, 16-18.

Allen, Pat, "The Verdicts' in: Crooks Are Out," *Savings Institutions*, March 1989, 36-42.

Allen, Michael, "Texas Insurer's Demise Raises Fear of Reprisal of State's S&L Fraud," *The Wall Street Journal*, February 17, 1989, A1, A9.

American Institute of Certified Public Accountants, *Internal Control*, New York, AICPA, 1949.

Apcar, Leonard M., "Loose Lending: Texas S&L Disasters Are Blamed by Regulators Partly on Feewheeling Operations," *The Wall Street Journal*, July 13, 1987, 1, 8.

Argyris, Chris, *Strategy, Change and Defensive Routines*, Boston: Pitman Publishing, Inc., 1985.

Atkinson, Rick, and David Maraniss, wrote the following series of articles for *The Washington Post:* "For Texas S&Ls, a Long, Nasty, Corrupt Descent, June 11, 1989; "Only Ambition Limited S&L Growth," June 12, 1989; "Turning Anger into Action on Thrifts," June 13, 1989; "Hardening the S&L Battle Line," June 14, 1989; "Putting the Hammer to Lone Star Thrifts," June 15, 1989; "Gray the Re-Regulator and Wright Lock Horns," June 16, 1989, "Grappling with the Aftermath of S&L Debacle," June 17, 1989.

Audits of Banks, New York: American Institute of Certified Public Accountants, 1983.

Bank Failure: An Evaluation of the Factors Contributing to the Failure of National Banks, Washington, D.C.: Comptroller of the Currency, June 1988; Various phases of this study include: Susan F. Krause, Fred C. Graham, and James E. Horner, "An Economic Evaluation of the Factors Contributing to the Failure of National Banks," presented at the Conference on Bank Structure and Competition, Federal Reserve Bank of Chicago, May 13, 1988; Fred C. Graham and James E. Horner, "Bank Failure: An Evaluation of the Factors Contributing to the Failure of National Banks," appears in *The Financial Services Industry in the Year 2000: Risk and Efficiency*, Proceedings of a Conference on Bank Structure and Competition, Federal Reserve Bank of Chicago, May 11-13, 1988, 405-435; "An Evaluation of the Factors Contributing to the Failure of National Banks," Office of the Comptroller of the Currency, January 1988.

"Bank Fraud and Embezzlement," *FBI Law Enforcement Bulletin*, February 1975, revised February 1978.

"Bank Fraud: Bulletin of Fraud and Risk Management," Rolling Meadows, IL: Bank Administration Institute, Vol 4., No. 2, March 1989.

Barth, James R., Philip F. Bartholomew, and Carol J. Labich, *Moral Hazard and the Thrift Crisis: An Analysis of 1988 Resolutions*, Research Paper # 160, Federal Home Loan Bank Board, May 1989.

Bartholomew, Philip F., Economist, Federal Home Loan Bank Board, statement before the United States Sentencing Commission, April 7, 1989.

Benston, George J., *An Analysis of the Causes of Savings and Loan Failures*, Monograph 1985-4, New York: Salomon Brothers Center for the Study of Financial Institutions, New York University, 1985.

Berton, Lee, "Audit Firms Are Hit by More Investor Suits for Not Finding Fraud," *The Wall Street Journal*, January 24, A1, A12.

Berton, Lee, "An S&L in California Dumped Peat Marwick for Congenial Auditor," *The Wall Street Journal*, May 9, 1989, A1, A11.

Black, William K., and William L. Robertson, "Statement of the Federal Home Loan Bank submitted by William K. Black, Deputy Director, FSLIC and William L. Robertson, Director

ORPOS, before the Subcommittee on Financial Institutions, Supervision, Regulation, and Insurance of the Committee on Banking, Finance, and Urban Affairs, House of Representatives, 100th Cong., June 9, 1987.

Blade, Joe, "Owner of Credit Card Servicer Cited for Diverting Money," *American Banker*, June 20, 1989, 2.

Booth, David E., Pervaiz Alam, Sharif N. Akham, Barbara Osyk, "A Robust Multivariate Procedure for Identification of Problem Savings and Loan Institutions," *Decision Sciences*, Vol. 20, 1989, 320-333.

Bork, Robert, Jr., "Never Give A Sucker an Even Break," *Forbes*, July 15, 1985, 72, 77.

Borrowed Money, Borrowed Time: The Fall of the House of Butcher, A collection of 27 articles by *The Tennessean and The Knoxville Journal*, November 18, 1983.

Brady, John, "Foreigners Jailed in Credit-Card Theft Ring," *The Atlanta Journal*, January 27, 1984.

Brannigan, Martha and Gregory Stricharchuk, "Court in Ohio Overturns Marvin Warner's Conviction," *The Wall Street Journal*, November 16, 1989, B8.

Pete Brewton, wrote the following articles for *The Houston Post*: "Bank Fraud Investigators Looking for a National Plot," February 11, 1988; "S&L Probe Grew - and Grew Again," March 13, 1988; "Major Break Foreseen in Bank Fraud Probes," May 3, 1988; "Mafia's Involvement in S&L Failures Probed," October 8, 1988; "Bentsen Says He Has No Objections to Probe of Mob Role in S&L Failures," October 9, 1988; "Conviction Won't Stop Probe into Bank Fraud," November 9, 1988; "Links to Mob Figures, Suspect Offshore Companies Abound," December 8, 1988, "Meyerland Deals: Missing Money, Bogus Notes, December 8, 1988; "Brokered Deposits Case Produces

Prison Term, March 1, 1989; " `Secret' Meeting of S&Ls Part of Probe," February 12, 1989; "He Saw the S&L Crisis Coming," May 14, 1989.

Capeci, Jerry, "He Straddled the Fence," *New York Daily News*, date unknown.

Cauchon, Dennis, "S&L Fraud Trial Opens in $136M Vanishing Act," *USA Today*, February 22, 1989, B1.

————, "FBI Probes Jury in Big Texas S&L Trial," *USA Today*, Sept. 27, 1989.

Clark, Robert L., Comptroller of the Currency, Correspondence to The Honorable Doug Barnard, Jr., in response to Committee on Government Operations report, March 10, 1989.

Comptroller of the Currency, "Criminal Referral Form (Short Form) 1557-0069.

Comptroller of the Currency, "OCC Advisory," November 21, 1989; "OCC Advisory," 1989; "Banking Issuance," November 21, 1989.

Comptroller's Handbook for National Bank Examiners, Washington, D.C.: Comptroller of the Currency, Loose-leaf, various dates.

Cookingham, Vincent P., "Organized Crime: The Corporation as Victims," *Security Management*, Vol. 29, No. 7, July 1985, 28-31.

Council of Economic Advisers, *Economic Report of the President*, Washington, D.C.: Government Printing Office, 1989.

Cox, Rebecca, "3 Colorado Bank Firms Report Credit Card Fraud," *American Banker*, June 15, 1989, 3, 13.

Cox, Rebecca, "Con Men Turn to Phone Scams to Fleece Credit Card Banks," *American Banker*, May 18, 1989, 1, 10.

Cox, Rebecca, "Bankers Urged to React Quickly to Card Fraud," *American Banker*, May 24, 1989, 11.

Cox, Rebecca, "Florida Police Break Up Credit Card Fraud Ring," *American Banker*, June 20, 1989, 2.

Cox, Rebecca, "Orange Bank Suit Claims Card Fraud by Telemarketer," *American Banker*, June 27, 1989.

"Cultural Crime Ring," International Association of Credit Card Investigators (IACCI) *News*, May/June 1989, 5-6.

Dalebout, Richard S., and K. Fred Skousen, "RICO and Accountants," *CPA Journal*, August 1987, 83-87.

Davis, James R., "Ambiguity, Ethics, and the Bottom Line," *Business Horizons*, May-June 1989, 65-70.

Day, Kathleen, "S&L Fraud Seen Going Largely Unpunished," *The Washington Post*, February 4, 1989, A1, A14.

Dorfman, Paul M., and Steven K. Buster, "Drafting a Code Lender Conduct: Guidelines and Suggestions" *The Journal of Commercial Bank Lending*, July 1989, 4-12.

Drucker, Peter F., *Management: Tasks, Responsibilities, Practices*, New York: Harper & Row, Publishers, 1974.

"Ex-VSL Officer to Plead Guilty to Fraud Charges," Vernon, Texas, *Record*, May 23, 1989.

Evaluating Internal Control: Savings Institutions, A Guide for Management and Directors, Cleveland, Ohio: Ernst & Winney, 1983.

Eavenson, Harold W., Vice President and Manager of Investigations and Special Services, NCNB, Texas National Bank, Dallas, "Investigating International Fraud," April 10, 1989.

Faludi, Susan, "Calls Pour in on Nigerian Mafia's Credit Card Ring," *The Atlanta Journal*, February 1, 1984.

Faludi, Susan, "Credit Card Ring Charging Millions," *The Atlanta Journal*, February 1, 1984.

"FBI: Jury Tampering May Be Cause of Mistrial," Bryan, Texas *Eagle*, Sept. 26, 1989.

Federal Deposit Ins. Corp. v. *Renda*, 692 F.Supp 128 (D.Kan. 1988).

Federal Deposit Ins. Corp. v. *Jennings*, 615 F.Supp. 465 (D.C., Okl. 1985).

Federal Deposit Insurance Corporation, *1987 Annual Report*, Washington, D.C.: FDIC, 1988.

Federal Deposit Insurance Corporation, News Release, "FDIC Considers Requiring Prior Notice from Bankers Embarking on Rapid Growth," PR-63-89, March 21, 1989.

Federal Deposit Insurance Corporation, *Manual of Examination Policies: Appendix A - Bank Fraud and Insider Abuse*, March, 1987.

Federal Home Loan Bank of Atlanta, "Supervisory Bulletin, Factors Contributing to the Current Savings and Loan Industry Problems," September 18, 1987.

Federal Home Loan Bank Board, "Directors' Responsibilities: FHLBB Guidelines; Procedures for Obtaining Information to Support Directors' Decisions," Memoranda #R 62, November 1988, 2689.

Federal Home Loan Bank Board, "News," (FHLBB Places Texas Thrift into Management Consignment Program), March 20, 1987.

"FDIC Sues Under RICO, Securities Acts for Broker Scheme in Bank Failure," *Washington Financial Reports*, Vol. 44, April 15, 1985.

Focer, Ada, "Bank Insiders Who Bend to Greed," *Bankers Monthly*, September 1988, 14-19.

"Former Bank Chairman Sentenced to Prison," *Times*, Kerville, Texas, July 21, 1989.

"Fraud Charges Filed Against Florida Man Over Loan Scheme," *The Wall Street Journal*, January 12, 1989, C11.

Gajewski, Gregory R., *Bank Risk, Regulator Behavior, and Bank Closure in the Mid-1980's: A Two-Step Logit Model*, Unpublished dissertation, George Washington University, 1988.

Galtney, Liz, and Thomas Moore, "The Judicial Aftermath," *U.S. News and Word Report*, January 23, 1989, 43.

Gifford, Dan, Special Report on Financial Fraud, Public Broadcasting System, Houston, February 2, 1989.

Gillam, Carey, "Credit Card Operation Could Hit Bank for Up to $500,000," *Kansas City Business Journal*, March 20, 1989.

Gillam, Carey, "Credit Card Scam Could Cost Area Banks $1 Million Plus," *Kansas City Business Journal*, March 13, 1989.

Gray, Edwin J., "It Didn't Have to Happen," an address before the Rotary Club of Miami, Miami, Florida, September 8, 1988.

Gray, Edwin J., "Statement of Edwin J. Gray, Past Chairman, Federal Home Loan Bank Board, before the Committee on Banking, Housing and Urban Affairs, Senate, August 3, 1988.

Grunewald, Alan E. and Richard B. Foster, "Bank Directors' Liability for Negligence and the Business Judgment Rule," *Journal of the Midwest Finance Association*, Vol. 12, 1983, 109-132.

Harris, Byron, S&L Stories, 1987-1988, WFAA Television Inc., Communications Center, Dallas, TX 75202.

Hays, Fred H., Daniel L. Enterline, and Probir Roy, "Community Bank Directors: Should Your Bank Have an External Loan Review?" *Journal of Commercial Bank Lending*, April 1989, 21-28.

Hellerman, Michael and Thomas C. Renner, *Wall Steet Swindler*, New York: Doubleday & Company, 1977.

Jackson, Brooks, and Paulette Thomas, "As S&Ls Crisis Grows, U.S. Savings League Loses Lobbying Clout," *The Wall Street Journal*, March 7, 1989, A1, A18.

Jordan, Herb, "Local Bank, Harvard's Estate Sued," *The Mobile Press Register*, February 11, 1988. And various other articles in October 1987, dealing with the Harvard case.

Kilpatrick, Andrew, "Central Bank Worker Sent $175,000 to Self," Birmingham Post Herald, March 8, 1989.

LaGesse, David, The following articles by LaGesses appeared in *American Banker*, on the dates shown: "FSLIC Charges Vernon Savings Was `Looted,'" April 28, 1987; "FSLIC Alleges Vernon's Officers Lived High at Thrift's Expense," April 29, 1987; "Politicians Flew on Plans of Texas Thrift That Collapsed," June 18, 1987; "'Vernon S&L's Yacht Was Used for Fund-Raisers," June 19, 1987; "'Daisy Chain' Loan Swapping Described by Ex-Thrift Exec," August 28, 1987.

Langley, Monica, "FDIC Using Racketeering Law in Suit Seeking Damages in Bank Failure Case," *The Wall Street Journal*, April 9, 1985.

Lewis, Holden, "Judge Rules Mistrial in I-30 Condo Case with Jury Deadlock," Jacksonville, TX, *Daily Progress*, Sept. 17, 1989.

Lindquist, Robert J., and James E. Baskerville, "To Catch a Thief," *World*, July-August 1985, 32-35.

Lindsay, Sue, "Aurora Gold Dealer Goes on Trial," *Rocky Mountain News*, November 29, 1987.

———, "Final Chapter Opens in Bank's Downfall," *Rocky Mountain News*, November 29, 1987.

———, "5 Indicted in Fraud Scheme That Felled Aurora Bank," *Rocky Mountain News*, April 23, 1987.

Lodge, Bill, "I-30 Defendants Prepare Case; Toler Set to Testify," *Morning News*, Dallas, TX, July 3, 1989.

Lodge, Bill, "Witness Says I-30 Figures Got Bogus Appraisals," *Morning News*, Dallas, TX, June 26, 1989.

Management Fraud in Banks, The Netherlands: Klynveld Peat Marwick Goerdeler, 1989.

Mastercard International Inc., etc. et. al. v. Daryl Wayne Jay, etc. et al., United States District Court for Northern District of California, C-88-20629 RPA, Filed September 23, 1988, October 6, 1988.

Mautz, R. K. and Hussein A. Sharaf, *The Philosophy of Auditing*, Sarasota, Florida: American Accounting Association, Monograph No. 6, 1961.

Merchant, Kenneth A., *Fraudulent and Questionable Financial Reporting: A Corporate Perspective*, Morristown, N.J.: Financial Executives Research Foundation, 1987.

"Money Laundering," A Special Report, *American Banker*, July 24, 1989, 7-29.

Moore, Thomas, "The Bust of '89" *U.S. News & World Report*, January 23, 1989, 36-43.

Near, Janet P., "Whistle-Blowing: Encourage It!" *Business Horizons*, January-February 1989, 2-6.

Nich, David L., and Robert D. Miller, "White-Collar Crime," *The Internal Auditor*, December 1984, 24-27.

Patriarca, Michael, "The Role and Responsibilities of a Savings Institution Director," *Perspectives*, Federal Home Loan Bank of San Francisco, Fall 1988, 2-6.

Peterson, Richard L., and William L. Scott, "Major Causes of Bank Failures," appears in *Proceedings, Bank Structure and Competition*, Federal Reserve Bank of Chicago, May 1-3, 1985, 166-183.

Pizzo, Stephen, Mary Fricker, and Paul Muolo, *Inside Job: The Looting of America's Savings and Loans*, New York: McGraw-Hill, 1989.

Powell, Bill and Daniel Pedersen, "Loan Stars Fall in Texas," *Newsweek*, June 20, 1988, 42-45.

President's Commission on Organized Crime, Interim Report to the President and the Attorney General, *The Cash Connection: Organized Crime, Financial Institutions, and Money Laundering*, October 1984, Washington, D.C.: U.S. Government Printing Office.

President's Commission on Organized Crime, Report to the President and the Attorney General, *The Impact: Organized Crime Today*, April 1986, Washington, D.C.: U.S. Government Printing Office.

Pusey, Allen, "5 Named in 1st Charges of Texas S&L Inquiry," *Dallas Morning News*, February 9, 1988, 1A, 7A.

Pusey, Allen, "Problems, Players Surfaced in '70s Scandal," *Dallas Morning News*, December 4, 1988, 31A.

Pusey, Allen and Lee Hancock, "Network Fueled $10 billion S&L Loss," *Dallas Morning News*, December 4, 1988, 1, 30A, 31A.

Pusey, Allan, "I-30 Juror Tells Why He Voted for Acquittal," *Dallas Morning News*, October 26, 1989.

Re Franklin National Bank Securities Litigation, 445 F.Supp. 723 (1978).

Report of the National Commission on Fraudulent Financial Reporting, National Commission on Fraudulent Financial Reporting, October 1987 (No city shown).

Ringer, Richard, "FDIC Awarded $8.7 Million in Linked Finance Case," *American Banker*, March 4, 1986.

————, "Investigation of Linked Financing Deals Grow," *American Banker*, December 17, 1984.

————, "Linked Financing Leads to Failure of Kansas S&L, *American Banker*, March 3, 1987.

————, and Bart Faust, "How Financings Linked to Brokered Deposits Entice Some Banks into Disastrous Loan Deals," "A Tale of Brokered Deposits and a Busted Bank," "Attempts to Save Indian Springs Were Too Late to Overcome Bad Loans and Brokered Deposits," and "FDIC Allows Convicted Felon to Serve as Indian Springs Officer," *American Banker*, November 15, 16, 19, 1984.

Robertson, Jack C., and Frederick G. Davis, *Auditing*, 3rd ed., Plano, Texas, Business Publications, Inc., 1982.

Rose, Robert L., "A Credit Union Fails, and Omaha Wonders: Was it Bamboozled?" *The Wall Street Journal*, February 8, 1989, A1, A11.

Rose, Robert L., "Ex-Manager of Franklin Community is Accused of Embezzling $12 Million," *The Wall Street Journal*, May 22, 1989.

Rosentein, Jay, "Stiffer Penalties for S&L Crimes are Challenged at House Hearing," *American Banker*, March 23, 1989, 7.

Rudolph, Patricia M. and Bassam Hamdan, "An Analysis of Post-Deregulation Savings-and-Loan Failures," *AREUEA Journal*, Vol. 16, No. 1, Spring 1988, 17-33.

Sawicki, Michael and Ross Ramsey, "5 Charged With Banking Fraud in Probe of Texas Institutions," *Dallas Times Herald*, February 9, 1988.

Singer, Mark, *Funny Money*, New York: Albert Knopf, 1985.

Sinkey, Joseph H., *Problem and Failed Institutions in the Commercial Banking Industry*, Greeenwich, CN: JAI Press, Inc., 1979.

"Speaking for the Speaker," *Bankers Monthly*, May 1988, 87.

Sprague, Irvine H., *Bailout: An Insider's Account of Bank Failures and Rescues*, New York: Basic Books, 1986.

Statistics on Banking, 1987, Washington, FDIC, 1988.

Statement on Auditing Standards No. 53, *The Auditor's Responsibility to Detect and Report Errors and Irregularities*, AICPA, April 1988.

Statement on Auditing Standards No. 54, *Illegal Acts by Clients*, AICPA, April 1988.

Statement on Auditing Standards No. 55, *Consideration of the Internal Control Structure in a Financial Statement Audit*, AICPA, April 1988.

Statement on Auditing Standards No. 59, *The Auditor's Consideration of an Entity's Ability to Continue as a Going Concern*, AICPA, April 1988.

Statement on Auditing Standards No. 60, *Communication of Internal Control Structure Related Matters Noted in an Audit*, AICPA, April 1988.

Statement on Auditing Standards No. 61, *Communications with Audit Committees*, AICPA, April 1988.

Stedman, Michael J., "Doing Time: Advice from a Jailed Banker," *Bankers Monthly*, November 1988, 17-22.

Strasser, Fred, "Racketeering Law in the States is Starting to be Felt," *National Law Journal*, March 20, 1989, 1, 34.

The Director's Book: The Role of a National Bank Director, Washington: Comptroller of the Currency, August 1987.

The Director's Guide: The Role and Responsibilities of a Savings Institutions Director, Federal Home Loan Bank of San Francisco, 1988.

The Mobile Press Register, Various articles concerning F. Ray Harvard, by Tom Jennings, Herb Jordan, and others that appeared October 1987 - February 1988.

Thomas, Paulette, "Over Half of Lincoln S&L Reported Net Since '84 Said to Be from Sham' Deals," *The Wall Street Journal*, November 15, 1989, A3.

U.P.I., "Jake Butcher Indicted for Fraud in Florida," *American Banker*, Sept. 1, 1989, 2.

U.S. Department of Justice, U.S. Attorney, Middle District of Florida, Press Release, August 30, 1989.

U.S. Department of Justice, *United States Attorneys' Manual, Criminal Division, Title 9.*

U.S. Department of Justice, Federal Bureau of Investigation, "Bank Crime Statistics (BCS), Federally Insured Financial Institutions," various dates.

U.S. General Accounting Office, *Bank Failures, Independent Audits Needed to Strengthen Internal Control and Bank Management,* GAO/AFMD-89-25, May 1989.

U.S. General Accounting Office, *Bank Regulation, Information on Independent Public Accountant Audits of Financial Institutions,* GAO/GGD-86-44FS, April 1986.

U.S. General Accounting Office, *Banking: Conflict of Interest Abuses in Commercial Banking Institutions,* GAO/GGD-89-35, January 1989.

U.S. General Accounting Office, *CPA Audit Quality: Failures of CPA Audits to Identify and Report Significant Savings and Loan Problems,* GAO/AFMD-89-45, February 1989.

U.S. General Accounting Office, *CPA Audit Quality: Status of Actions Taken to Improve Auditing and Financial Reporting of Public Companies,* GAO/AFMD-89-38, March 1989.

U.S. General Accounting Office, *Commercial Banking, Lending to Troubled Sectors,* GAO/GGD-88-126BR, September 1988.

U.S. General Accounting Office, *Thrift Failures, Costly Failures Resulted from Regulatory Violations and Unsafe Practices,* GAO/AFMD-89-62, June 1989.

U.S. General Accounting Office, *Failed Financial Institutions: Reasons, Costs, Remedies and Unresolved Issues,* Statement of Frederick D. Wolf before the Committee on Banking, Finance, and Urban Affairs, House of Representatives, GAO/T-AFMD-89-1, January 13, 1989.

U.S. General Accounting Office, *Failed Thrifts: Internal Control Weaknesses Create and Environment Conducive to Fraud, Insider Abuse, and Related Unsafe Practices,* Statement of Frederick D. Wolf before the Subcommittee on Criminal Justice Committee on the Judiciary, House of Representatives, GAO/T-AFMD-89-4, March 22, 1989.

U.S. General Accounting Office, "The Need to Improve Auditing in the Savings and Loan Industry," Statement of Frederick D. Wolf before the Committee on Banking, Finance and Urban Affairs, House of Representatives, February 21, 1989, GAO/T-AFMD-89-2.

U.S. General Accounting Office, *Thrift Failures: Costly Failures Resulted From Regulatory Violations and Unsafe Practices,* GAO/AFMD-89-62, June 1989.

U.S. General Accounting Office, *Thrift Industry: Forbearance for Troubled Institutions 1982-1986,* GAO/GGD-87-78BR, May 1987.

U.S. House, *Adequacy of Federal Efforts to Combat Fraud, Abuse, and Misconduct in Federally Insured Institutions,* Hearing before the Commerce, Consumer, and Monetary Affairs Subcommittee of the House Committee on Government Operations, 100th Cong., 1st Sess., November 19, 1987.

U.S. House, *Adequacy of Federal Home Loan Bank Board Supervision of Empire Savings and Loan Association,* Hearing before the Commerce, Consumer, and Monetary Affairs Subcommittee of the Committee on Government Operations, 98th Cong., 2nd Sess., April 25, 1984.

U.S. House, *Adequacy of the Office of the Comptroller of the Currency's Supervision of Franklin National Bank,* Committee on Government Operations, House Report 94-1669, September 23, 1976.

U.S. House, *Combating Fraud, Abuse, and Misconduct in the Nation's Financial Institutions: Current Federal Efforts are Inadequate,* 72nd Report by the Committee on Government Operations, House Report 100-1088, 100th Cong., 2nd Sess., October 13, 1988.

U.S. House, *Federal Home Loan Bank Board Supervision and Failure of Empire Savings and Loan Association of Mesquite Tex.,* 44th Report by the Committee on Government Operations, House Report 98-953, 98th Cong., 2nd Sess., August 6, 1984.

U.S. House, *Federal Regulation of Brokered Deposits in Problem Banks and Savings Institutions,* Committee on Government Operations, House Report 98-1112 (Committee on Government Operations Report No. 52), September 28, 1984.

U.S. House, *Federal Regulation of Brokered Deposits: A Followup Report,* 38th Report by the Committee on Government Operations, House Report 99-676, 99th Cong., 2nd Sess., July 16, 1986.

U.S. House, *Federal Regulation of Direct Investments by Savings and Loan Associations,* Committee on Government Operations, 1985, House Report 99-358.

U.S. House, *Federal Response to Criminal Misconduct and Insider Abuse in the Nation's Financial Institutions,* 57th Report by the Committee on Government Operations, House Report 98-1137, 98th Cong., 2nd Sess., October 4, 1984.

U.S. House, *Federal Response to Criminal Misconduct by Bank Officers, Directors, and Insiders, Part 1,* Hearing before the Commerce, Consumer, and Monetary Affairs Subcommittee of the Committee on Government Operations, 98th Cong., 1st Sess., June 28, 1983.

U.S. House, *Federal Response to Criminal Misconduct by Bank Officers, Directors, and Insiders, Part 2*, Hearings before the Commerce, Consumer, and Monetary Affairs Subcommittee of the Committee on Government Operations, 98th Cong., 2nd Sess., May 2 and 3, 1984.

U.S. House, *Federal Supervision and Failure of the Penn Square Bank, Oklahoma City, Okla.*, Hearing before the Commerce, Consumer, and Monetary Affairs Subcommittee of the Committee on Government Operations, 97th Cong., 2nd Sess, July 16, 1982.

U.S. House, *Federal Supervision and Failure of United American Bank (Knoxville, Tenn.)*, Hearing before the Commerce, Consumer, and Monetary Affairs Subcommittee of the Committee on Government Operation, 98th Cong., 1st. Sess., March 15 and 16, 1983.

U.S. House, *Federal Supervision and Failure of United American Bank of Knoxville, Tenn., and Affiliated Banks*, 23rd Report by the Committee on Government Operations, House Report No. 98-573, 98th Cong., 1st. Sess., November 18, 1983.

U.S. House, *Financial Institutions Reform, Recovery and Enforcement Act of 1989*, Report of the Committee on Banking, Finance and Urban Affairs, Report 101-54, Part 1, 101st Cong., 1st Sess., May 16, 1989.

U.S. House, *Financial Institutions Reform, Recovery and Enforcement Act of 1989*, Report 101-222, Conference Report to Accompany H.R. 1278, 101st Cong., 1st. Sess., August 4, 1989.

U.S. House, *Fraud and Abuse by Insiders, Borrowers, and Appraisers in the California Thrift Industry*, Hearing before the Commerce, Consumer, and Monetary Affairs Subcommittee of the Committee on Government Operations, 100th Cong., 1st. Sess., June 13, 1989.

U.S. House, *Impact of Brokered Deposits on Banks and Thrifts: Risks Versus Benefits,* Hearing before the Subcommittee on General Oversight and Investigations of the Committee on Banking, Finance and Urban Affairs, 99th Cong., 1st. Sess., July 16, 1985, Serial No. 99-36.

U.S. House, *Impact of Faulty and Fraudulent Appraisals on Real Estate Loans by Federally Insured Financial Institutions and Related Agencies of the Federal Government,* Hearings before the Commerce, Consumer, and Monetary Affairs Subcommittee of the Committee on Government Operations, 99th Cong., 1st Sess., December 11 and 12, 1985.

U.S. House, *Oversight Hearings into the Effectiveness of Federal Bank Regulation (Franklin National Bank),* before the Commerce, Consumer, and Monetary Affairs Subcommittee of the Committee on Government Operations, 94th Cong., 2nd Sess., February 10, May 25, 26, and June 1, 1976.

U.S. House, *Real Estate Appraisal Reform Act of 1988,* Report 100-1001, Part 1, together with dissenting views, 100th Cong., 2nd. Sess., September 28, 1988.

U.S. House, *The Market for Bank Stocks,* Subcommittee on Domestic Finance, Committee on Banking and Currency, 88th Cong., 2d Sess., 1964.

U.S. Senate, *Bank Supervision, Bank Directors, and Conflicts of Interest,* Hearings before the Committee on Banking, Housing, and Urban Affairs, U. S. Senate, 95th Cong., 1st. Sess., May 24 and 25, 1977.

U.S. Treasury, Nicholas F. Brady, Secretary, Testimony before the Committee on Banking, Housing and Urban Affairs, Senate, February 22, 1989.

U.S. v. *Arthur Young & Co.*, 465 U.S. 805, 817-818 (1984).

U.S. v. *Herman K. Beebe, Sr.*, Northern District of Texas, Dallas Division, CR 3-88-124-D, Filed April 29, 1988.

U.S. v. *Martin Schwimmer and Mario Renda*, Eastern District of New York, CR 87-00423, Filed January 28, 1988.

U.S. v. *Tyrell G. Barker*, Northern District of Texas, Dallas Division, CR 3-88-017-D, Filed February 8, 1988.ts

U.S. v. *Woody F. Lemons*, Northern District of Texas, Dallas Division, CR3-88-234-T, Filed November 10, 1988.

U.S. v. *Rapp*, 871 F.2d 957 (11th Cir. 1989).

U.S. v. *Schwimmer and Renda*, 692F. Supp. (E.D.N.Y. 1988).

U.S. v. *Larry K. Thompson*, Northern District of Texas, CR-5-88-002, CR 5-88-024, Filed May 20, 1988.

Villa, John K., *Banking Crimes*, New York: Clark Boardman Company, Ltd., 1987.

Violano, Michael, "The High-Tech Future of Foiling Fraud and Forgery," *Bankers Monthly*, April 1989, 35-40.

Wall, M. Danny, "Statement of M. Danny Wall, Chairman, Federal Home Loan Bank Board, before the Committee on Budget, U.S. Senate, October 5, 1988.

"Warning Lights for Bank Soundness: Special Issue on Commercial Bank Surveillance," *Economic Review*, Federal Reserve Bank of Atlanta, November 1983.

Weld, William F., Assistant Attorney General, Criminal Division, U.S. Department of Justice, Remarks before The Banking

Law Institute, 4th Annual Bank and Savings & Loan Supervision, Enforcement, and Compliance Conference, Washington, D.C., September 21, 1987.

Wells, Joseph T., "Red Flags: The Key to Reducing White-Collar Crime," *Corporate Accounting*, Spring 1987, 51-53.

Wells, Joseph T., "White-Collar Crime: Myths and Strategies," *The Practical Accountant*, August 1985, 43-45.

"Wright, Coelho and the S&L Fiasco," *U.S. News and World Report*, June 12, 1989, 21-22.

"Wright's Troubles Seem Unrelenting," AP, Sherman, Texas, *Democrat*, May 7, 1989.

Zipser, Andy, and Christi Harlan, "Flashy Federal Posse Pursuing S&L Abuses Bungles Effort in Texas," *The Wall Street Journal*, February 10, 1989, A1, A4.

ABOUT THE AUTHOR

Dr. Benton E. Gup received his undergraduate and graduate degrees from the University of Cincinnati. At present, he holds the Robert Hunt Cochrane/Alabama Bankers Association Chair of Banking at the University of Alabama. He has also held banking chairs at the University of Virginia and the University of Tulsa. Dr. Gup is the author of 10 books, including *Commercial Bank Management* (with Fraser and Kolari), *Cases in Bank Management* (with Meiburg), *Financial Intermediaries, Management of Financial Institutions*, and others. His articles on financial subjects have appeared in the *The Journal of Finance, Journal of Money, Banking, and Credit, Journal of Retail Banking, Journal of Financial and Quantitative Analysis*, and elsewhere. Dr. Gup is a nationally known lecturer in executive development programs and seminars and has served as a consultant to government and industry.